Human Resources Kit

4th Edition

by Andrea Butcher
CEO of HRD — Human Resources Development

A Wiley Brand

Human Resources Kit For Dummies®, 4th Edition

Published by: **John Wiley & Sons, Inc.**, 111 River Street, Hoboken, NJ 07030-5774, www.wiley.com

Copyright © 2023 by John Wiley & Sons, Inc., Hoboken, New Jersey

Media and software compilation copyright © 2023 by John Wiley & Sons, Inc. All rights reserved.

Published simultaneously in Canada

For general information on our other products and services, please contact our Customer Care Department within the U.S. at 877-762-2974, outside the U.S. at 317-572-3993, or fax 317-572-4002. For technical support, please visit https://hub.wiley.com/community/support/dummies.

Wiley publishes in a variety of print and electronic formats and by print-on-demand. Some material included with standard print versions of this book may not be included in e-books or in print-on-demand. If this book refers to media such as a CD or DVD that is not included in the version you purchased, you may download this material at http://booksupport.wiley.com. For more information about Wiley products, visit www.wiley.com.

Library of Congress Control Number: 2023931111

ISBN: 978-1-119-98989-9 (pbk); ISBN: 978-1-119-98991-2 (ebk); ISBN: 978-1-119-98990-5 (ebk)

SKY10042699_021323

Contents at a Glance

Table of Contents

Introduction

A company's ability to grow and stay on top of customer demand has always depended heavily on the quality of its people. Today, this relationship is even more relevant with a focus on creating an employee experience that meets the changing needs of the workforce. Businesses are now, more than ever, recognizing that a highly skilled and motivated workforce is mission critical — the talent within the business *is* the business.

Here are two overarching themes that form the foundation of this book:

>> The people who work within your business *are* your business.

>> Their needs and expectations are shaped by the dynamic, evolving environment in which we live.

As you peek into the world of human resources (HR), it's important to focus more on the human and less on the human as a resource, in an effort to understand the motivators and preferences that the people within your business bring to their work and the workplace.

About This Book

Leaders and business owners who are intentional about building a strong organizational culture with engaged teams that consistently delight customers aren't hard to spot. They're the people who know how to attract and nurture these teams. In short, they're very good at leading the people and talent processes within their business and creating an employee experience that's meaningful and rewarding. In other words, they're good at leading human resources.

But doing this well is no small feat. In any job market, competition exists for the most desirable candidates, and once hired, these top performers are only a click away from leaving you. Not only that, but the HR and talent function now encompasses everything from creating a strategic workforce plan to ensuring a competitive total rewards strategy, launching effective learning and development initiatives, interpreting federal and state codes, and implementing people policies and benefits that safeguard team members while protecting company interests. And the stakes are high. The legal and economic consequences of a major HR misstep can be enormous.

As a business owner or leader, you've probably already faced these and other challenges. You may not think of yourself as an "HR person," but you recognize that you need to attract the best talent you can and motivate them to do their best work for you. In the past, you likely took on some aspects of finding and keeping top talent, with perhaps someone else on your team handling the details. Now, as your organization has grown, you're no doubt finding that your company's HR responsibilities have become more complicated. Whether you're a business owner who wants to make sure that you're up-to-date on employment regulations and HR best practices, or you're a leader within the business who has been asked to take on HR-related duties, you're going to need a resource and guidance along the way. Even if you attend conferences or network with others who are leading talent/HR functions in their businesses, you won't remember everything you hear. Ultimately, you need a straightforward yet comprehensive resource with information, insights, and tools to help align your company's HR practices and policies with the overall objectives of your business. That's the purpose behind the fourth edition of *Human Resources Kit For Dummies.*

Some companies are lucky enough to have their own HR professional or even an entire HR department. Most of these HR specialists have developed their skills through years of education and on-the-job experience. In writing this book, my aim is not to pretend that I can magically turn you into a seasoned HR professional by the time you read the last page. I *do* believe, though, that I can give you a fair representation of the issues HR leaders navigate, best practices for approaching these challenges, and enough background to help you better oversee or handle the HR/ talent activities within your organization — both today and as you continue to grow.

What can you expect to gain from this new edition? For starters, you'll be better able to

>> Recognize how remote work and changing employee expectations are affecting the workplace of the future — and make the necessary long-term plans for success.

>> Examine what today's most successful and progressive companies are doing with respect to basic HR areas as recruiting, total rewards, learning and development, performance management, and employee engagement and retention.

>> View recruiting as an ongoing sales process and continually market your employer brand to hire the best talent.

>> Gain insight into practices (leading in a virtual environment and providing a competitive total rewards package) to create a meaningful and positive employee experience for your team members.

>> Understand the key regulatory issues that apply to many business owners and leaders, thus putting yourself in a better position to navigate the risks involved in hiring and leading team members.

This book provides general guidelines on how to set up and implement successful HR practices, as well as actual tools — templates — that you can use right away. In other words, *Human Resources Kit For Dummies*, 4th Edition, isn't simply a book to read; it's a book to use.

This edition has moved the helpful online documents from a CD to online at www.dummies.com/go/humanresourceskit. From sample job descriptions to sample employee policies, you get a variety of tools you need to implement solid HR practices and procedures. Some of these forms are turnkey — ready to use immediately. Others are sample templates that you may want to adapt.

The collection of forms is comprehensive, but your situation may be unique. When in doubt, the best practice is always to contact a knowledgeable and experienced lawyer who specializes in this area.

Foolish Assumptions

In writing *Human Resources Kit For Dummies*, I had to make certain assumptions about you, the reader. Because I'm not sure exactly what your background and needs are, I wrote the book with two broad audiences in mind:

>> Business owners who find that their growing companies are demanding a greater portion of their time and attention in managing one or more of the most common HR functions, such as recruiting, benefits administration, performance management, learning and development, and regulatory issues

>> Individuals in small to mid-size companies who have only a limited knowledge of HR functions but who have been asked to take on some or all of these roles

First and foremost, I want to address you as a businessperson — someone who, after reading the book, is knowledgeable not only about the nuts and bolts of HR but also about how to approach the function with the goal of becoming a major player in helping to run your company.

Icons Used in This Book

When I want you to pay close attention to a specific piece of information, I place little pictures, called *icons*, next to the text in the margin. Here's what the icons mean:

This icon flags what I consider to be good and practical advice.

I flag important conceptual information with this icon.

This icon indicates something that is particularly sensitive and could get you into legal trouble if not handled properly. Always contact an attorney if you're unsure whether something is legally risky (regardless of whether it's flagged by a Warning icon).

This icon flags legal jargon and technical discussions.

Whenever I mention a document that you can reference within the online tools, I use this icon. You can access the documents at www.dummies.com/go/ humanresourceskit.

Beyond This Book

This book is full of information in plain English about human resources. If you want some additional pieces that you can refer to on a regular basis, check out the book's Cheat Sheet at www.dummies.com. Just search for "Human Resources Kit For Dummies Cheat Sheet."

Where to Go from Here

Every chapter in this book covers a topic of importance to the HR function. But you'll likely find that some chapters have greater relevance to your situation than others. If you're completely new to the HR role, for instance, you'll want to start with Part 1 to build your baseline knowledge. If you have some experience hiring and managing staff, you may instead choose to start with the later chapters to discover the finer points of these activities. You don't have to read this book from start to finish to get the most out of it. Look through the table of contents and index so you can find those chapters or sections that address the issues you currently face.

1

Embracing the Evolving Role of HR

Understand the basics of human resources, also referred to today as the *talent* or *people* function.

Grasp the fundamental categories of HR responsibilities and walk through the steps involved in attracting the best talent.

Examine some of the most important trends in the HR and talent space, such as creating a positive employee experience, leading in a virtual environment, and ensuring HR and talent processes are equitable and inclusive.

Focus on the continued effect of technology, which is so rapidly changing the dynamics of the way in which human resources equip and support the workforce role.

Chapter **1**

Peeking into the World of HR

Whether you're a business owner building an organization, a leader within an organization supporting the success of your team, or a human resources (HR) or talent professional creating processes and systems that maximize the strengths and talents within your workforce, it's important to recognize that the people within your business *are* your business. You get more from the talent within your organization when you're clear about what success looks like, care for people, provide an experience that allows people to bring the best of who they are, and create processes and systems that support their needs and their ongoing growth and development.

No matter what products or services a company offers, the talents and abilities of every team member are what ultimately determine how well it performs and serves customers. Whether you call them team members or employees (I use both interchangeably throughout this book), these human beings differ from physical or financial assets of the company because each human being has unique talents and needs that collectively shape the culture of your organization. The world of HR exists to leverage their individual and collective potential, and because the focus is on the human (more so than the human as a resource), many organizations are rebranding human resources to better reflect a focus on people, culture, and talent. Regardless of the name, the impact of strong talent and people processes in an organization is clear, particularly in today's complex work environment.

In order to best support the people within your organization, you have to understand what makes them tick — their preferences, their needs, their expectations, and their humanness, and in this volatile, uncertain, complex, and ambiguous (VUCA) world, their humanness is front and center. Team members no longer "leave their personal lives at the door" as many are working from home — the line between personal and professional has blended as HR leaders promote life/work integration and focus on the holistic well-being of the workforce.

As organizations adapt to the shifting landscape, HR plays a critical role. This chapter provides an overview of how you can navigate the changing landscape and best support your team members (and ultimately, your business) in the process.

Recognizing Key HR Responsibilities

Overall, the HR or talent function within an organization leads the decisions, activities, and processes designed to support the needs and performance of employees in today's dynamic environment. The most common responsibilities falling within the HR function include the following:

>> **Attracting talent:** Strategically attracting, sourcing, recruiting, and onboarding the talent needed to accomplish business goals

>> **Creating a positive employee experience:** Ensuring a safe environment and retaining team members

>> **Providing a total rewards package:** Establishing legally compliant, effective, and attractive compensation, benefits, and recognition

>> **Developing employees and providing opportunities for growth:** Ensuring that team members grow in knowledge and experience, and that their skill sets support the goals of the business

>> **Navigating risk:** Complying with the ever-increasing complexities within the regulatory environment

Regardless of the number of employees within your organization, a people-focus is important in order to get and keep the talent necessary to serve your customers. After they reach a certain size, most organizations find it more efficient to establish a team focused on people and culture — even if it consists of only one person.

Because of the increasing complexity of HR issues, larger organizations have boosted the size of their departments and typically employ specialists in areas such as talent acquisition, learning and development, and total rewards, but smaller organizations that don't have the resources for such specialization must ensure that the people who handle their HR functions (or they themselves) possess skills in several areas of HR rather than in one particular specialty.

REMEMBER

The HR profession has undergone enormous changes in the past 20 years . . . even the last 2 years, in the wake of the Covid-19 pandemic. HR and talent activities are an integral part of a business (remember, the people in the business *are* your business). Rather than creating and executing a talent strategy in a vacuum, HR leaders work cooperatively with leaders at all levels of the business to determine the most effective ways to meet team members' needs.

Building Your Team: Attracting Talent

One of the primary jobs of an HR professional is recruiting and hiring the best people for the organization. It all starts with developing an overall talent strategy. This involves putting your current employees in the right places to best address the organization's most critical task, as well as attracting additional people with the talent and attributes that complement both your short- and long-term business goals. At the heart of a talent strategy is taking advantage of the strengths of your people and augmenting their talent and capabilities in a thoughtful, focused way. (See Chapter 4 for more on creating a talent strategy.)

REMEMBER

A carefully crafted job description (or *position success profile* as I encourage you to think of it as) — and job postings based on it — are critical to bringing the best people onboard. Both should focus on a job's expected outcomes to attract the best applicants possible. The key to a good position success profile is clearly defining what success looks like (hence the name). (See Chapter 5 for more on creating a position success profile.)

From there, you have a broad array of potential candidate sources. These include referrals from your current team members, online job boards, social media and online networking sites, and your own company website. (See Chapter 6 for more on your sourcing strategy.)

Now comes the process of narrowing the candidate pool and assessing talent. The goal is to choose the prospective candidates who are in the best position to achieve the outcomes of the position, so it's critical to look for specifics about their experience and history of achievement in the focus areas that have been defined. You may use a video or phone interview as an initial way to determine those who are likely to be most successful in the position. When it's time for the all-important in-person or more detailed virtual interview, you need to use effective interview techniques and strategies, with a special emphasis on nondiscriminatory interview questions. (See Chapter 7 for more on evaluating applicants and Chapter 8 for tips on interviewing.)

As you near the final hiring decision, it's important to set up a system to help select the right candidate, including how and when to conduct background and reference checks (refer to Chapter 9). Final considerations include ways to craft and present a job offer, and from there, techniques to negotiate a total rewards package to be competitive and win over an attractive candidate.

Retaining and Engaging Talent: Creating a Positive Employee Experience

Recruiting and hiring great talent is obviously the first step but represents only one side of the talent strategy coin. Creating an environment and a culture that keep employees onboard is no less critical to the long-term growth of your organization. Employee retention begins the moment you connect with the prospective candidate in the recruiting process and is heightened on their first day with your organization (see Chapter 10). Upon joining the organization, one of your first responsibilities is to get to know your team member to best set them up for success. It's not a one-size-fits-all approach. Your employee handbook will provide general guidelines and expectations for all employees, but each manager should connect with individual employees regarding any individual needs or expectations. Communication and clarity are the keys to setting up new hires for success.

It's also important to leverage onboarding strategies to help new team members engage quickly, get off to a strong start, and have some quick wins. The onboarding process is ongoing and should include regular check-ins and follow-up about what the employee is learning through the process.

Every business needs an effective rewards and motivation system that includes how much and by what means employees are compensated (see Chapter 11). A first step for all organizations is to determine an overall compensation philosophy that can help establish pay levels and wage plans throughout the company. Your compensation philosophy also applies to raises, bonuses, and other forms of incentives. Next, of course, are the benefits themselves. It takes a high-level understanding of (and access to experts who can provide detailed expertise on) health insurance, retirement packages, workers' compensation, employee wellness, and on-the-job safety (refer to Chapter 12).

Creating a great employee experience encompasses other elements that are important contributors to a motivated and satisfied workforce. Get to know the essentials of alternate work arrangements (for example, hybrid working arrangements and flexible work hours) and their value in retaining top performers (see Chapter 13). Consider, too, the importance of good corporate citizenship and getting ongoing feedback from team members via surveys — two components that boost employees' sense that they work in a business that does the right thing and values team members' perspectives.

Developing Talent: Providing Opportunities for Growth

Developing talent is another way to retain and engage team members on an ongoing basis. Providing opportunities for growth is no longer a nice-to-have feature within organizations — employees *expect* opportunities for growth during their tenure. It bears repeating — your employees *are* your business, so connecting your learning and development goals to your business goals ensures a win-win for the employee and the company (see Chapter 14). Recognize the importance of both technical skill development and leadership development, and leverage innovation in educational activities and the variety of options available — microlearning, traditional classroom learning, coaching, and mentoring.

Whereas learning and development programs typically are about skills improvement, career development emphasizes longer-term qualities and expertise that employees need to enrich their careers in general (see Chapter 15). Understand the role of coaching and mentoring relationships to foster personal growth, as well as leadership development and succession planning efforts to identify and groom future leaders.

Employers need to provide recognition and offer feedback if they expect the people working for them to accomplish what's needed — and improve on their performance. Consider implementing a performance management process that's ongoing and built on the success needed in the position. (See Chapter 16 for details on assessing talent through a performance management process.)

Minimizing Organizational Risk

There's no substitute for the guidance of a trusted employment attorney, but HR professionals need to have a basic understanding of the legal issues and challenges that come with hiring and managing employees — and with terminating the employee relationship.

REMEMBER

Throughout this book, the legal-related information provided is the result of a collaborative effort with the law firm of Ogletree, Deakins, Nash, Smoak & Stewart, P.C., and the information is presented to increase your knowledge of employment-related law, but I strongly recommend consulting a knowledgeable and experienced lawyer regarding anything you encounter in your work that is legally complex.

First and foremost, proactively put processes and systems in place (and create a culture) that minimizes charges of discrimination and other employment-related legal claims. Be sure to understand the concept of disparate impact and the steps you can take to keep your business as compliant with employment laws as possible. And, although your lawyers should take the lead in any formal legal actions or responses, you also need to be well acquainted with issues and situations covered by Title VII of the Civil Rights Act; the Americans with Disabilities Act; the Family and Medical Leave Act; the Fair Labor Standards Act; and other important federal, state, and local laws that can impact your business.

A successful business takes an ethical approach to all its interactions with customers, as well as its employees. As a business leader, you need to know how to handle — sensitively but firmly — what are undoubtedly the least pleasant aspects of your role. These include, but aren't limited to, dismissals, layoffs, and sexual harassment or hostile work environment claims. (See Chapter 17 for a discussion of key HR-related laws and Chapter 18 for more on the specifics of termination and other difficult situations.)

IN THIS CHAPTER

» Focusing on the hybrid model

» Creating new skills by upskilling

» Using analytics and data

» Ensuring a diverse, equitable, and inclusive environment

» Making employee well-being a priority

Chapter **2**

Setting the Stage: Trends in the HR and Talent Space

Picture yourself in the offices of a business 50 years ago. It may be a major corporation or a modestly sized startup (although they wouldn't have used the term "startup" back then). Another term you probably won't be able to find on any company directory or office door is "human resources." After a few minutes of searching, you stop a passing employee and ask them for the department that handles job applications. The answer: "Personnel is down the hall, third door on the left."

This imaginary anecdote speaks volumes about the revolution that has occurred in the field of human resources and the world of work. I'm going far back to paint this picture because it's helpful for someone new to HR to see the vast changes that have taken place in the field. It's also helpful to recognize the changes in the way companies of all sizes view the people who work for them. In one respect, this shift has been the result of more-comprehensive labor laws and a much better employee experience. The more the government requires of a workplace, the more pressure on the organization to implement whatever steps are mandated and ensure they're maintained. But the shift also reflects how today's businesses value the people they employ and the importance of creating an experience that is meaningful and engaging.

Enter the modern field of human resources with a focus on the talent within the business. Today's HR functions are often referred to as "The People Function" or "Talent Function" for this reason. It's a continually maturing, evolving discipline, one where significant changes have completely reinvented what it means to be an HR professional and a leader in any business focusing on getting the most from your team members. As valuable as it is to know how HR has changed, it's just as important to know where it's headed. You need a clear sense of the trends that will continue to change the field in the future.

In this chapter, I outline the current trends that are impacting how HR and Talent leaders support the businesses they serve. Shifting employee expectations and needs are at the forefront of the changing dynamics within an organization, and organizational systems and processes must adapt to meet the needs of the current workforce and prospective employees. If organizations and HR and Talent leaders don't keep up, organizations will suffer, employees will leave, and ultimately the business will not be able to deliver to customers.

Working from Anywhere: The Hybrid Work Model

Changes in how employees work, where they work, who they work with, why they work, and the technologies they use are in continual flux. Many of these changes started prior to the pandemic, were accelerated by it, and have become permanent aspects of the workplace. HR and Talent leaders must adapt processes and systems to align with the new expectations. It's important that organizations create an employee experience that's aligned with the changing workforce expectations.

REMEMBER

Hybrid work (having the flexibility to work from home or in the office) is what the majority of workers want, so it's here to stay. Because many workers shifted to a hybrid model or even a full-time work at home (or work from anywhere) model during the pandemic, organizations quickly learned how to drive productivity and serve customers remotely, and this change was welcomed by the workforce overall. Employees view this freedom to work from anywhere as an important benefit of their job. A 2022 *Accenture* survey reported that 83 percent of workers prefer a hybrid work model and that 63 percent of high-growth companies have already adopted a "productivity anywhere" workforce model, so employees can choose between remote or on-site work.

Recognizing different types of hybrid work

The trend of a hybrid office offers a versatile approach to organizing a workplace and is flexible in design. Here are the different iterations the hybrid model can take:

>> **Partially remote:** This type implies some of the workforce working remotely and others on-site. It's a typical scenario for companies that can't move some of their processes to remote work due to security or hardware limitations, or the nature of the work being performed.

>> **Flexible remote:** Employees can manage their workflows and work some of the time (either days or hours) out of the office.

>> **Coworking:** A coworking-like organization of the office occurs where employees don't have a dedicated desk or a workplace. They book the workspaces in advance after they decide to work on-site.

Making the hybrid model work for all employees

Hybrid work policies are typically driven from the top, but in many organizations, leaders have autonomy to make decisions about how to lead and engage their teams. Regardless of where the decision is made, it's important for leaders to understand the importance of hybrid work and to seek opportunities for flexibility for team members.

REMEMBER

For both employees and employers, a hybrid work experience is about owning results, regardless of where or when work happens, so defining successful hybrid work policies and work from anywhere (WFA) practices is critical for employers. For example, employers are creating WFA policies that ensure virtual collaboration, mentoring, and asynchronous communication and brainstorming. These range from creating virtual communities of practice for remote workers to ensuring everyone who works remotely has the right set of collaboration tools as well as online whiteboards. Here are a few examples of a few widely used collaboration tools and applications:

>> **Asana:** Good for project management, communication, tracking and monitoring progress, and workload management

>> **Slack:** Good for creating shared channels for messaging, voice and video chats, and document management

>> **Trello:** Good for digital whiteboarding, team collaboration, and task management

Because HR leaders are focused on the employee experience and creating connection between team members, they're often leading the charge for encouraging the use of collaboration tools within their businesses. Most tools are inexpensive and the employer will invest in these tools to support team and employee success. These tools are easy to administer and use across the organization. An organizational administrator would be responsible for assigning access and setting team members up to use these tools.

In addition, it's important for leaders to communicate how their approach to management evolves as hybrid work opportunities expand. That means clearly defining how they'll create a fair and equitable workplace for all employees regardless of location, how leaders will manage employees they never physically see and who may live in different time zones, and how teams will achieve work flexibility while meeting their goals. Leaders must re-imagine how the post-pandemic business landscape will operate for their organization and communicate this to every team member.

Workplace Skills: Upskilling

Because of the shifting expectations within the workforce, HR and Talent leaders must ask themselves: Am I anticipating the development of new skills and capabilities for my team members and how am I doing this? To stay agile and adapt to external market challenges, organizations will implement upskilling initiatives to help their workforce stay competitive in the job market.

REMEMBER

Upskilling is the focused development that helps an individual become better at the job they're already doing. Upskilling helps employees acquire new skills that make them adaptable forces that can bend and shift with any new changes in your industry.

In fact, upskilling has become one of *the* key HR trends because it's a sustainable and lean approach to developing your workforce. Upskilling initiatives help HR professionals retain employees, boost morale, and cut costs on recruiting and onboarding. Chapter 14 addresses upskilling in more detail by providing best practices for providing the right growth experiences for all team members.

Leveraging People Analytics and Data-Driven HR

As organizations adapt to new workplace realities, there's an uptick in using data to improve performance and boost employee engagement. In a socially distanced work setting, data becomes even more important for HR decision-making. Known as *people analytics*, this branch of data discovery focuses on using information typically collected and stored by HR to deliver a better understanding of what employees are doing, why they're doing it, and how it impacts the organization. Industries such as finance have been leveraging data for years, and while their outcomes often focus on profit more than people, the basic principle is the same: Metrics matter.

The focus on data analytics in HR supports the shift to HR as a strategic business partner and away from HR as an administrative function.

Shifting HR leadership from administrative to strategic

Although many dynamics are driving the shift of HR as administrative to strategic function and there are many different examples of this shift, below are three ways in which that is happening within organizations:

» **The rise of the Chief People Officer (CPO) or head of HR's role in the company's processes:** To stay competitive within an organization, HR executives are adopting a data-driven mindset to assess current and future workforce demand, skill gaps, diversity in the workplace, and more.

For example, a venture capital firm has grown through acquisition and is experiencing a high level of turnover. Recognizing the need for change, the CEO brings in a new CPO to lead the strategy and processes related to building and retaining an exceptional team. Very quickly, the new CPO realizes that outdated systems and a lack of tracking key people metrics are foundational issues that need to be addressed. By acting as an adviser and consultant to the business and rallying the HR team, the new CPO builds relationships with other key senior leaders to drive change and execute solutions quickly.

» **Technologies that make a candidate's experience more engaging and dynamic:** These include AI-powered chatbots, screening tools, and recruitment automation tools. The growth and advancement of HR technologies are making it possible to gain better insight and allow HR to influence the business in new ways.

>> **Rapidly changing market forces:** Building more agility into the workplace and moving quickly is important for business leaders, given rapidly changing market forces. Coupled with an increasingly competitive market for talent, HR leaders are required to use analytics to make better decisions more quickly.

Recognizing what you can do

HR and Talent leaders who want to track the right metrics can take two key actions:

>> Define the key questions to answer for *your* business.

>> Ensure your systems and the business processes they support are capturing data that represent reality.

For example, a key metric that many organizations struggle to track is new-hire turnover. *New-hire turnover* is the percentage of employees who leave after the initial onboarding period (such as one week, one month, or three months). Tracking this metric measures the success of your recruiting (finding the right people) and onboarding processes (getting them productive and engaged). To ensure the metric is calculated effectively, you also need to inspect how data is being entered during recruiting, hiring, and termination processes to make sure the numbers are accurate, as well as to understand the why behind the numbers.

By starting with data and managing critical metrics, you can better position yourself to develop actionable insights that support the work of your colleagues and business. Business savvy HR leaders rely on data and metrics for decision-making because they know that data is the language of business. If you aren't currently doing so, it's time to take a more data-driven approach to your people strategy.

Leading Diversity, Equity, and Inclusion (DEI) in the Workplace

Diversity, equity, and inclusion (DEI) is a term used to describe policies and programs that promote the representation and participation of different groups of individuals, including people of different ages, races, ethnicities, abilities and disabilities, genders, religions, cultures, and sexual orientations. Creating an environment that leverages the diversity within the team and is inclusive and equitable is just good leadership.

Here I delve deeper into DEI and discuss what the benefits are to your organization and what you can do to ensure your workplace is diverse, equitable, and inclusive.

Considering the pros to a DEI workplace

In addition to being the right thing to do, research shows that a DEI workplace and financial performance are linked. According to a McKinsey & Company study, gender and ethnic diversity are correlated with profitability, and companies committed to DEI can attract top talent, enhance customer and employee satisfaction, and improve decision-making.

McKinsey & Company's study also found that on a global scale, the top-quartile companies on executive-level gender diversity had a 21 percent likelihood of outperforming their fourth-quartile industry peers on earnings before interest and taxes (EBIT) margin and had a 27 percent likelihood of outperforming fourth-quartile peers on value creation. The study also found that companies with the most ethnically diverse executive teams are 33 percent more likely to outperform their competitors on profitability. You can see more details of the study at www.mckinsey.com/business-functions/people-and-organizational-performance/our-insights/delivering-through-diversity.

DEI matters. A financial impact exists because equitable employers create diverse and inclusive workplaces where employees share unique perspectives, respect one another's individual needs, and reach their full potential without barriers. In addition to enhanced financial performance, successfully delivering diversity, equity, and inclusion in the workplace can lead to the following:

>> A more extensive talent pool

>> Increased employee engagement and satisfaction

>> Higher retention and lower turnover

>> Better decision-making

>> Greater innovation

>> Ability to outpace the competition

Creating a DEI workplace

You may be wondering what you can do to deliver DEI in the workplace. DEI practices should be woven into every HR and talent practice, including:

>> **Redefined hiring strategy:** Hiring is the first step to ensuring a diverse workforce. Diversity sourcing, blind hiring processes, and AI-powered candidate screening are common recruitment techniques that help organizations build diversified teams.

>> **Education and development initiatives:** Creating awareness and building skills that create a more inclusive environment. For example, Starbucks initiated anti-bias training for employees in the United States and Canada to fight race and ethnicity bias.

>> **Analytics and accountability:** People analytics help organizations set SMART (specific, measurable, achievable, realistic, and time-bound) diversity goals, measure impact of DEI initiatives, and create an inclusive workplace. With automated diversity tools, HR leaders are able to gain key insights across the employee lifecycle such as diversity of applicant pools and employees by function or level to find opportunities for improvement with actionable data at hand.

Even though I'm calling out diversity, equity, and inclusion in the workplace as an important HR trend, DEI should *always* be top-of-mind for leaders, and change doesn't happen overnight. Leaders must continuously revisit the state of diversity, equity, and inclusion in the workplace to assure employees that improvement is happening. Diversifying leadership teams is essential to ensure people from various backgrounds lead teams to a more equitable workplace. In most business settings, change starts at the top, and the right leaders have the power to inspire teams to champion DEI in the workplace.

For more information, check out *Diversity, Equity, & Inclusion For Dummies* by Dr. Shirley Davis (John Wiley & Sons, Inc.).

Prioritizing Employee Well-Being and Workforce Health

Employee well-being has expanded beyond physical well-being to a more holistic definition that encompasses the overall mental and emotional, physical, and economic health of your employees. Social, career, and community aspects, as well as having a sense of purpose, also influence well-being.

Here is additional information on each of the areas of focus and examples of how organizations and leaders are prioritizing the well–being of their team members:

» **Promoting mental health and emotional well-being:** Today's employees are stressed, living in a post-pandemic era with heightened social and political unrest and full of uncertainty. In addition, a hybrid work environment has blurred the line between work and life, so it's imperative for HR leaders to prioritize mental health. This focus is critical to developing workplace resilience and supporting success in all aspects of employees' lives.

Many companies use an employee assistance program (EAP) to support the mental health of team members. This confidential service provides direct access to mental health professionals over the phone, online, or in-person, and often, this resource is available to employee's immediate family members, as well. But promoting an environment that supports the mental health of all team members goes well beyond an EAP — it's important that executives and leaders communicate the importance of mental health and emotional well-being. Promote mental health benefits and resources in organizational communications. Chapter 12 discusses EAPs in greater detail.

» **Promoting physical well-being:** One of the best ways to improve mental health is to improve physical health, and although the importance of physical activity and a healthy lifestyle are well known, it can be difficult for employees to fit physical activity into their daily routines. But by doing so, employees will actually increase their productivity. Research shows that physical activity is associated with improved cognitive processing, which has big impact on productivity and performance.

Many organizations use policies such as offering flextime and paid activity breaks to employees to encourage physical activity. Leaders can also encourage short bursts of activity throughout the day or start team meetings with a quick stretch break. In addition, a common practice is to subsidize employee's gym memberships to encourage regular activity.

» **Promoting financial well-being:** Financial wellness has a significant effect on overall well-being and is likely to impact both physical and mental health, and yet, according to the Guardian's 2022 Annual Workplace Benefits Study, only one in five employees strongly agree that their employer does a good job at educating them on financial planning and how to achieve their financial goals.

A good start to increasing the economic health of your workforce starts with communicating your benefits offered to team members in a clear and focused way. Many employees don't understand the benefits their organization offers and miss out on programs and resources designed to improve their financial situation. In addition to communicating your benefits offerings, providing educational content that can be shared with employees to help increase their financial literacy around their benefits and other financial products helps to expand their awareness and sets them up for financial success.

>> **Promoting other influencers of well-being:** Many additional factors affect the well-being of team members, including the following:

- Their relationships with coworkers

- The decisions they make

- The tools and resources they have access to

- The level of flexibility that exists in their work

- Their sense of purpose

- The state of working for an organization whose values match their own

- Connection to the broader community

The pandemic has given employers increased visibility into the life struggles of their employees and has shifted the focus from just organizational issues to individual human life experiences. Leaders now view well-being not just as an employee benefit but as an opportunity to support employees in all aspects of their personal and work lives. In other words, it's a call for focusing much more on the *human* and much less on the human as a resource.

Chapter **3**

Leveraging HR Technology

The world of HR technology is booming, as leaders navigate the management of a remote workforce, identify solutions to match the pace of the environment, and solve business problems. In addition, integrating technology into HR operations helps to organize talent processes and ensure efficient delivery. HR leaders wear a lot of hats and are traditionally overworked and under-resourced, so technology eases the burden of administrative activities, captures key data, and boosts efficiency.

HR technology is an umbrella term for all of the technology that HR and business leaders use to strengthen the people processes within an organization and ultimately support business goals. The field of HR technology is evolving every day as work becomes increasingly technology enabled.

HR processes are an integral part of the business. As a result, a wide variety of technology tools and software helps different functions. However, the purpose of all HR technology is the same — to improve the employee experience and ensure an effective and strategic HR function.

Most businesses have implemented HR technology solutions into their work in recent years, but some organizations still have manual processes. Regardless of the scenario that you're in or the maturity of your business, this chapter provides key insight into how to best leverage HR technology to support your goals. I provide tips for staying up-to-date on the latest in HR technology, outline three categories of HR technology that are used within organizations, provide tips for sourcing HR technology for your business, and outline key technology skills for HR leaders.

Looking at the Growth of HR Technology

The world of HR technology can feel overwhelming, and many times HR leaders don't know where to start or how to keep up. New technologies and tools hit the market every day, and the trend is expected to continue. According to a 2022 report by Verified Market Research, the HR technology market is expected to reach $38.36 billion by 2030 (valued at $23.32 billion in 2021), growing at a compound annual growth rate of 5.7 percent from 2022 to 2030.

TIP

Don't be afraid of technology. Rather, recognize how helpful it can be for you and your business. Stay focused on your business goals to determine the right technology and tools to support your team members' success, and leverage the following ideas to remain in the know on what's happening in the world of HR technology:

>> **Network to build and maintain relationships.** Focus on other HR leaders both within and outside of your industry to know what others are doing to enable their HR and talent processes. Do one coffee chat a month with a peer you respect and ask how they're using technology and what new technology they're considering.

>> **Find out what other organizations are doing.** Look at others that are vetting HR technology objectively — SelectSoftware Reviews is an organization dedicated to simplifying the world of HR technology. As their founder, Phil Strazzulla (who provided input on this chapter as an expert in this area) says, "Our goal at SSR is to make sure you focus on the best HR and recruiting software vendors, with the right frameworks to make the best decision for your business." You can find out more about them on their website at www. selectsoftwarereviews.com

>> **Attend an HR technology–focused conference.** Go in-person or virtually to network with other leaders and experience many different technologies. These conferences also provide valuable education around how to best use technology to support business goals. Conferences such as HR Executive's HR Technology Conference host thousands of attendees each year in various locations around the country (see www.hrtechnologyconference.com).

>> **Use social media.** Search "#HRTech" on social sites (such as LinkedIn) to identify technology influencers and ensure HR tech news is a part of your feed.

>> **Participate in a demo a month on an HR technology tool you don't know anything about.** Experience is the best teacher, and this practice helps to ensure you stay up-to-date on tools in the market and the features they offer.

>> **Pay close attention to emerging technologies.** For example, look at artificial intelligence (AI) and how it may impact HR tech in the future.

>> **Talk to your colleagues in other departments.** Start with marketing/sales/products to discover the new technologies they're adopting that should have an HR equivalent (for example, chatbots came out in marketing a few years before they hit recruiting).

HR systems also can afford your business legal and financial protection. Consider the following:

>> **Wage and hour claims:** In some cases involving wage and hour laws, time and attendance systems may provide you with the means to rebut or mitigate claims of failure to pay for all time worked, failure to provide compliant meal periods, and other claims.

>> **Failure to hire:** Applicant tracking systems can help you implement a more consistent application and interview process. That can head off claims stemming from rejected job applicants.

>> **Wrongful termination:** Similar to providing data on applicants who don't make the cut, empirical documentation of employee performance can defeat allegations of unjustified dismissal.

HR TECHNOLOGY SYSTEMS AND SMALLER COMPANIES

In this chapter, I provide an overview of HR technologies even though not all of them will prove practical or affordable for companies of every size. I do this here — and with other HR tools and practices elsewhere in the book — because I feel it's part of the job for anyone in an HR role to have a current view of the entire landscape.

That said, it's only fair to point out that HR systems have become increasingly affordable as they become more modular. This scaling is made possible by cloud computing, which enables users to access applications or data stored on servers at a remote location (the cloud) through a web browser or mobile application. The arrangement not only reduces the hardware you have to maintain on-site but also allows you to purchase only the capabilities you need now, with the option of easily adding to them later.

Identifying the Categories of HR Tech

Technology applications within the HR field were initially focused on employee administration and recruitment, allowing for more efficient maintenance of employee records and automation of routine HR tasks and processes. And while these applications still exist, HR technology systems and platforms have matured to become critical tools in a number of decision-making processes central to a business. They're making efforts such as talent development and measurement more accurate and easier to manage.

Meanwhile, social tools are having a wide-reaching impact on the HR function, as HR professionals increasingly turn to them to achieve efficiencies in responsibilities ranging from hiring and training to internal collaboration and process improvement.

To map the HR technology ecosystem and keep it simple, I outline three categories of HR technology to consider: human resource information systems (HRIS), applicant tracking systems (ATS), and employee experience systems (a broad category including multiple subcategories such as engagement software, employee recognition systems, succession management systems, and so forth).

Human resources information systems

A human resources information system, or HRIS, (sometimes referred to as a human resources management system or HRMS) is a software solution used to collect, process, and store employee and organizational data and combines a number of features to help HR leaders at every level do their jobs more effectively. There are hundreds of HRISs on the market with different features and functionality. The key is to identify the needs of your organization (today and tomorrow) and identify a tool that works for you.

Although features of HRIS solutions vary, core functionality includes the following:

>> A centralized database to collect and store employee information

>> Payroll administration and compensation management

>> Benefits administration

>> Workflow, scheduling, and timekeeping

>> Recruitment processes and onboarding

>> Performance management

>> Workforce analytics (such as retention)

Here are the key benefits of using best-in-class HRIS, whether you're a small business or Fortune 500 company:

>> **An HRIS keeps everything organized.** If you're collecting and storing employee data manually, using an HRIS eliminates spending time sifting through paper files to find the information you need. An HRIS creates an easily searchable database of all employee-data points that administrators can access in seconds.

>> **It frees up time for HR leaders to handle more important tasks and add greater value to the business.** By automating recurring tasks such as benefits and payroll administration, employee onboarding, and time tracking and attendance management, your HRIS helps make tedious HR processes quick and simple. By automatically managing the tedious aspects of HR, an HRIS saves valuable time and allows HR leaders to work on more strategic initiatives to benefit your overall company. A strategic HR department can react to employee trends more easily and work on fostering a company culture that increases well-being and employee retention rates.

>> **It provides valuable data.** An HRIS can provide valuable insight on organizational data such as head count, salaries, retention rate, employee satisfaction, and the effectiveness of business initiatives. Leaders can then use this data to identify opportunities for improvement.

>> **It ensures regulatory compliance.** As a business leader, you're responsible for ensuring compliance with local, state, and federal regulations. An HRIS can help HR professionals comply with regulations and can also make the process of compiling information and reports much less painful and time consuming.

Applicant tracking systems

An applicant tracking system (ATS) offers a central location and database for an organization's recruiting efforts. Information can be gathered from internal applications as well as from external candidates from sources such as job boards. An ATS enables the review and management of applicant information and status. Other features may include the creation and administration of job requisitions, automated résumé ranking and evaluation, customized online applications, pre-evaluation questions, and response tracking. It also can generate interview requests to candidates via email.

There's no question that AI is rapidly changing the world of recruiting. Already, AI-powered applicant tracking systems are screening résumés, identifying potential candidates, and even conducting screening interviews. As AI continues to evolve and become integrated into the solution, it's likely that ATS software will become even more sophisticated and automate additional aspects of the process.

If you have more than 100 employees, you should be familiar with equal employment opportunity parameters. If you're considering applicant tracking systems, ask about features that automatically address Equal Employment Opportunity Commission (EEOC) compliance. That way, you stay as up-to-date as possible.

When you're ready to review résumés for a particular position, e-recruiting systems pre-evaluate them to identify appropriate experience, skills, education, and other credentials. The systems scan for keywords, work history, years of experience, and education. The technology identifies likely candidates and ranks them. Candidates who place poorly are weeded out from further consideration.

Applicant tracking systems can integrate with email solutions and text messages to more easily handle résumés that are submitted electronically. This allows for automated follow-up with candidates who have been screened out.

REMEMBER

Don't look to an ATS to take the human touch out of the hiring equation. They're designed to make your involvement more time efficient and more effective, but taking their results at face value in every case is risky.

When reviewing résumés, question vague descriptions of skills, such as familiar with and was involved in — if the skill is critical for the role, you may want to focus on digging further in that area during the interview process to ensure the candidate has the level of experience needed. Also, ask references to confirm basic information you see on a résumé, such as the candidate's employment history, job titles, responsibilities, and salary. You also can work with a reputable staffing firm that is skilled at identifying experienced job candidates for your business.

Employee experience systems

Employee experience systems form a broad category of HR technologies supporting multiple aspects of the employee experience — setting team members up for success, managing performance, providing motivation and encouragement, and so on. An employee experience system is less about the administrative part of HR and more about developing and better utilizing an organization's people, its talent.

Following is an overview of the types of systems that many organizations are using to assess and improve their employee experience (please note that there is overlap within many of the tools/systems I note because many tools offer multiple features).

Performance management systems

Performance management systems are designed to measure as accurately as possible how well an employee is meeting the responsibilities and challenges of their particular position. A key advantage is the capacity to minimize any subjectivity in the overall review of an employee. For instance, some systems include comprehensive position success profiles/competencies that allow an accurate and empirical picture of whether an employee is, in fact, fulfilling the requirements of that particular job. That makes it easier to provide ongoing coaching and support to employees to set them up for success.

In a nutshell, many performance management systems let managers view employee goals and objectives and, from there, enter information and feedback as to whether that person has met those goals. At the same time, the employee is completing a similar form. From there, similarities and discrepancies can be identified. It creates important, ongoing visibility for both managers and team members.

Employee engagement software

Assessing team member engagement is an important activity for business leaders because employee engagement affects every aspect of your organization, including profitability, revenue, customer experience, and employee retention. To stay on top of the pulse of the business and engagement levels at all levels, organizations use employee engagement software.

These tools help leaders solicit and track feedback from their employees, recognize employee achievements, and promote positive activity. Most important is the data that employers can glean — leaders can use the data to act on areas of improvement to increase engagement.

Learning management systems

A learning management system (LMS) offers a centralized structure for a company's learning and development efforts. In effect, it streamlines employee access and content delivery as well as the tracking and reporting of your educational programs. Another key function is to help you analyze what's working and what may need your attention with regard to your learning initiatives. LMS technology gives you access to specifics about a person's progress and other data.

As with most HR technology, there are many LMS vendors to choose from. A good system allows you to administer and capture data tied to all aspects of your learning programs, including mobile platforms for employee learning on the go and social components, which involve learning from facilitators or even peers through informal online channels such as blogs, podcasts, or video content.

An LMS also can help you coordinate other efforts, such as mentoring and performance reviews, with your learning and development efforts.

Employee recognition software

Employee recognition goes a long way in boosting the morale of team members and creating a culture of community and connection. Setting up an organization-wide recognition system can be challenging, especially if your managers and HR department oversee a lot of people, so employee recognition software can help to streamline and encourage employees' efforts.

To evolve and improve the employee experience, employee recognition software focuses on identifying employees' successes in the workplace as well as noting any significant benchmarks. This type of system works to improve the workplace culture by recognizing what employees do well and by supporting employees to recognize each other in different ways — for doing great work, for exhibiting company values, and for wishing them well on important personal dates like birthdays. Furthermore, this type of software tracks peer recognition and reward options — by managing things like points, gifts, certificates, gift cards, and more. Although someone in your HR department oversees the software, any employee can access it.

In addition, these systems are often integrated with internal communication tools such as Slack, Teams, Outlook, and other technology that employees use every day, making access to such tools easier.

Succession management systems

Succession management systems can automate many of the tasks associated with succession planning. These can include laying out the necessary leadership and experience prerequisites for certain positions as well as hosting checklists that allow you to track when employees have reached specific benchmarks. Some applications also let you map out what-if scenarios. For instance, if a particular leader were to leave the company unexpectedly, who (if anyone) in the developmental process would be best positioned to immediately assume those new responsibilities?

Succession software also can remove or, at the very least, mitigate some of the subjective forces that can negatively impact succession management.

Choosing the Systems That Are Right for You

When selecting HR systems, take the time to really understand your needs and identify the system that will best support your goals. Speak with enough vendors to give you an adequate overview of the differences from product to product. And don't be shortsighted with the questions you ask. Does the proposed system have the capacity to grow as your business grows? What level and quality of support can you expect from your vendor? In short, which system best fits your specialized needs — now and in the future?

A key consideration in choosing any new system is integration. According to Gartner, 68 percent of software implementations fail, and often it's because the organization didn't choose the right software for their needs. Other considerations include how well it matches up with any current systems you may be using and how well it integrates with other tools employees are using on a regular basis that may not be HR system. Whether going with an all-in-one or an a-la-carte approach, it's important to start with the end result in mind. You need to have an idea of what the finished solution is going to look like in order to understand the implementation phases and what you're going to be asking users to work with.

A key consideration in deciding whether to go with the a-la-carte approach is that a substantial integration effort often is required. A company already using one system for payroll and benefits, for example, may want to implement another one for recruiting. These systems have different user interfaces, system designs, and approval flows, all of which end-users have to learn and manage on a daily basis. That fragmentation needs to be weighed against the feature set of a certain application or vendor.

Sometimes vendors will have already taken care of integration (an example includes SuccessFactors, which is designed to "talk with" Jobvite for applicant tracking). But generally, a core HRIS stores the majority of the HR data and is considered the system of record for the other tools. Links must be established to any a-la-carte applications you want to add. For instance, when you hire a new employee, you may add their information to the core HRIS. It then must interface with your payroll administration system, benefits administration system, LMS, and so on in order for the new employee's data to carry over to those systems as well. These integrations can become complex and should be factored into the decision process.

Given the speed at which technology changes, you may want to consider engaging a specialized HR technology consultant when deciding on a first system or a system upgrade for your organization. There are solid reasons to consider external expertise. Technology isn't a cosmetic issue. It's a vital part of your business and should be approached in that manner. If you lack some of the technical know-how to properly integrate HR systems with your primary business needs, an external resource can provide valuable insight. Regardless of whether you hire a consultant, it pays to do some research on your own.

Sourcing and Purchasing HR Technology: The How-To

Here are key steps in the sourcing and purchasing process. Remember that you have the power as the person purchasing the technology. Rather than deferring to others, lead the process and engage other stakeholders (such as other key business leaders, external expertise, and vendors) throughout the process.

1. Make the business case for the technology.

If you can't make the case, you don't need the tool. Take the time to define the pain you're trying to alleviate and determine the return on investment (ROI) by considering the before and after state. This highlights the value the new technology can bring to the business.

2. Get buy-in and align with relevant parts of the business.

Determine who needs to be involved in the process and involve them early to ensure alignment on the needs outlined in the business case. In particular, partner with IT and legal leaders within your business given the ever-increasing importance of data privacy and security. Involve them early to leverage their expertise throughout the process.

3. Evaluate the vendors.

Evaluate five to seven vendors that can solve your pain points. The primary question to ask these vendors is how they can solve the problem you outline in the business case (see Step 1). Send them your must-haves so that they're clear on your needs. This helps to ensure that you don't get dazzled by their favorite bells and whistles, but instead, you stay focused on your needs.

4. Organize the vendor information.

Keep track of what you find out and make notes on each of the vendors so that you can share and use this information at the right time. In particular, make notes about the systems' ability to provide your "must haves" as well as the "nice to haves."

TIP

In addition, take notes on your interaction with the vendor teams and how well you connect with and engage with them — these relationships will be important should you choose to purchase their system.

5. Narrow down your list to two or three systems to demo.

Ask vendors to create a dummy profile for you so you can actually test how well the system does the things you need it to do. Recruit people who are going to use the system to practice using it and create a process for them to provide feedback on the tools they demo. Do the demos within a short time frame so you can easily compare user experiences across the systems you test.

6. **Regroup with internal stakeholders to ensure alignment.**

Following the demos, reconnect with the key stakeholders whose buy-in is most important. During this meeting, review the business case again to ensure that the solutions you're looking at solve the problem you've defined. This discussion will help you identify which vendors to move forward with.

7. **Negotiate the contract.**

Don't be afraid to negotiate pricing for HR technology — there's always wiggle room. The smarter the buyer you are and the more research you've done, the more vendors will respect you and the pricing they offer will reflect that. Ensure that you get the best price and terms you can without delaying the buying process by starting negotiations before determining the specific vendor you will work with. It's also important to engage legal counsel in the contract review to look for red flags.

8. **Conduct final vendor vetting.**

Based on your check-in with stakeholders, demos, and contract negotiations, narrow your search to two vendors. Ask to speak to a current customer and try to find a customer that wasn't recommended by the vendor to talk to and probe into their experience. Connect with your network to identify successes and challenges others have had with the systems you're exploring. Ask specific questions about how you'll use the tech to ensure the vendor is able and willing to get into the weeds with you.

Communicating the Value of HR Tech

An important final step for purchasing new HR technology is capturing and communicating the value that it adds to the organization after implementation. Go back to your business case and show the impact of the technology by highlighting the before and after states.

This applies not only for new technology but also for all the tools and systems you're using to fuel talent and HR processes. Utilize the reporting capabilities within your HR systems. Identify the right opportunities to communicate this information on an ongoing basis with key leaders. This gets you more internal credibility and support to reinforce other new initiatives and efforts. It also provides evidence that HR and talent processes are key for business success.

Identifying Technology Skills You Need

Many HR leaders struggle to keep up as new technologies are coming out on an almost daily basis. HR needs to be more agile now more than ever before, but the key isn't to know all of the technologies — it's to have a technology-enabled mindset and continually be thinking about how to best leverage and integrate technology into your ways of working.

In today's world, technological skills are no longer a bonus, but a necessity for HR leaders. For example, all HR and Talent leaders need to be able to do the following:

>> **Know how to use social media platforms.** Use them to promote the business and team member accomplishments and successes and to communicate key information about the business.

>> **Integrate gamification into HR and talent processes.** Connection, collaboration, and motivation become that much better when elements of competition and fun are woven into HR and talent processes. Examples are real-life simulations built into learning and development efforts and a values-based puzzle or game included to determine fit with the culture and environment.

>> **Develop HR data analytics skills.** HR technology provides data that reflect important insights into the workforce. Knowing how to harness the data to make business decisions is key. HR data analytics is the process of examining the data to identify trends and drawing conclusions. This helps HR leaders to focus their efforts on those that best support business success.

2

Putting the Right People in the Right Roles

Align talent needs with the business strategy to determine the skills and expertise you need to move your business forward.

Leverage contract and contingent talent to round out specific talent needs beyond current and full- or part-time talent as your business flexes or expands.

Get clear on the talent you need and develop position success profiles that define what success looks like.

View recruiting as an ongoing sales process.

Source, screen, and hire talent aligned with the outcomes of the position you're hoping to fill.

IN THIS CHAPTER

» **Defining your employer brand, starting with core values**

» **Grasping the basics of workforce planning**

» **Being cognizant of worker classifications**

» **Leveraging a contingent workforce**

Chapter **4**

Creating a Talent Strategy Aligned with Business Strategy

B ecause the people within your business are your business, ensuring the *right* people is a must for business success. That's where a talent strategy comes in. Simply put, a talent strategy ensures that you get and keep good talent. This chapter addresses the foundational aspects of your talent strategy, and because getting and keeping the right talent isn't one-size-fits-all across organizations, always consider what is most helpful for your organization, given your organizational goals and vision.

Talent processes have changed dramatically with advances in technology and people's evolving relationship with work. For example, gone are the days in which organizations posted open positions and received hundreds of qualified applicants. Acquiring talent is a marketing and sales process that starts with your employee value proposition and an understanding of how the open position can move the organization forward. Only then are you able to attract the right talent for your business.

Attracting the right talent starts not with unrelated, ad hoc efforts to close a perceived gap, but rather with a comprehensive approach based on your overall organization priorities and an understanding of what's happening in the talent market. In short, you want to get a big-picture view of your workforce needs, understand your employee value proposition, and create a systematic, cost-effective plan to attract the right talent. That's what this chapter is all about.

Getting Clear on Your Employer Brand

The traditional hiring notion of finding the best people to fill job openings has been replaced by a much more dynamic concept that starts with what the organization has to offer prospective employees. It's generally referred to as *employer brand* and includes two parts:

>> An employer's reputation as a place to work

>> The employee value proposition

REMEMBER

Companies and organizations are at war for finding the best talent, and the workforce has never had a greater choice, so in order for your organization to attract the best talent, you must be clear on what you offer employees as opposed to the more general corporate brand or customer value proposition.

The good news is that your organization already has an employer brand — it's the company's reputation as a place to work. The key is to name and document it so that you can use it with prospective employees, and the best place to start is with your organizational values. Here I touch on these two facets to help you clarify your core values.

Recognizing what core values are

Core values are the guiding principles and beliefs that underpin a company and its employees. For example, I lead a professional services business (HRD — A Leadership Development Company). Key components of our employer brand include growth and service. At HRD, our core values are growth, service, and connection, and we've defined specific behaviors for these values in actions with clients (externally) and with each other (internally). The values guide all of our decisions and shape our culture.

We offer employees variety — the opportunity to work with many leaders across large, global organizations. We offer a work-from-anywhere model that allows flexibility for employees to integrate work and life activities. Because of our mission, vision, and values, our employer brand is different from a large production organization whose value proposition includes stability, career pathing, and an attractive total rewards package.

Figuring out your organization's values

Here's a simple five-step process for determining (or validating) your organization's values. *Note:* Many organizations overcomplicate this process. Your organization already has a brand, and similarly, you have values, so this process is about exploring and documenting them. I encourage you to engage key leaders/team members in this process to get different perspectives:

1. **Identify four to five top performers/superstars in your organization and write down their key leadership attributes.**

   Determine what about these leaders differentiates them and the value they bring to the business and your customers.

2. **Identify four or five employees who haven't been successful in your organization.**

   Write down the attributes/characteristics that most hindered their success in the business.

3. **Identify three to five key themes across both lists and notice connections.**

4. **Based on your observations, identify three to five core values.**

   Limit these values to no more than five to keep the process simple and focused.

5. **Over a period of time (one to three months) use the core values as a guide in your decision-making to validate and/or shift the final list of values.**

After you determine your organization's values, you can use them in the recruiting process to define your employer brand and the culture.

Workforce Planning: Aligning Talent Needs with Business Strategy

With a clear employer brand, you're in a good position to attract talent. Before you do that, however, you need to take the time to review where your organization is going and what its needs are — in other words *workforce planning,* which I discuss here. The goal of workforce planning is to have the right people in the right roles at the right time. That happens by knowing the current workforce capabilities, planning future scenarios based on your company's business goals and strategy, determining the desired workforce, and taking steps to align the future workforce with this desired workforce.

Being strategic with workforce planning

The idea is to begin thinking in terms of need rather than job, long term rather than short term, and big picture rather than immediate opening. To succeed, you need a firm understanding of your organization's goals and priorities.

A strategic workforce plan ensures that you get the most out of your current workforce while preparing for the changes to come. The place to start is your organization's vision and goals — what are you trying to achieve? Then, identify the skills necessary for success and the talent you'll need to support those goals. Table 4-1 shows the difference between the traditional approach to acquiring talent and a strategic approach based on workforce planning.

TABLE 4-1 Paradigms: Old and New

Old Staffing Paradigm	Strategic Workforce Planning
Think job.	Think competencies and outcomes that drive business goals and enhance a company's ability to compete.
Create a set of job specs.	Determine which competencies and skills are necessary to produce outstanding performance in any particular function.
Find the person who best fits the job.	Determine which combination of talent can best handle the tasks and responsibilities that need to be carried out.
Look mainly for technical competence.	Find people who are more than simply technically qualified but who also can carry forward your company's mission and values.
Base the hiring decision primarily on the candidate interview.	View the candidate interview as only one of a series of tools designed to make the best hiring decision.
Hire only full-time employees.	Consider a blend of full- and part-time employees and contingent workers to meet variable workload needs.

Looking at your company's overall priorities, your job is to determine the staffing implications. You need to make sure that any staffing decision clearly supports these business priorities. To do so, look beyond the purely functional requirements of the various positions in your company. Focus instead on what skills and attributes workers need to perform those roles exceptionally well as well as skills gaps that exist within your current workforce.

Unless you're a sole proprietor or run a very small business, you can't adopt a strategic staffing approach all by yourself. Make it a priority to reinforce the concept with other managers in your organization. You need their input to better understand company and departmental priorities — and they need your help in guiding them through the process and adopting this mindset as well.

To get you started, here are some of the key questions that you and other people in your organization should answer before you make your next move:

>> What are your organization's long-term strategic goals or those of departments seeking your assistance in hiring?

>> What are the key competitive threats in your industry? In other words, what factors have the greatest bearing on your organization's ability to compete successfully?

>> What kind of culture currently exists in your organization? And what kind of culture do you ultimately want to create? What are the values you want the organization to stand for?

>> What knowledge, skill sets, and general attributes are required to keep pace with business goals and, at the same time, remain true to your organization's values?

>> How does the current level of knowledge, skill sets, and attributes among today's workforce match up with what will be necessary in the future?

>> How reasonable is it for you to expect that, with the proper support and development, your current employees will be able to develop the skills they're going to need for your organization to keep pace with the competition? In addition to on-the-job experience within an employee's current role, would programs such as job rotation help reach these objectives?

Change is the name of the game in business. Organization priorities will undoubtedly shift over time as leadership innovates and identifies ways to keep the firm competitive. As a result, you should consider performing a needs assessment on an annual basis. That helps ensure that you're still on track with the assumptions and priorities that are guiding your staffing strategy. Workforce planning is an ongoing activity, not an event.

Developing potential within the current team

Workforce planning isn't just about hiring more employees. It involves making the best staffing choices available to address the core business needs you and the hiring manager have identified.

For some needs, you may not have to hire at all. Your job is to help company hiring managers strategically — and honestly — evaluate projects and focus their teams' efforts on only those that grow revenues, increase efficiency, reduce expenses, or meet other company priorities.

If a line manager you support is thinking of filling an existing position, encourage them to consider how their group's most critical needs may have changed since the last time the job was open instead of immediately searching for a candidate to fill the vacant position. Is a full-time individual still required in this role? And should a potential replacement have the same skills and experience as their predecessor?

In some cases, employees may have full work schedules, but their expertise isn't devoted to the right projects. Ask the hiring manager to focus here:

» Analyze their work group's daily activities to better understand how current resources are allocated. Needs identified as crucial may be handled in a variety of ways to best utilize the team.

» Suggest the idea of creating project teams to focus on critical, but temporary, activities to the manager of a group who feels that there is a case for new staff. These groups could then be quickly disbanded or reassembled, depending on changing needs.

» Look at current positions and consider combining the responsibilities of two less critical positions into one to free up a staff member who can help out elsewhere.

TIP

Encourage line managers to look at their group's projects and attempt to match staff members with assignments best suited to their talents, even if some tasks fall outside their traditional job duties. Better utilizing the skills and experience of each person can help teams operate more efficiently.

Also, discuss with hiring managers whether it makes sense to provide targeted learning and development to current team members. Organizing a development session to help a team better utilize a common software program, for example, may be a cost-effective way to increase the group's efficiency and develop the potential within the current team.

Finding Inner Peace: Filling Jobs from within the Organization

Redeploying full-time staff may partially address rising demands, but this step alone isn't likely to be the answer to all your company's staffing concerns. At some point, you'll need to replace people who leave your organization. And you'll also need access to fresh ideas and perspectives to help your company grow by bringing in new staff. These sections discuss how you can fill those open positions from within your organization.

Recognizing the pros (and cons)

Before seeking outside talent, consider whether refilling positions or creating new ones by using internal resources may best serve your workforce plan. In other words, first consider promoting from within. Here are the key reasons:

>> **Increased efficiency:** Filling jobs from within usually takes less time and is generally less costly (in the short term, at least) than hiring from the outside.

>> **Increased morale:** Hiring from within sends a message to team members at all levels of your organization that good performance gets rewarded.

>> **Shorter adjustment period:** Everything else being equal, an existing employee requires a lot less time to acclimate to the new job than an employee who's never been with your organization.

The drawbacks of filling positions from within? Only two, really.

>> Limiting your search to internal candidates limits the pool, and you may end up promoting someone who isn't as qualified or doesn't have the future potential of an external candidate.

>> Whenever you recruit from within, you always run a risk that otherwise important and valuable employees who don't get the job may become resentful and even eventually decide to leave the organization.

That's why it's essential to establish an atmosphere of trust when looking to existing employees for available positions. Make it clear that employees can be comfortable applying for open internal positions. No employee should be concerned about repercussions, such as a manager or supervisor being frustrated that they want to change jobs when they're doing "just fine" in their current position.

REHIRING FORMER STAFF MEMBERS

Don't discount the idea of rehiring former staff members who left on good terms. You already know the person, so recruiting and hiring expenses can be low. And, when you rehire a former staffer, you already have a pretty good sense of what you're getting.

However, be as selective with former employees as you would be with any other hire. Focus on those with outstanding performance records, both with your company and in their endeavors since. If your company culture or values have changed since the employee left, make sure the former employee is still a suitable fit.

Creating a successful internal hiring process

Key procedures you need to put in place to set up a successful internal hiring process include establishing a way to communicate job opportunities to your team members and a procedure they can use to submit applications. Go out of your way to ensure that everyone understands the scope and basic duties of the job as well as the hiring criteria you're using. You also must make sure that whatever system you use to alert team members to job opportunities in the company everyone gets a fair shot at the opening. This is an important aspect of creating a culture of equal employment opportunity.

Developing an employee skills inventory

If you see yourself hiring internally at some point down the road, a dynamic *employee skills inventory* that you plan for in advance can be a great help when the time comes. This inventory is exactly what the name implies: a portfolio of the human capital in your company — a catalog of the individual skills, attributes, credentials, and areas of knowledge that currently exist.

See the online tools for a Blank Skills Inventory Form and a Sample Skills Inventory Form.

FIND ONLINE

Knowing where to look for internal talent

When beginning your search for internal candidates, you don't have to search far. Most organizations have traditionally maintained a personnel file or job history file for each employee. The difference lies in how the information is categorized. Conventional job histories tend to focus on accomplishments. An employee skills inventory focuses on the skills and attributes that led to those accomplishments — and that can be called upon once again.

You may assume that this practice is one that is suitable only for big organizations. And you may assume, too, that the process is more bother than it's worth. Neither assumption is necessarily true.

Even if your organization is relatively small, it still may be worth the time and effort to develop the capability of pulling an employee skills inventory. The chief benefit is that, instead of picking your way through reams of folders to compile a list of people who may be logical candidates for an opening, you simply search your employee profile database using specific categories.

REMEMBER

Some of the categories you may want to pull from the employee profile include the following:

>> **Skills/knowledge areas:** Business-related functions or activities in which the employee has either special knowledge or a proven record of proficiency.

>> **Second-language skills:** Anything other than English. Emphasize that familiarity with another language isn't enough; the candidate must be fluent if they're going to assist customers or work with suppliers who communicate in that language.

>> **Special preferences:** Requests the employee has made about their own aspirations, other jobs in the company they want to pursue, or areas of the country (or world) to which they may be interested in relocating.

>> **Educational background:** Schools, degrees, and subjects in which the employee majored and minored.

>> **Job history at your organization:** Include the title, department, organizational unit, and actual job duties the employee has performed.

>> **Previous job history:** Include the same general information as for the preceding category but for the employee's prior employers.

>> **Learning & Development courses and seminars:** List the program, topics covered, and, if applicable, the format and timing of the development experience.

>> **Assessment results:** Key results, if applicable, of any company-sanctioned assessments or other types of measurement activities that the employee has formally undergone during their tenure at the organization.

>> **Licenses, credentials, and affiliations:** Obviously, all these categories should be work related and logically linked to the tasks and responsibilities of the job. (A warehouse employee who's going to operate a forklift, for example, doesn't need a certificate from a stunt-driving school, and the person you hire to supervise the kitchen of your company cafeteria doesn't need to belong to an international wine society.)

REMEMBER

The preceding list is meant to be a set of recommendations, nothing more. You can incorporate into your own employee skills inventory anything that you consider relevant. Just be careful that, as you develop your inventory (and the employee profile that drives that inventory), you don't inadvertently violate any equal employment opportunity (EEO) laws. If you have any question about any category, check with legal counsel.

The more in touch you are with the existing talents, skills, and attributes of your people, the easier time you'll have getting the most out of their expertise. Your employee profiles and skills inventory is a valuable tool.

New Horizons: Attracting Talent from Outside Your Organization

For all its virtues, a workplace plan that's built almost entirely around promoting from within isn't always the best way to go — especially if your organization has never taken the time and effort to develop a well-structured career development program (see Chapter 15).

Bringing in new talent to assist you (or other company managers) in running the business is a large part of your responsibility in your HR role. Likewise, it's a major concern of this book. Here are the basic arguments for looking outside your organization to locate talent:

>> **A broader selection of talent:** Basic mathematics shows that if your search is confined solely to your current team members, the pool of likely candidates will be a lot smaller than if you're looking outside the company.

>> **The "new blood" factor:** Bringing in outside talent can go a long way toward diminishing the "We've always done it that way syndrome." Recruiting from outside helps to foster creativity, innovation, and a new way of thinking.

>> **The diversity factor:** Workforce diversity (or the effort to allow and encourage diversity in the workplace) enables an organization to draw on the resources, expertise, and creativity of people from the widest possible range of backgrounds: gender, age, color, national origin, ethnicity, and other factors. It also makes good business sense (see Chapter 6).

A Wide World of Talent: Understanding Worker Classification

When looking outside the company for talent, you have a number of options.

If core team members are at full capacity and you have new tasks that must be handled on an ongoing basis, hiring additional full-time or part-time employees probably makes the most sense. Much of the advice in this book concerns this option — hiring and managing a core team of employees — and I address the best ways to go about this in upcoming chapters.

If, however, upcoming projects are of limited duration or you need specialized skills unavailable internally, then a mix of full-time employees and contingent workers may be your best bet. Here, I delve a bit deeper into planning your workforce strategically from a practical standpoint.

There's a wide world of talent in the market, and you don't have to approach tapping into it the same way for every individual or job. You can engage workers in different ways that depend on your particular needs at the time you're recruiting. But you have to know what you're doing when you engage workers who are not employees of your company in the traditional sense.

The relationship of various workers to your organization is of key concern to federal and state governments, in particular the agencies responsible for collecting payroll taxes. Confusion around these relationships drives a large number of lawsuits, and it's critical that you understand the differences. The three factors determining how workers serve an organization are as follows:

» Their relationship to the company in need of their services (the capacity in which they work)

» The duration of their engagement (short term or long term)

» The schedule they work (part time or full time)

Of these three, relationship is most important from a legal standpoint. The following sections discuss the three basic types of worker relationships: employee, contingent worker, and independent contractor (IC). Factoring in duration and schedule, workers in all three relationship categories may be full time, part time, short term, or long term.

FIND
ONLINE

See the Worker Classification Quick Reference Table online for a printout you can keep handy that explains the major differences between these three.

Employees

Companies hiring *employees* are required to pay whatever payroll taxes are required by law and must also withhold applicable state, federal, and local taxes. Employees can be either full time or part time, and they may be hired either on a short-term basis or on an ongoing, indefinite basis. Regular part-time employees enjoy many of the same benefits (usually on a prorated scale) and the same federal and state protections as full-time employees.

Contingent workers

Contingent workers are employees of a staffing firm, which for a fee assigns them to client companies to augment the client's employees or provide skills and knowledge not available internally to the client. This category includes temporary to full-time staffing but not ICs. Staffing firms employing contingent workers are required to pay whatever payroll taxes are required by law and must withhold applicable state, federal, and local taxes. As with all three of the worker relationships, contingent workers can be either full time or part time and either short term or long term. Companies can conceivably hire contingent workers on their own, but using a staffing firm is strongly advised.

Correctly defining contingent workers can be tricky for someone beginning in an HR role (or anyone, for that matter) because there are no uniform, commonly understood terms used to describe them. In fact, contingent workers often are described collectively and interchangeably as temporary, contract, interim, leased, or project-based workers; consultants; or other designations.

Contingent workers represent a large segment of the workforce, and the tasks they perform are varied ranging from administrative to strategic, specialized support. For this reason, I discuss contingent workers in more detail in the section, "Benefitting from Contingent Workers," later in this chapter.

REMEMBER

For clarity with regard to worker classification, I consistently use the term *contingent workers* throughout this book whenever I refer to individuals employed by a staffing firm and assigned to a client company — even when the workers are professional-level specialists, an increasingly likely scenario in today's business world.

Independent contractors

Strictly defined, an *IC* also referred to as a *freelancer* controls the methods and means of performing their tasks and is responsible to the organization they're working with only for the results. The organization engaging the IC has no tax liability and almost no other administrative responsibility other than paying the invoice and reporting payments on 1099 forms.

WARNING

You can't be too careful when working with ICs. There is a significant risk that the Internal Revenue Service (IRS) may not agree with your interpretation of an IC or contingent worker and may declare that the proper classification of the worker is as an employee. Likewise, the person in question may claim that they never should've been treated as an IC but, instead, should've been treated as an employee, entitled to the various financial and other benefits associated with an employer/employee relationship. You must understand the specific distinctions between ICs and employees. Seek the advice of a knowledgeable and experienced lawyer for help in this sensitive area.

Benefitting from Contingent Workers

In today's *gig economy* (a labor market characterized by the prevalence of short-term contracts or freelance work as opposed to permanent jobs), contingent workers are a significant part of the workforce. More and more talented people are drawn to contingent work because of the flexibility and opportunities this arrangement provides. It enables them to pursue personal and professional goals and, at the same time, explore a variety of industries. Contingent assignments allow job seekers to try out work in different firms and office cultures, and, in fact, many times a contingent engagement may become a full-time employment opportunity. This group includes working parents who want more time to devote to their children, team members acting as caregivers to elderly parents, and people at retirement age who still want to be active but perhaps not on a full-time basis. For these and many others, contingent work fills the bill.

New thinking about contingent working arrangements is evident not only among these workers themselves but also among the businesses that engage them. A 2020 Intuit Study found 80 percent of large U.S. corporations plan to increase their use of flexible workforces, with contingent workers making up more than 40 percent of the total workforce. In addition, 62 percent of enterprises perceive contingent labor as a vital component of their overall workforce, according to research firm Ardent Partners. Organizations are increasingly attracted by the labor cost flexibility they can gain though a combination of full-time or part-time employees and contingent workers.

Given the importance of this topic, in the next two sections, I outline the key advantages to addressing your talent needs with contingent workers and how to determine when contingent talent is the right approach for your business.

Noting the pros to contingent workers

The flexibility of variable-cost labor provides an advantage to organizations that seek greater control over their HR budgets and appreciate having access to skilled talent when and for as long as they need that talent. In fact, as companies continually rebalance their workforces to remain profitable in both good and difficult times, many are discovering that a *year-round* mix of core employees and contingent workers is their best bet for ultimate flexibility.

Here are some advantages to using contingent workers in your workforce mix:

>> It allows departments to adjust staffing levels to the ebb and flow of business cycles, thus helping to keep overhead costs under control.

>> It eases the work burden on employees who may already be spread too thin because of business demands or duties added to their roles from prior layoffs or downsizing.

>> It offers departments a way to handle special projects — or special problems — that lie beyond the expertise of current staff members.

>> It gives the organization an opportunity to engage — on a short-term basis — high-level specialists it can't afford for the long term.

>> It creates job stability for a core group of full-time workers in highly cyclical businesses. Otherwise, those sorts of businesses need to subject their workforces to constant nerve-racking cycles of hiring and layoffs as the demands of the business fluctuate.

>> It provides what amounts to a trial period for potential new employees. If, as your needs evolve, you decide to consider converting a contingent worker to employee status, you have the advantage of already knowing some of the individual's capabilities and personal attributes.

>> It allows an organization to grow and scale more quickly, especially when in-demand skill sets are required.

Determining whether they're the right fit

The more proactive and strategic you and hiring managers are in approaching your talent needs, the bigger the payoff. However, before you use contingent workers, answer these threshold questions:

>> **What specific tasks do you need someone to perform and over what time period?** The shorter the time period, the more inclined you should be to seek contingent help.

>> **What skills or expertise are necessary to perform those tasks?** Generally speaking, the use of contingent workers enables you to tap into a knowledge base that's far broader than you can find in your current staff.

>> **Can people who are on the organization's payroll perform those tasks — without affecting other aspects of their job performance and without creating excessive overtime costs?** Balancing basic responsibilities with additional tasks isn't easy. To answer this question, departmental managers will likely look to you and your HR colleagues because you're probably more familiar with the skills and workloads of people in all parts of the company.

>> **Can the department and company afford the extra cost involved to engage highly skilled supplemental staff?** Think overall value, not just immediate expense.

>> **Can I build a team with this skill set in the time frame needed?** It's important to understand market availability and costs associated with specific skill sets to determine whether it would be more cost effective and also feasible to bring the skills into your organization in a needed time frame.

You can engage many types of contingent workers on your own without going through a staffing/recruiting firm. You also can run a marathon in a pair of sandals.

The case for using a firm to help execute a contingency staffing strategy is strong. Firms that specialize in providing contingent workers already have a pool of experienced people they can assign to your company. They understand the complex legalities (including tax-related issues) of contingency staffing. They handle all the paperwork. The cost is a little more than the average pay rate for people in that particular specialty, but the staffing firm handles preliminary evaluation of the candidate and government-mandated benefits and assumes responsibilities as the employer of record.

Your company has a number of options, as staffing firms expand their services in efforts to remain competitive. But with so many options available, making the right choice can be a challenge. Reputation is important. The best job candidates — and these are the people you want access to — work for the best staffing firms. Specialization is a key factor in attracting skilled talent, so look for staffing firms that focus on the types of positions you're looking to fill or individuals with the types of skill sets or experience you need.

Asking the right questions

To help you on your way, the following checklist offers several questions you may want to ask whenever you're checking out potential partners:

>> Does the firm specialize in the areas where you need help?

>> How long has the firm been in business?

>> How does the firm recruit and retain a highly skilled set of candidates?

>> How does it evaluate and select its talent?

>> How broad and deep is its candidate base?

>> How does the service match needs with skills?

>> Does the firm guarantee its workers? Does it provide replacements?

>> Is a contact person available after hours?

FIND ONLINE

The Staffing Firm Evaluation Checklist in the online tools can serve as a quick reference when evaluating staffing firms.

Make sure you nail down all the costs ahead of time. Clarify this information with the departmental supervisor who's going to be managing the worker(s). A reputable firm is always willing to communicate its fee structure in writing.

REMEMBER

The more familiar a staffing firm is with your organization — how it operates, who your employees are, the needs of various departments — the greater its ability to provide you with the right talent.

Engaging a contingent workforce

All of the workers serving in your business, including contingent team members, represent your business. Each individual, regardless of classification, is adding to the environment and culture, so it's important that contingent workers feel a connection to the business and as if they're part of the team. Create an environment where they feel connected. Here are some ideas:

>> **Communicate to your internal team.** You're inviting misunderstanding if you don't communicate beforehand to your internal staff the rationale behind your strategy of engaging contingent workers for a project. Failing to do so can cause trouble on two fronts:

- It leads to needless confusion or even tension among your full-time employees who may wonder why the individual has been engaged, what that person's role is to be, and what may be amiss that caused the need for a contingent worker in the first place.

- It creates unnecessary pressure for the contingent staff who must work with or near a group of people who are puzzled by their mere presence.

Instead of merely announcing that a contingent worker has been engaged, involve employees weeks earlier in the staffing process to help you clarify the scope of the department or project team's workload. Internal team members can offer input about specific tasks that require attention or skills that are needed and creative solutions, such as reassigning certain activities among themselves and carving out a particular function for the supplemental worker.

>> **Create a plan for successful execution.** You need to have a clear idea — before the contingent worker arrives — about the scope of the project, when it should be completed and, as appropriate, matters related to quality. Just make sure that your expectations and those of other managers are realistic, particularly regarding the difficulty of the task. Also, factor in the reality that even seasoned contingent workers need time to acclimate themselves to a new working environment.

>> **Ensure that equipment and resources are available.** Verify that the contingent worker has the equipment and materials needed to be successful, including the provision of any necessary logon IDs and passwords.

>> **Make safety a priority.** Provide appropriate safety and health training, particularly for workers in manufacturing or other nonoffice settings.

>> **Create a friendly atmosphere.** The more at home a company can make contingent workers feel, the more productive they're likely to be.

Either you, their manager, or someone in the department to which the worker has been assigned should conduct a mini-onboarding session.

>> **Be explicit.** One of the concerns that contingent workers who have unsatisfying work experiences voice most often is that they're not given enough direction at the start of the assignment. Here's a general rule: The lengthier and more complex the assignment is, the more time you or a line manager needs to spend on orientation and explaining the nature of the assignment.

>> **Provide adequate leadership and management.** Regardless of how busy your company is, make sure that hiring managers stay connected with the work of the contingent workers you engage. They're working under your direction. Check in with managers and make sure that they're communicating well with contingent staff.

>> **Intervene early.** As important as it is for managers to provide clear direction to contingent staff, sometimes the work simply isn't getting done properly. Let managers on your team know that if they're not pleased with the quality of a contingent worker's contributions, they should contact you or the staffing firm immediately.

WHAT MOST CONTINGENT WORKERS NEED TO KNOW

One of the best things you and the line managers you work with can do to ensure that contingent workers are as productive as possible is to anticipate their information needs. Here's a list of the questions they're likely to have the first day they show up for work:

- What's expected of me?
- What does success look like?
- What are your policies and ways of working?
- What does your company do?
- What's the culture like?
- Who will provide feedback and direction?
- Where do I go if I run into a problem?

To save time, consider preparing a one-page document that covers these issues and provides space for notes. You should share this information with your staffing firm before the assignment, too, so it also can prepare the contingent workers who will be assigned to your company.

>> **Don't settle.** A reputable staffing firm won't argue with you if the person who's been sent to your firm isn't doing a good job. The firm simply sends a replacement and handles communication directly with the individual (the contingent worker is their employee, after all) regarding termination of the assignment. For everyone's sake, however, try to be as specific as you can when expressing displeasure. If you do a good job of telling the firm where the individual fell short, you're more likely to get a suitable replacement.

Documenting performance and offering feedback to the staffing firm

When contingent workers finish their assignments, document their performance. Depending on whether your experience was positive or negative, you may want to ask the staffing firm for a particular person again — or ask that they never return!

Sharing your assessment with the staffing firm helps the firm do a better job of meeting your company's needs. (*Note:* Many staffing firms offer evaluation forms after an assignment to solicit this type of feedback.) As you go through this exercise, you and line managers who have used contingent staff should ask yourselves whether the contingent worker:

>> Met your expectations

>> Finished the job on time and professionally

>> Required little, some, or too much daily instruction

>> Worked well with others

Additionally, ask your line managers:

>> What could the contingent worker have done differently? Done better?

>> Would you hire this person as a full-time or part-time employee? If no, why not?

WARNING

Be aware that your assessment isn't to be used as a performance evaluation. Your records should be treated as internal documents only and shared only with internal staff and with the staffing firm. Under no circumstances should you share what may be perceived as a formal performance evaluation with a contingent worker. Why? Doing so is one of the criteria the courts use to determine whether the worker was really working on a contingent basis or directly for you. If you're sued, and the decision goes the wrong way, you could be liable for back payroll taxes and other expenses.

That's not to say that you can't offer feedback, including words of encouragement ("Good job!") to a contingent worker or point out when your expectations aren't being met during the course of the assignment ("I need you to improve your performance"). Just don't formalize the encounter or offer anything in writing.

At the end of the assignment, ask for feedback from contingent workers about your company or department and its procedures and approaches.

Looking at your legal responsibility

Apart from whatever strategic benefits the use of contingent workers offers, their growing presence in the workplace introduces some thorny legal issues as well. One key question: To what extent are companies that hire temporary or project workers directly (instead of relying on staffing firms) obliged to provide these workers with the same benefits and protections that regular employees receive?

Equal coverage

The Equal Employment Opportunity Commission (EEOC) believes that discrimination is discrimination — regardless of whether the victim of discrimination is working for you as an employee on a full-time, part-time, or interim basis. The bottom line is that contingent workers have many of the same fundamental rights with respect to EEO legislation as do regular employees — and this fact holds true for all forms of discrimination, including sexual harassment. Even when it comes to leave laws, such as the Family and Medical Leave Act (FMLA) or state or local supplemental laws, contingent workers may have rights, irrespective of "temporary" status.

Workplace injuries

Even if a staffing service employs someone working for your company on a contingent basis, your firm may be responsible for that individual's health, safety, and security while on the job at your company. Check with your staffing firm to determine whether your workers' compensation package adequately protects you. And remember: You can always face a lawsuit from anyone who's injured while working on your premises.

Chapter **5**

Kicking Off the Hiring Process

I f you've determined that the needs in your workforce plan are best addressed by hiring additional full-time employees, it's time to find this talent! This chapter outlines the foundations of a successful hiring process — engaging the right people in the process and ensuring that you (and everyone involved) are clear on what success looks like.

Nearly everything else you do with respect to HR policies and practices becomes easier if you're making good hiring decisions. If you don't have to spend the bulk of your time each day helping leaders resolve people issues, you can concentrate on the big picture: where you or your senior management want the organization to go in the years ahead.

That's the benefit of good hiring decisions. A bad hiring decision produces just the opposite result. You spend more time as a firefighter and less time as a leader and strategic planner.

Engaging the Hiring Manager

Ensuring the right talent is a team sport, so when the organization needs to source talent for an open position, the first step is to involve the *hiring manager*, the individual who will lead this new team member. The quality of a recruiter's relationship with the hiring manager makes a world of difference.

When a recruiter and hiring manager aren't aligned, the process *will* take longer than it should. The recruiter will bring in candidates whom the hiring manager doesn't think are a fit; candidates may suffer from a poor, unorganized interview experience; and chances are decent that the search will end back at square one. So the first step is a well-run intake meeting with the hiring manager. This meeting sets the stage for collaboration and clear communication between the recruiter and the hiring manager throughout the process.

REMEMBER

All intake meetings should include conversation on the following:

>> **Position success profile:** Also known as the *job description,* the *position success profile* is a document that outlines success in the position that you're hiring for. It encourages maximum fit between the employee and the expected outcomes of the role and allows you as the employer to quickly and accurately identify the competencies and motivations needed for successful job performance. Ensure that it's current and reflects the outcomes that define success in the position (see the next section).

>> **Time to fill:** *Time to fill* measures the time between when a job is opened and when a candidate accepts the offer. It's the most common recruiting metric because it indicates how much time is needed to hire for the role and how long it takes to find the right candidate.

>> **Time to hire:** This metric indicates how fast you're moving candidates through the hiring process. Just like time to fill, it's an important metric, but more indicative of the recruiting team's ability to move qualified candidates through the process after they've been identified.

>> **Recruitment and interview process:** Your recruitment process can be broken down into several stages: screening, phone/virtual interview, assessment, in-person interview, and so forth. By breaking down your time to hire, you can also find out how long it takes for an average candidate to move from one stage to the next.

>> **Logistics:** Save yourself huge headaches down the line by sorting out logistics like compensation, equity, and target start date at the very first hiring manager intake session.

>> **Assessment tests:** *Assessment tests,* also known as *pre-employment tests,* help hiring managers determine whether a candidate has the skills, work style, knowledge, or personality to succeed in a job. Companies use assessment tests to make good hiring decisions, often during the early parts of the interview process. Before using any assessment in the recruiting process, ensure reliability and validity for selection. Any assessment used should yield consistent results that predict success on the job without any unintended discriminatory impact.

>> **Sourcing strategies:** Ask your hiring manager to help you build a list of sourcing channels where your ideal candidates may have a presence and a list of role-specific keywords to search.

REMEMBER

Consider the environment/culture. Remember that the recruiting process is a sales experience, but it's also important to provide the candidate with a realistic preview of the role and your organization. It's important to consider the aspects of the role that will be most important to candidates, which includes the people and the environment they will be working in. Consider how people work to ensure that you're prepared to talk to candidates about the environment and help them determine whether it will be a good fit.

Creating the Position Success Profile

An important outcome of the intake meeting is the development of a success profile for the position you're recruiting for. Traditionally and often still referred to as a job description, the updated terminology of the success profile reflects what it does: *defines success in the position.*

REMEMBER

Job descriptions merely focus on tasks, whereas position success profiles focus on the *outcomes* that are most important for this position. In addition to outcomes, a position success profile also includes the core competencies necessary to accomplish the desired outcomes of the position. The goal is to shift your recruiting conversations away from just the job duties to provide specific, measurable goals that tie back to your business needs and company objectives. The position success profile helps to ensure that connection.

The position success profile is where your hiring criteria are first formally set forth, so it should be airtight. Why? Because the position success profile eventually drives the communication of the position, the candidate selection process, and a new employee's first performance check-in or review.

Think of the position success profile as your blueprint. Do a good job of constructing it, and all the subsequent pieces of the hiring process will more easily fall into place.

The following sections dive deeper into creating the position success profile and ensuring the correct elements. Because it's the foundation of many of your Talent and HR processes, it must be done thoughtfully.

Laying the foundation: Why you need to create a position success profile

There are a number of reasons to create a position success profile, and when done well, it serves as the foundation for all talent processes. For example, success profiles do the following:

>> Establish performance expectations and core competencies necessary for success in the role

>> Support the recruiting and hiring process

>> Highlight the essential functions of a position in the event the company needs to accommodate an individual with a covered disability under federal or state law

>> Differentiate between jobs that are exempt versus nonexempt from legal overtime and other requirements

Throughout this book, I focus on how position success profiles are essential tools for the purposes of effective recruiting, hiring, and performance management. At the same time, to ensure that your position success profiles are written in a way that carries out your reasons for having them, you may want to consult a lawyer before finalizing and using them.

Knowing what to include

Just like the blueprint of a home ensures the correct layout for the builder (and eventually the homeowner), the position success profile ensure clarity on the outcomes of the position. It sets the organization and the employee up for success, so it's important that it includes the right information. The following elements are most often included in a well-written position success profile:

>> The job or position title.

>> The department within the organization in which the position exists.

>> The reporting structure for the position, both up and/or down, as applicable. For example, the title of the person(s) to whom the position reports and any position(s) and/or numbers of employees over whom this position has supervisory responsibility.

>> A brief summary (one to three sentences) of the position and its overarching responsibility, function, or role within the organization and how it interrelates to other functions within the organization.

>> A list of the expected outcomes (what success looks like).

>> Whether the job is exempt or nonexempt. (Refer to Chapter 11.)

>> A qualifying statement that the list of outcomes isn't exhaustive and may be revised from time to time per business needs.

>> The qualifications for the position (the specific knowledge, skills, employment or other experiences, training, language, or aptitudes required).

>> The educational requirements for the job, if any, such as degrees and licensing. (Refer to the section, "Considering educational requirements and qualifications," later in this chapter for more vital information.)

>> Core competencies (qualities or attributes that contribute to superior performance in the position — check out the section, "Defining Core Competencies for Success in the Position," later in this chapter to help you figure out these core competencies).

>> If appropriate, a statement of the physical demands of the position (for example, lifting or mobility requirements).

>> A statement that the position also includes "such other duties as assigned" to protect your company's ability to add duties as needed.

>> A statement that your organization is an equal employment opportunity employer.

Apart from everything else, a well-written position success profile reflects your organization's hiring practices and terms and conditions of employment — which are areas subject to federal and state laws prohibiting your organization from unlawful discrimination. As such, any references to race, ethnicity, color, religion, sex, national origin, age, physical or mental disability, genetic information, sexual orientation, or other status protected by state or local law can expose your company to a possible discrimination suit.

In rare cases, an employer can rely on certain protected statuses in hiring (or in other employment practices) when doing so is a bona fide occupational qualification (BFOQ). One frequently cited example is recruiting only women for a position as a live-in counselor in a female residence hall. Rarely does a discriminatory hiring criterion qualify as a BFOQ, however, and BFOQs are very difficult for an employer to prove. So, before you include such criteria in a success profile, consult an experienced and knowledgeable lawyer.

Looking ahead, not behind

You may be thinking, "This is a piece of cake. I already have on hand the job descriptions we've always used for the positions I want to fill." But consider this: The outcomes and responsibilities that constitute most jobs today are a far cry from what they were as recently as a few years ago. You may have a job description that outlines job duties, but to ensure that it adequately describes success in the role, it must include outcomes — what's expected in the role. What's happened in most organizations is that tasks and responsibilities that were formerly regarded as jobs unto themselves are now consolidated with other functions. The overall result is that many existing success profiles are pretty much obsolete, or they are written as job descriptions with more of a focus on tasks and duties rather than outcomes.

Jobs today are generally broader in scope than those of the past. Position success profiles, therefore, now need to consider the expanded skill sets that employees need to handle greater responsibilities. Focus on success in the position now and in the near future (18 to 24 months out), based on your company's current needs and longer-term objectives.

Aside from establishing the priority of job duties from a business needs perspective, this distinction can be legally significant. The Americans with Disabilities Act (and many analogous state laws) protects disabled employees who are able to perform "essential" (which has a special legal definition) job duties, with or without a reasonable accommodation. Courts and agencies like the Equal Employment Opportunity Commission (EEOC) investigating a charge of disability discrimination consider which duties the employer treated as primary or essential in determining whether they're "essential" within the meaning of the statute. Although the employer's characterization of a duty as "essential" isn't conclusive, it's evidence of which duties are most important.

Considering educational requirements and qualifications

Educational requirements like degrees and licenses are formal acknowledgments that a candidate has completed a specific field of study or passed a particular test. Credentials like these, or qualifications like certain work experiences or fluency in particular languages, are absolute necessities in some jobs. The person who delivers pizza for you, for example, must have a driver's license; the appropriate medical boards must license the surgeon you hire. Be thoughtful about the credentials for your position to ensure that they accurately reflect the needs of the position.

Make sure that the credentials are necessary. Sure, every manager wants someone with an MBA and maybe a PhD and probably some sort of industry certification, too. But unless these are actually required for the job, they shouldn't make it into the success profile or be used as hiring criteria because they can limit the potential talent that you attract.

WARNING

Educational requirements or qualifications may discriminate by eliminating candidates with protected characteristics. An attorney can help you address this area.

Making sure that outcomes are doable

The job you describe must truly be realistic. Some job descriptions work beautifully until the person you hire actually tries to perform the job. One factor to consider is the compatibility of a job's various duties. Some people who are creative may be less adept at tasks that require attention to detail.

By the same token, some people who are at their best when they're working by themselves on complex, analytical tasks may be content to work independently and not as part of a tight-knit team. The takeaway here is to make sure that when you're lumping several tasks into the same job description, you're not creating a job very few, if any, people could fill.

Accurately describing success outcomes

Outcomes are the results. They're the most valuable and important part of the position you're focused on filling and the most important aspect of the position success profile. The activities the position engages in and the outputs produced should be geared toward these results. These results should be measurable (preferably with numbers), directly lead to objectives being met, and be of real value. Following are some examples of types of outcomes that should be noted in the position success profile:

» Meeting or exceeding revenue, profit, and/or growth targets

» Delivering products and services to customers who meet their needs or delight them

» Process changes in operations and/or product areas resulting in savings of time and/or money

>> Culture improvements shown to increase employee morale, productivity, and retention

>> Other measurable improvements that can be directly or indirectly attributed to the position

>> Better collaboration or relationships among distinct teams leading to quicker and higher-quality product/service delivery

Being specific

You don't need to be William Shakespeare to write a solid position success profile, but you definitely need to appreciate the nuances of the language. For example, use clear and concise language and, when possible, words with a single meaning. And you want to make sure that the words you choose actually spell out what the job entails. "Good communication skills," for example, is too general; more specific would be: "Ability to communicate technical information to nontechnical audiences."

Setting a salary range

Before you start the recruiting process and look at options for how and where you can find the ideal candidate for the job you're designing (see Chapter 6), you should establish a salary range for the position. In Chapter 11, I discuss the details of salary and what constitutes an effective compensation structure. Your ideal candidate may come at a hefty price, so know the market compensation for people with the skills you seek.

Being Clear When Writing Job Titles

Job titles are meant to be meaningful, relevant, and clarifying. If you want to attract and retain the best talent, be thoughtful about naming the job carefully and appropriately whenever possible.

REMEMBER

The goal of a job title is to describe in a few words what the position entails in terms of responsibilities or expectations. Job titles can also indicate where a particular position fits into the overall work hierarchy (you can check out Indeed's advice on making this determination at www.indeed.com/hire/c/info/establishing-a-company-hierarchy?hl=en&co=US). C-level job titles, such as CEO and CFO, indicate that the individual is part of senior management, while titles with words such as assistant or junior may indicate that the job is an entry-level position.

An inaccurate or overblown job title can create false expectations and lead to resentment, disappointment, or worse. Now that the majority of positions in most companies involve multitasking, some job titles are probably outdated. If your office manager left, for example, does "office manager" accurately describe the job they were doing, and is that the title you should still use for your opening? Or is "operations manager" now more accurate for the position as it has evolved?

Consider the following guidelines when determining the right job title:

>> **Choose a job title that is industry-relevant.** Make it clear from the title what the specific job requires based on industry norms and language. Ask yourself, "Does this job title clearly indicate this person's role at the organization and level of industry-relevant expertise?"

>> **Avoid industry jargon and uncommon abbreviations.** Because not every job seeker uses the same abbreviations or knows specific industry terms, steer clear of jargon and such in job titles unless they're extremely well known. Commonly used acronyms, such as RN, HR, or VP, are okay because most job seekers already know what they mean.

>> **Indicate the level of seniority required, as appropriate.** Words such as senior, junior, and assistant help target your job posting so people who aren't qualified, or who are overqualified, don't waste their or your time. If the position works externally with vendors, partners, or customers, the title should be aligned with their level of influence to ensure credibility.

>> **Be wary of informal wording.** Informal or creative wording in a job title can bring out your brand personality but wreak havoc when it comes to fitting your job description or position success profile into a search engine. A job title that seeks a "director of first impressions" or "IT rock star" may seem to present a fun vibe that supports the culture you're trying to create, but it also keeps your listing hidden when people search for marketing consultant or IT analyst positions. If the ideal job candidate never sees your posting, you may miss out on good talent. Informal or creative titles can also create organization confusion, unintended sexism, and ambiguity regarding both responsibilities and compensation.

>> **Leave out unnecessary information.** Job titles have two main functions: to appear in job searches and to attract high-quality applicants. Extraneous details such as numerical job codes, salary information, and location can be conveyed in other parts of your posting instead of in the job title.

>> **Avoid outdated job titles.** Many common job titles have changed over the years to reflect changing attitudes. As an example, the job title of "clerk" is

now "office assistant" or "clerical associate." Modern job titles also tend to avoid gendered terms, such as using "server" instead of "waitress" and "camera operator" instead of "cameraman."

>> **Match the job title to salary expectations.** To keep your applicant pool properly qualified, avoid mismatching job titles and salary expectations. Title inflation creates career trajectory problems and salary confusion. You'll waste time interviewing candidates who have the wrong impression about the job and likely will turn down an offer during negotiations.

Job titles are helpful beyond the hiring process, so it's important to be thoughtful and get it right. They can help others within your organization understand a particular employee's role, and a change in title can indicate when an employee has taken on more responsibility. Outside contacts, such as vendors and clients, use job titles to determine who they need to talk to when they have specific questions or needs.

Defining Core Competencies for Success

Every job has a set of technical requirements, but a success profile isn't complete without those broad-but-telling aspects of a candidate known as *core competencies*, which are the soft skills, interpersonal abilities, or simply qualities and attributes that support success in the position.

These include an aptitude for communicating with people at all levels, abilities, and backgrounds; the capacity to work well in teams (as both a leader and a team member and both in person and virtually); and other factors, such as a strong sense of ethics and a talent for efficient and creative problem-solving. Candidates who are weak in these areas — even while having solid hard skills and work experience — may prove unable to grow as your organization goes through changes that are part of today's work environment.

For example, if you're recruiting an outbound sales rep for your home security business, one way to market your service is to solicit potential customers by phone. The basic job of an outbound sales leader is, of course, to generate leads by calling people on the phone. Some sales leaders, however, are clearly much better at this than others. They have a knack for engaging the interest of the people they call. They don't allow repeated rejections to wear them down.

REMEMBER

Some consulting companies specialize in helping businesses identify core competencies or *success drivers* for key functions or positions. The following can help you gain insights on success drivers for your organization's positions:

>> **Interview your own top performers.** Assuming you have a group of people who perform the same job — and assuming one or two of those people are clearly the "stars" of the group — sitting down with your key people or their immediate supervisors to determine what makes them so successful at what they do is certainly worth your time.

Try to answer the following questions:

- What special skills, if any, do these outstanding performers possess that others don't?

- What type of personality traits do they share?

- What common attitudes and values do they bring to their jobs?

>> **Talk to your customers.** One of the best — and easiest — ways to find out which employees in your company can provide the basis for determining your desired soft skills is to talk to people with whom your staff interact on a regular basis: your customers. Find out which employees your customers enjoy dealing with the most, and, more important, what those employees do to routinely win the affection of these customers.

WARNING

Hiring decisions that rely on subjective criteria are particularly susceptible to being challenged as discriminatory. Applicants may argue that unconscious stereotypes can be injected into the decision via subjective criteria. If subjective criteria are used, be sure that your company's hiring decision-makers can articulate a clear and reasonably specific factual basis for assessing whether a candidate possesses those criteria. For example, to support a conclusion as to whether a candidate "exercises initiative," ask them to describe times when they've spearheaded work projects and record how they respond to that question. Base your conclusion about whether the candidate exercises initiative from the examples they provide.

FIND
ONLINE

See the online tools for a blank Position Success Profile and Sample Position Success Profiles that you can use as a starting point and modify to align with your particular jobs.

IN THIS CHAPTER

» **Recognizing recruiting as a process**

» **Maximizing the job posting**

» **Exploring various recruiting sources**

» **Recognizing the importance of diversity**

» **Tracking your progress**

Chapter **6**

Attracting Great Talent

Getting good talent is at the core of a strong HR function, so in this chapter I provide insight into the recruiting process and how to best navigate and manage the process. Strong execution is at the heart of an effective recruiting process, so I highlight the keys to execution to help you get it right. It starts with recognizing the importance of intentionality throughout the process because each touchpoint with the candidate is informing them about what your organization has to offer. To ensure you're attracting a diverse candidate pool, I highlight best practices to maximize the job positing. And finally, I provide insight into how to best track progress throughout the process. Here's to you attracting the best talent for your business!

Being Intentional throughout the Process

To attract the best and brightest, you need to convince potential recruits that yours is a great organization to work for. Recruiting is a sales job that requires important selling skills. How you show up and interact throughout the entire process is important. That's why it's key to be deliberate and purposeful about each interaction with candidates and communicate with them throughout the process. Remember the following:

> » **Represent your organization as professionally as possible.** That also includes paying attention to your organization's web presence.

>> **Make it clear to everyone in your business who may interact with a candidate how important it is to demonstrate your organizational values throughout the process and to be warm and courteous.** You're competing with many other prospective employers, so make sure that each part of the process is seamless and clear. After all, today's job seeker may be tomorrow's desired employee or even a potential customer, and every single interaction sends a message about what their employee experience will be should they join your organization. From their initial contact with you to each update to the final decision on employment, they're building (or losing) a connection with your business.

WARNING

At a time when a candidate can spread news of their poor experience at your company like wildfire via social media, your reputation can be affected overnight. And the last thing you need when you're searching for top talent is a bad reputation.

REMEMBER

Recruiting for your organization doesn't mean exaggerating your positive qualities either. If you misrepresent your business's scope or capabilities, you'll feed false expectations to employees who decide to join you. That can lead to job dissatisfaction and mistrust after they're onboard. Clearly communicate what the company is as well as what it wants to become; your employee value proposition; and why you need capable, committed employees to help the business reach its goals.

Kicking Off the Process

Aligned with the hiring manager, have a plan for conducting and managing the process. Based on the time to hire, you have a deadline for when, ideally, you want to see the position filled. After the deadline is in place, you can establish a sequence of steps, each with its own deadline. You may decide, for example, that you're going to look inside your company for a certain period of time — say, two weeks — and if unsuccessful, you'll post the opening externally, start sourcing external candidates, or seek the services of an outside recruiting firm.

REMEMBER

No one plan is right for everyone, so keep your options open at all times. Don't become so locked into one strategy that you become unable to see that it's not working for you.

Be systematic. Ensure that all the administrative aspects of the process are managed and tracked. Leverage recruitment software tools (see more information in Chapter 3) as much as possible to streamline and automate the process. Before you start the search, ensure you have a specific protocol — a predetermined, systematic procedure — for taking in, evaluating, sorting, and tracking the many résumés you'll attract.

If you're using an outside recruiter, make sure that someone in the company — either you or the hiring manager — has a direct line to the individual who's handling the search. If you're seeking candidates online, you'll need to secure a consistent process for taking in, evaluating, sorting, and tracking the résumés you'll attract. Chapter 3 provides more insight into the use of recruiting systems to help with this.

Identifying Key Considerations for the Job Posting

Writing a good job posting is a critical step in the hiring process, but the task is often more difficult than many people think. You're not trying to win a literary prize, but you are trying to attract job candidates (just as your competition and other organizations are) — and the right candidates at that.

REMEMBER

Keep in mind the following two considerations in writing a job posting:

>> **Help your firm stand out by focusing on *your* employee value proposition.** When you're recruiting, you're also putting out the word that your company is a great place to work. In effect, you're advertising a product — your company. Every aspect of your posting must result in a favorable impression of your organization and what you have to offer.

>> **Focus on quality, not quantity.** Your goal is not only to generate responses from qualified applicants but also to eliminate candidates who are clearly unqualified. You're better off getting only five responses, each from someone who clearly deserves an interview, than 100 responses from people you'd never dream of hiring.

If you've done a good job of preparing the position success profile (see Chapter 5 for more about developing a profile), then you've very nearly accomplished this task. In fact, you should think of the posting as a brief synopsis of the success profile albeit with a little flair added to get your job noticed. Recruiters refer to this as "sizzle" — something to ensure your job positing stands out.

Include these elements:

>> **Job title:** The *job title* serves as the headline, which is why getting the title right is so important. Many job seekers are turned off by vague or confusing job titles. Ensure the title describes the role (and level) accurately (see Chapter 5 for more information on the job title).

» Position summary: Use two or three sentences to describe the main duties. This should help job seekers understand the position at a quick glance. Use these questions as a guide:

- Is this a new role? What created the need for this position?

- Who is it reporting to?

- What kind of work will this person spend most of their time doing?

- What do you want the person in this role to help you achieve over the next 6 to 12 months?

- How will this role support other roles in the organization?

» Organization information: A description of your organization helps job seekers decide whether it's a place they want to work. For example, some people decide to only apply to organizations of a certain size, whether that's a small one or a large company with multiple departments.

You may want to include some of this type of information:

- An overview of your company's product or service offering

- Your organization's mission statement and/or purpose

- Your organization's values

- Your organization's size

- A description of the team or department you're hiring for

» Your ideal candidate: In a short paragraph, describe the qualities that make a great job candidate. This shows what traits make your employees successful while giving job seekers a glimpse into your company culture.

» Job qualifications: Specify the level of education and experience and relevant attributes and skills (per your success drivers or competency model) required to do the job.

» Salary range: The pay range. Pay transparency in the job posting is a hot topic; in 2022, New York City passed a law requiring businesses to list the minimum and maximum salary range for a job on any printed or online posting.

» Additional information: Depending on your organization and the job position, you may decide to add any of the following:

- A roadmap of the interview and application process

- Any tools or training that you'll provide

- Whether you conduct any screening or testing pre-employment and during employment (drug tests, driving records, or a criminal background check)

- Include instructions for how people should apply, such as by emailing you a résumé and cover letter. If your job posting is on an online job board with their own application system, you can probably skip this.

Bear in mind, too, the following key points:

>> You want to convey some sense of your culture and values with a few phrases (for example, *fast-paced, ethical,* or *client-centered*).

>> Use the active voice and action words throughout the posting. Make it move, not just sit passively on the screen or page.

>> Create sizzle — a buzz or a sense of enthusiasm — to pique applicants' interest. Highlight your employer brand and give applicants a glimpse of what it would be like to work within your organization.

>> Ensure you have included key words to support SEO (search engine optimization) efforts so that your job posting is visible to candidates who are most likely to be interested in the position you are recruiting for.

See the Sample Job Posting for examples that take into consideration the preceding criteria.

FIND
ONLINE

Implementing Sourcing Strategies

The next step is figuring out where to post the job to attract the most qualified applicants, a process called *sourcing*. Implementing an effective recruiting sourcing strategy can make it easy to find a large pool of qualified applicants for open positions. A strong recruiting sourcing strategy can lead to efficient hiring processes, higher retention rates, and positive candidate engagement experiences. When choosing the best sourcing strategies for you, consider factors like the types of candidates needed for open roles, available recruiting resources, and results from previous recruiting methods. As Chapter 5 discusses, have this important conversation with the hiring manager. The following sections identify specific ways and places you can implement sourcing.

Establish a system to keep track of your recruiting success by using any of these sources. How many candidates did each source produce? How qualified and skilled was each applicant? These metrics can help you determine the return on your investment in a variety of recruiting channels.

REMEMBER

Current team members/employee referrals

Your current workforce is an important sourcing opportunity. In addition to the potential that exists within your team, their network is a great place to source talent. Think about it — the talent within their network already knows someone who works at your organization. They already have a connection, so today *employee referrals* (when current employees refer qualified candidates for employment at your organization) are considered one of the most effective recruiting sources. Few employees would risk their own reputation by recommending someone who may turn out to be a source of embarrassment.

Many organizations have instituted employee referral programs with rewards (extra vacation days, trips, cash bonuses, or other goodies) for employees who recommend a person you eventually hire and who stays with the company for a specific period of time. Employee referrals can be especially effective in helping to locate candidates for critical or hard-to-fill positions.

WARNING

As with other elements of your recruiting program, keep in mind that your employee referral program can pose legal issues in the areas of discrimination and wage and hour law. Consult an experienced attorney for assistance with analyzing the legal risks of your recruiting program.

Before you launch a program, consider all the ramifications and establish a systematic process for administering it. Here are some questions to answer:

>> Is everyone eligible to receive a referral award, or are certain positions not eligible, such as executives, officers, board members, recruiters, and hiring managers (in the case they may refer candidates for the position they're hiring for)?

>> What incentives are you offering to the employee who refers someone? Are you going to vary the incentives based on the importance of the job?

>> How long does any referred employee need to remain with your organization before the person who makes the referral becomes eligible for the incentive? (The norm in most companies is three to six months.)

>> What procedure must any employee who's making a referral follow?

REMEMBER

After you set up an employee referral program, don't keep it a secret. Publicize it every way you can — through posters, emails, and newsletters, for example. Your objective is to generate as many quality referrals as possible, and reminders always help. Finally, make sure that everyone knows when an employee receives a bonus for a referral.

Online job boards

Job boards are the best way for employers and job seekers to find each other online. You have many options, ranging from general boards to narrowly focused niche boards that cater to specific industries and jobs. The landscape is constantly changing, with old boards being phased out or bought by competitors, and new ones sprouting up. The key is to find two or three that give you the most reach and job seekers a trustworthy collection of the best jobs.

Here are four online job boards that employers and job seekers widely use:

>> **Indeed:** Indeed initially began as a job search engine and job aggregator and has become the biggest and most popular board worldwide. It's available in more than 60 countries and is currently the most visited job site in the United States. The platform offers free, subscription-based, and pay-per-click pricing models to suit various recruitment needs, as well as access to an extensive résumé database of more than 200 million professionals across the world.

>> **LinkedIn:** LinkedIn is the world's most popular social network for professionals. It's a great place to post jobs because of its enormous reach and growth in active users. LinkedIn mostly caters to professional jobs and senior roles. With the rise of social recruiting, LinkedIn fulfills a prominent role. It can be used to search for great candidates, or employers can buy advertising on the site to promote their open positions.

>> **ZipRecruiter:** ZipRecruiter is a job board that allows employers to post jobs to hundreds of job boards, including ZipRecruiter itself. ZipRecruiter has gradually changed from an applicant tracking system into a job board that competes primarily with Indeed.

>> **CareerBuilder:** CareerBuilder is a general posting site and is one of the most trusted and high-traffic job sites in the United States. It has direct relationships with 92 percent of the Fortune 500 companies. Job post pricing is based on the number of posts purchased. Bulk discounts are available.

In addition to these four widely used platforms, many others exist, including Monster, Google for Jobs, Craigslist, and Mashable. You can be confident that by the time you're reading this, many others will have joined their ranks — or replaced them as the technology is constantly evolving.

WARNING

Online job boards come with a number of legal implications that you need to understand and properly manage. Title VII of the Civil Rights Act of 1964 (Title VII), the Americans with Disabilities Act (ADA), and the Age Discrimination in Employment Act (ADEA) stipulate that employers can't discriminate in any aspect of the employment process. This rule, of course, includes online interactions. In other words, you must make sure that you offer avenues to candidates who don't own computers or have access to email to apply for an open job. This requirement is particularly important given the fact that some candidates may not only send you résumés electronically but may also direct you to web pages that extensively showcase their accomplishments and qualifications. Keep in mind that those without access to such online tools deserve an equal chance to be considered for a position as those who do have access.

FIND ONLINE

Being responsive to job applicants is simply good business practice. Anyone who comes in contact with your company forms a perception that can influence the firm's reputation. A simple, straightforward message sent to all applicants is a good way to showcase your organization's professionalism. For a good example of an Acknowledgement of Receipt of Résumé or Job Application, see the online tools.

Your company website

Your organization's website provides valuable information for prospective team members about your organization and your mission. Just as you and the hiring managers you're supporting are now able to find out more about candidates who may be applying, job seekers can uncover in-depth information about your company. Although the savvy ones review a variety of sources — articles, discussion groups, industry analyst reports — your website is a great place to communicate your unique culture and most appealing characteristics.

Well executed, your website can give job seekers a glimpse into the employee experience — what it's like to work in your company. Today, even the smallest of companies have websites describing what they do, and often, the advantages of working for them. Your website gives you an opportunity to explain why your company is an employer of choice. If properly outfitted, your website also can receive applications directly from interested job seekers and potentially use this information to create employee profiles that can be used later as new hires join your organization. The implications of these changes for HR professionals are twofold:

>> With information now so much more accessible than ever, you want to make sure (to the extent that you can) that your company's website accurately showcases your firm's strengths and range of capabilities. After all, you want the best people to be drawn to your company. A website that's outdated, difficult to navigate, or lacking relevant information can reduce your chances of attracting top-notch candidates.

>> Because of all the available information about companies, expect candidates to be well prepared in the interview process. You also need to be prepared and raise your expectations for the discussion. The topics you cover can relate more specifically to business priorities and issues affecting your industry and company. (I discuss interviewing in detail in Chapter 8.)

Social media and online networking

Job seekers go where the jobs are. Because of the sheer number of openings they list, job boards and company websites are among the first stops on a typical candidate's itinerary, but social media is also an important part of sourcing options. Because of the prevalence of social media and the integration of work and life, job candidates have an incredibly large online network of friends they contact for insight on various jobs and companies. Jobvite's 2019 Job Seeker Nation Survey reports that 50 percent of respondents heard about jobs from friends; 37 percent said they also learned about positions from professional networks, and 35 percent found out about jobs from social media.

Even prospective candidates who didn't grow up using computers (and this is a shrinking group) engage in active social networking. Because of this, a social media and online networking strategy is an essential part of your overall recruitment program, so it's important to create a strong presence and remain active on the social media sites where your prospective candidates spend time.

According to Monster.com, 80 percent of employers are using social media as a recruitment tool. Jobvite's 2020 Recruiter Nation Survey reports that the social media platforms most used for recruiting prospective talent are LinkedIn (72 percent), Facebook (60 percent), Twitter (38 percent), Instagram (37 percent), Glassdoor (36 percent), and YouTube (27 percent).

Listing your job openings on social networks, either directly or through a third party, has many pros. Perhaps the most important benefit is the ability to reach a wide audience. The most popular social networks have millions of users and information can be shared among individuals quickly. Before you realize it, your job ad may reach someone who otherwise wouldn't have known about it (or your organization).

You also may be able to communicate your vacancy to highly targeted groups of professionals. Communities of like-minded individuals exist within every social network. For example, LinkedIn features groups for people who share the same profession, job title, alma mater, or interests.

One of the defining characteristics of social media is that they encourage interaction. The whole point is to talk to other members — virtually, of course — and share links, photos, videos, news, and other tidbits. As a result, you can take an active role in recruiting. Sending a message or tweet or changing your status ("Looking for a new A/P supervisor") quickly lets everyone you're connected to know about your opening and encourages them to share the news with their own connections. You also can easily search people's profiles (especially on LinkedIn) and identify professionals with certain skill sets. Many sites offer tools to help you do this. This can be an effective way of locating *passive job candidates* (those not active in the job market but who would consider a job change if the right opportunity came along).

Making info available to candidates in the early stages

Just as you may reach out to prospective candidates, job seekers may want to contact you directly and ask questions about the company or position, enabling you to address concerns they may have and highlight aspects of your organization that may appeal to potential employees. Of course, candidates also can identify people who work for you — and reach out to them for candid thoughts on the company. Do employees know how to respond or whom to forward requests to? Do you want them to respond at all? You may want to prepare your workers for these types of inquiries by providing education or drafting social media guidelines that outline acceptable behavior.

TIP

Recognize the potential benefit of giving workers the freedom to share their experiences with the firm with their online networks. You may find that, with the right guidance, your employees can aid your recruiting efforts and help spread the word about why your company is a great place to work. Sincere and unfiltered insight into the organization, provided by actual employees, can be a powerful draw for job seekers.

Making your presence known on social media

It's becoming more and more expected that all organizations have a presence on social media. Those who don't may be seen as being behind the times, especially by workers who've embraced social media or younger people who've grown up with it. In some ways, an organization's Facebook page or Twitter feed is becoming the new web page. In fact, some companies have a Facebook page only and no traditional company website at all.

An additional advantage of establishing a presence on LinkedIn, Twitter, Facebook, or any other social platform is that you can build a large community of people who are actively engaged with your company — including potential hires. By sharing news about your organization, fostering interaction among your followers and fans, and addressing inquiries from users, you can create a virtual "open house," where interested job candidates are able to find out about the business, its culture, and its people. When it comes time to make your next hire, you can tap a group of individuals who are already familiar with your company and invested in it.

It's important to realize, however, that doing this takes time and effort. Users expect regular postings and open communication from the brands they follow, as well as a high level of interaction with real people inside those firms. If you aren't willing or able to make that type of commitment, you may not be ready to launch your online open house just yet.

TIP

Keep in mind that social media also include review services where individuals can rate your company across various categories; Yelp (www.yelp.com) is perhaps the best-known example. Of particular interest to those in a recruiting role may be Glassdoor (www.glassdoor.com), which provides company reviews from the employee's perspective. Visitors can access candid feedback about an organization's culture, management, and pay practices and even uncover the questions potential hires can expect to be asked during a job interview. Such reviews can bolster — or greatly harm — your firm's reputation among in-demand candidates. My advice: Monitor what's being said about your company on these sites and be prepared to counter a comment or claim you disagree with.

Technology moves very quickly, and I can't offer you specific advice in this area, but you may want to think about whether you need a social media presence. Yes, there's a lot to consider — which social networks you'll join, who will run the sites, what resources will be needed to maintain an active presence — but it's worth addressing these types of questions now if you haven't done so already.

REMEMBER

As with all technology-based tools, keep in mind that, although social networking sites such as LinkedIn can be useful in recruiting, they are no substitute for the value of in-person networks and reputable recruiters. No technology, no matter how popular, is a cure-all for your recruiting challenges. It can be an important part of your efforts, but it can't entirely replace all other recruiting methods.

Candidates who previously applied

Because you're spending so much time finding and recruiting talented candidates, you may attract some with impressive credentials who may not be the right fit for any of your currently open roles. Store all of the candidates' information in a recruitment database and review them when you're hiring for a different role. See whether any of these previous candidates better fit the next available position's qualifications. It's as simple as reaching out to the candidate to share the opportunity.

Here is sample language you can use:

> I am reaching back to you because we have a new job opening, a [job title].
> I believe that your skills, characteristics, and experience would make you the
> perfect candidate for this position, so I decided to reach out. Would you be
> available for a call [include date and time] to talk about this exciting opportunity?

Consider other ways to stay connected to candidates who applied previously — they are your candidate pipeline, and just like you're staying connected to potential customers, you want to stay connected to potential future talent for your business. Invite them to open house events, continue messaging, and keep looking for organization opportunities to send them.

Recruiters

Anyone in an HR role who has unlimited time and resources can identify job candidates online, but sometimes engaging with an external recruiter is the best option. Recruiting professionals meet with the candidates they place to determine their suitability for various jobs and often provide skills testing and select reference checking. This is time you don't have to spend on these activities. The best firms also fill a consultative role, helping you develop an effective overall staffing strategy. Recruiters can be an invaluable part of your candidate search arsenal.

Yes, using external recruiters does have an associated expense, but if you know how to maximize their services, they can more than pay for themselves. Using outside recruiters has several key advantages:

REMEMBER

>> Outside recruiters generally have access to a large pool of applicants. After all, it's their job to continually locate quality candidates.

>> They handle such cumbersome administrative details of recruiting as sourcing, evaluating skills, and conducting preliminary interviews.

In the course of their evaluation process, the best recruiters check selected references from their candidates' past employers to gather skill proficiency information and job performance history. Employers should perform their own reference checks as well. This is because a preliminary check may or may not reveal all the information you want to consider in making your final decision as to whether to bring an individual into your company.

>> Recruiters often are a valuable source of talent acquisition advice. A recruiter who knows their stuff often can help you identify whether you need a contingent worker, full- or part-time employee, or a generalist or specialist. Recruiters also can provide feedback on what the market looks like right now to find the candidate you need. They can be particularly helpful in identifying passive candidates who may be interested in working for your firm.

Understanding who does what

If you at times have difficulty determining what makes a headhunter different from a recruiter and an employment agency different from a search firm or staffing firm, you're not alone. The names can be confusing. All these sources fulfill the same basic function, although the service approaches differ from firm to firm: They find job candidates for client firms for a fee. The difference between the various specialists in this large and growing industry is primarily how they charge and on which segment of the labor market they focus.

In describing how these players differ, it's only fair to point out that not everyone uses these terms in the same way.

EMPLOYMENT AGENCIES AND STAFFING FIRMS

You engage these companies to find job candidates for specific positions. What they all have in common is that you pay them a fee — but only after they find you someone you eventually hire. These firms recruit candidates in virtually every industry, and companies call on them to fill positions at all levels of the corporate ladder. If you want to hire a full-time employee, they typically charge you a percentage of the new employee's first year's salary. It can vary, depending on the level of the position you're filling and the skills required.

Employment agencies and staffing firms typically differ in the types of positions they help you fill. In most cases, employment agencies are generalists and focus on entry-level and mid-level jobs in a range of industries, whereas staffing or contingency search firms focus on mid- to upper-level positions. Specialized staffing firms can find you these types of roles in a shorter amount of time than the generalists because their candidate pools are focused on a particular field or profession — finance or marketing, for example. In another usage, a staffing firm can refer to a firm that provides contingent workers, whereas a recruiting firm places full-time employees. Again, usages vary.

EXECUTIVE SEARCH FIRMS OR HEADHUNTERS

Executive search firms or headhunters focus on higher-level executives, up to and including CEOs. Unlike employment agencies, most search firms charge a retainer regardless of whether they produce results. You also can expect to pay, in addition to expenses, a commission of 25–30 percent — or even one-third or more — of the executive's annual salary if the firm is successful in its search.

Why, then, go to an executive search specialist? The main value comes into play if you're seeking someone for a high-level job that's most likely to be filled by an executive who's already working for another company. A good search specialist usually has the contacts and the expertise to handle very targeted, high-level searches.

REMEMBER

The most general term for firms or representatives from firms that find job candidates for client companies for a fee is *recruiter,* and that's the way I describe these roles in this book. (Implied is that these firms and individuals are *outside* recruiters, not internal recruiters who are employees of a company, often residing in the HR department at mid-sized to larger businesses.)

Using recruiters — yes or no?

Most companies that rely on outside recruiters to fill positions do so for one of two reasons:

>> They don't have the time or the expertise to recruit effectively on their own.

>> Their recruiting efforts to date haven't yielded results.

True, using an outside recruiter involves an extra cost, but bear in mind that handling all aspects of recruiting yourself may not be the best use of your time in your HR role. Evaluating résumés, in particular, has become exceptionally labor intensive because of the number of applications received from internet postings. Perhaps most important, recruiters typically have wide networks they can tap on your behalf.

Finding the right recruiter

You choose a recruiter the same way you choose any professional services specialist. You take a look at what services are available. You ask colleagues for recommendations. You talk to different recruiters. And you leave it up to the recruiters to convince you why they're the best way to go. Ultimately, you want a recruiter you feel confident will be able to effectively articulate your company's mission, values, and culture to job prospects.

The following list provides some reminders that can help you make a wise choice:

>> **Check them out.** However busy you may be, make getting to know any recruiter who may be representing your company part of your business. Make sure that you feel comfortable about the way the recruiter works. (A good question to ask yourself when getting to know a recruiter: Would I, as a job candidate, like to work with this recruiter?) Don't hesitate to ask for references.

>> **Be explicit about your needs.** The cardinal rule in dealing with recruiters is to be as candid and as specific as possible about your needs. Make sure that the firm understands your business, your company culture, and what exactly you're looking for in a candidate. Extra bonus: A savvy recruiter often can tell you, simply by looking at the job description, how likely you are to find someone to fill the position.

>> **Clarify fee arrangements.** Make sure that you have a clear understanding — before you enter into a business agreement — of how your recruiter charges. Make sure that any arrangement you agree on is in writing. If you don't understand something, ask for clarification; a reputable firm is always happy to explain its fee structure.

>> **Ask about replacement guarantees.** Most of the leading recruitment firms offer a replacement guarantee if a new employee doesn't work out after a reasonable period of time. Just make sure that you understand the conditions under which the guarantee applies.

>> **Express your concerns openly.** Speak up if you're unhappy about any aspect of the proposed arrangement with a recruiter. Tell the recruiter exactly what your concerns are. If you don't feel comfortable expressing your concerns with the recruiter you're considering, you're probably dealing with the wrong company.

As in any field, recruiting has its bad apples. Fortunately, the industry has done a very good job in recent decades of policing itself. Still, you need to be wary of any recruiter that

>> Is evasive about providing a list of satisfied clients it has worked with or unwilling to provide information about its procedures.

>> Is reluctant to provide progress reports or vague about fees and billing arrangements ("Don't worry about it — we're friends").

>> Charges applicants for services (résumé preparation, testing fees, and so on).

>> Has no track record or has a record of legitimate consumer complaints.

Campus recruiting

College campuses have long been fertile hunting ground for companies in search of entry-level talent. Smaller firms without well-organized college recruiting programs have always been at somewhat of a disadvantage. If you're a smaller company, here are some tips on how to level the playing field:

>> **Get to know the folks in the career center.** Campus recruiting is usually coordinated by the college career center. As long as your company has a reasonably good reputation, the people in the career center will be receptive to your recruiting overtures and are likely to steer good candidates your way. A big part of their job, after all, is getting good jobs for their graduates. The best way to build a strong relationship with career center personnel is to pay them a personal visit — or better still, invite them to your company to see what you have to offer. The career center is also the place to gain access to campus job fairs (see the next section).

>> **Get to know the students better in small groups.** You can target students pursuing a major or majors in the field in which you're seeking talent by contacting student organizations. This can take the form of cosponsoring study hours, community events, or other small activities with the student group where you can provide snacks, network, and sometimes even make a presentation about your company.

>> **Focus on topics that students are interested in.** When speaking to students at job fairs or student events, limit the time you touch on generalities about your company and instead focus on students' interest areas, such as opportunities for advancement in your firm or what to expect in the recruiting process. They don't want just a rehash of what they can read on your website.

>> **Be prepared to promote your organization.** The image projected by you (or anyone else in your organization who goes on a campus recruiting

mission) goes a long way toward determining how successful you are at attracting a school's top candidates. Make things simple for yourself. Put together a PowerPoint presentation that you can use repeatedly on your laptop, but don't stop there. Students want to hear your company's story in your own words. How did you build your own career there? They want real-life examples and testimonials.

» **Speak their language.** By speaking their language, I don't mean you need to actually talk like a student — unless you're cool enough to get away with it and not sound ridiculous. You just need to *think* like a student. Words like *opportunity, growth,* and *learn* will strike exactly the right chord. Yes, money still talks for most college students today, but students also want to know the nature of the job and the culture of the company.

» **Promote volunteerism.** If your organization is active in the community and provides volunteer opportunities, don't forget to mention it.

» **Follow through.** For certain positions, recruiting on campus can be very competitive with other companies, so you'll need to be a lot more than a dog-and-pony show. Students expect a short turnaround time in the recruiting process. Let them know when and how you'll be back on campus. And needless to say, follow through on your promise to be there.

Refer to the Cheat Sheet at www.dummies.com for more information about recruiting on a college campus. Just search for "Human Resources Kit For Dummies Cheat Sheet."

Job fairs — in person and virtual

Job fairs are recruiting events that bring together employers and job seekers. They present a great opportunity to connect with multiple job seekers at one time in a single location or at a single event and vary in size and scope. Some are quite large with a collection of employers from a variety of industries, and others are targeted to a particular audience, for example, job fairs targeted specifically to transitioning veterans and military spouses.

Just like the nature of work is becoming more virtual, so are job fairs, and one simple online search will yield a variety (both in-person and online) of regional and national job fairs for job seekers.

While it's helpful to connect with a variety of potential candidates, the primary downside of job fairs is their competitive aspect. Regional and industry specific job fairs — IT professionals in Boston, for example — tend to attract firms from your region who are looking for the same folks you're looking for. You may well end up with your company's booth or online presence right next to a competitor.

Regardless of the format, here are some suggestions for participating in job fairs to maximize your efforts:

>> **Put your best foot forward.** Whether you're going to be greeting applicants at a booth or online, you want to make sure that the general impression you're conveying is one of quality and professionalism. The promotional information you distribute doesn't necessarily have to be expensively designed and printed — and you don't have to invest vast sums in elaborate posters or audiovisuals. Just make sure that everything you do is substantive and well organized.

>> **Ensure that good company ambassadors represent your organization.** The people staffing your in-person or online booth should not only be able to handle all questions attendees are likely to ask about your company but also be enthusiastic and personable. Remember, too, that having senior people as part of your recruiting team tells applicants that your company takes potential candidates and the job fair seriously.

REMEMBER

Your diversity and inclusion efforts are also a way to ensure your recruiting efforts are ongoing and include a diverse candidate base. Participation in ethnic and cultural community fairs or events, for example, can serve both marketing and recruiting purposes.

Open houses

Open houses are most commonly held by companies in industries that experience high turnover and, thus, have an almost constant need for new employees: Mass market retailing or fast-food restaurants are examples. But open houses also can be an effective recruiting strategy for companies that are about to expand into a new region.

Conducting a successful open house hinges on several important factors. One key, certainly, is getting the word out by using a variety of media (social media, fliers, store posters, notices to local schools and colleges, commercials on local cable TV and radio outlets, and banner ads on your company website) to stir up interest.

Here are some other considerations:

>> **Choose the place carefully.** You can hold open houses at either your own premises or at some outside location, such as a hotel ballroom or conference room. Each has pros and cons. Holding the event on company premises gives attendees a firsthand look at what you have to offer, but your facilities — because of their location, configuration, or security considerations — may not lend themselves to this kind of an event.

>> **Think about timing.** Open houses are typically held after working hours and on weekends to attract potential applicants who are currently employed. Before you select the date, double-check to make sure that your open house doesn't conflict with other events that can hold down attendance, such as a popular sporting event or religious holiday.

>> **Be friendly and informal.** Not everyone who attends your open house will be a potential candidate, but they'll all come away from the event with an impression that they'll pass along to friends, relatives, and acquaintances. Make sure that the impression you make is as favorable as possible.

Direct applications (walk-ins)

Even though most employers prefer online application (via email or the company's website), some organizations still welcome direct, walk-in applications. This is especially true at retail businesses and restaurants, which often keep paper copies of their application on hand. Some even conduct on-the-spot interviews and think about it: Anyone who has the energy and the gumption to make a cold, face-to-face appearance is someone whose résumé probably deserves a review. Invite the person to fill out an application or either leave behind or send you a résumé, along with a cover letter.

Government employment services

Since the Great Depression of the 1930s, every state has operated a public employment service in conjunction with the Department of Labor. Employer-paid unemployment taxes fund these offices — in other words, you foot the bill. These agencies exist primarily to offer services to job seekers. They register the unemployed, determine and pay unemployment benefits, offer counseling and training, and provide labor market information.

In the past, state employment agencies have generally been considered a source for unskilled labor and lower-level clerical and industrial jobs. This perception, however, is not necessarily accurate anymore. Technicians and professionals are registering with these agencies, too, and as is true of many other aspects of the government, their operations are becoming less bureaucratic and more client oriented. Your local agency is always worth a try — after all, you pay for it.

The downside: Although all government agencies are subject to federal standards and guidelines, the quality and usefulness of the services they offer can vary widely from state to state.

Diversity Recruiting: Benefiting from a Diverse Workforce

In recent years, the terms *diversity, equity,* and *inclusion* have entered the business lexicon in a big way. Countless articles, papers, studies, and books talk about how to create a diverse workforce that's equitable and inclusive, and for good reason. The country's demographics are rapidly changing, and the workforce is becoming increasingly more diverse. Of course, workplace diversity entails more than the presence of racial or ethnic minorities. It also covers culture, gender, sexual orientation, disability, mobility, and many other characteristics.

Organizations and business leaders recognize that minorities will be the source of all growth in the nation's youth and working-age population and much of the growth in its consumers and tax base as far into the future as we can see. Here are some important statistics that reinforce this:

>> In 2019, most new hires of prime age workers (ages 25–54) were people of color for the first time, according to a *Washington Post* analysis.

>> In 2020, the U.S. population under age 18 became "majority minority" — where the number of individuals who are multiracial and racial and ethnic minorities exceeded those of whites. By 2044, the full population will reach that status. By 2060, the estimates are that 43.6 percent of the U.S. population will be white.

>> The Latino population is expected to make up more than 20 percent of the labor force by 2028, up from 17.5 percent in 2018, 14.3 percent in 2008 and 10.4 percent in 1998.

>> The share of Latinos in the workforce is projected to reach 9.2 percent by 2028.

>> An increasing numbers of individuals — 4.5 percent — identify as LGBTQ, with those in younger generations more likely to self-identify (56 percent of LGBTQ adults are under age 35 compared with 28 percent for the non-LGBTQ population).

Chapter 17 summarizes the laws that have been enacted to bar discrimination in hiring and other employment-related practices. These laws often are changed or updated, such as the addition of the Internet Applicant Final Rule of 2006, which requires federal contractors to collect and maintain data for use in enforcing nondiscrimination laws, and the Genetic Information Nondiscrimination Act, prohibiting consideration of a person's genetic information in the terms and conditions of employment.

But the need to nurture a diverse workplace is not limited to ensuring legal compliance. An organization isn't well served by employing only people who come from the same mold. Building a diverse workforce can enhance creativity and productivity. If everyone in your company thinks alike, you miss the opportunity for innovative ideas that often come from individuals from diverse cultures and backgrounds — input that can help you improve your products and level of customer service.

Diversity recruiting means *seeking out* people who can bring a greater variety of ideas and approaches to the workplace. There are other benefits to embracing diversity as well:

>> Your company can attract, retain, and maximize the contributions of all members of the changing workforce.

>> Exposure to diverse employee groups gives everyone on your team the chance to benefit from different ideas, cultures, and perspectives that can expand their thinking and attitudes.

>> Being known for maintaining a diverse workforce can prove attractive to potential job candidates.

When recruiting, consider whether your company reflects the demographic makeup of the communities in which you do business or the markets you serve. To address this, connect with local organizations, including churches, cultural and social institutions, and colleges. They can be great sources for building a diverse base of applicants.

Also, consider diversity, equity, and inclusion education. Make sure that leaders at all levels within your business understand and value the importance of diversity.

Last, although diversity is important, employees should understand that hiring decisions are based on finding the best candidate and not meeting diversity quotas. Making the recruiting process more transparent can help ease the minds of skeptical employees. Check out *Diversity, Equity, & Inclusion For Dummies* by Dr. Shirley Davis (John Wiley & Sons, Inc.) for a deeper dive into the topic.

WARNING

It may be prudent for certain employers to hire members of protected groups as part of an affirmative action plan. If your company doesn't have an affirmative action plan, a decision to hire a person based on their protected status may produce a *reverse discrimination* claim by an applicant outside that protected group.

Handling Helicopter Parents

What do hiring managers have in common with youth sports coaches, high school teachers, and college administrators? All these professionals are likely to encounter *helicopter parents* (parents who are hyper-involved in their kids' lives, holding their hands through every stage of growing up, whether the kids want them to or not). These parents are always "hovering," rarely out of reach in case guidance, advice, or a terse phone call is needed to help their kids.

Helicopter parents may have called sports coaches to argue that their kids deserved more playing time, enrolled their children in endless summer camps and academic prep courses, or lobbied with college admissions counselors for a spot at a preferred school. If you've ever met a mom who calls her son every day at college to make sure that he's eating well and doing his laundry, you've come across a helicopter parent.

It should come as no surprise, then, that as their sons and daughters enter the workforce, helicopter parents are nearby to help them land the jobs of their dreams. Helicopter parents have been known to submit their kids' résumés, attempt to negotiate salary and benefits, and even show up to sit in on job interviews. No kidding.

As surprising as this phenomenon may be to you, helicopter parents are a reality that hiring managers face. Here are several ways to address the issue:

>> State in your job posting that issues such as compensation and benefits can be discussed only with an applicant.

>> Even though you want to discourage too-close parental involvement in your hiring process, recognize, too, that a parent who thinks yours is a good company to work for will likely have an impact on the child's opinion of your workplace. To that end, some companies send the same recruitment package to parents that they send to the applicants themselves.

>> If parents appear at a job fair to present you with a résumé, diplomatically inform them that, although you appreciate their involvement, you'll likely get a better impression of their offspring if they submit the résumé themself.

>> If parents call you multiple times or attempt to go above your head, remain polite and keep your cool. Offering a curt response will only add to your headaches. Parents who feel dismissed or disrespected — whether for legitimate reasons or not — are apt to let others know about their poor experience with your firm. In the age of social media, you don't want to give anyone cause to complain about you or your company.

>> Assertive parents who insert themselves into the hiring process should give you reason to pause:

- Is the applicant mature and self-sufficient enough to conduct a job search on their own?

- If hired, will the parent continue to contact you and interfere?

- Will the applicant be able to perform the duties of the job if they had the help of a parent to write a résumé or cover letter?

These are reasonable questions to ponder. But don't rule out a promising applicant simply because of a parent's actions. Consider following up with the candidate to gain more insight. They may offer an apology or reassurances that the third-party intrusions will end. You may even find that the embarrassed applicant didn't know a parent had interceded.

Keeping Tabs on Your Progress

Monitor your recruiting efforts on a daily basis and evaluate your progress not only in terms of the number of inquiries you receive but also in terms of their quality. *Quality*, in this context, refers to responses from applicants who not only meet but also exceed your basic requirements. Depending on your sense of urgency, be prepared to intensify your efforts if you come up empty in the initial stages of the process.

Be flexible. If the initial response to your recruiting efforts produces poor results, you need to be prepared to revisit the job description or explore the possibility of restructuring the job to attract more (or better) candidates.

Companies known for their ability to attract and hire good employees are always recruiting — even if they have no current openings. If recruiting is, indeed, an ongoing process, and if you're the person in your company responsible for recruiting talent, you're always looking for people who can contribute to your organization's success, even if those people are working somewhere else now and you have no immediate need for them. At the very least, you want to keep an active database of names and résumés of people you've met or who've sent in letters or contacted you online expressing interest in your firm — assuming, of course, that they have the qualities you're looking for.

IN THIS CHAPTER

» Dissecting the résumé

» Making it easy for candidates to apply

» Setting up a candidate evaluation system

» Understanding the ins and outs of pre-employment assessment

» Conducting pre-screens via video or phone

Chapter **7**

Narrowing the Pool: Evaluating and Assessing Candidates

Traditionally, the interview has been perceived as the most important part of the hiring process, for good reason — it's the best opportunity to really get to know and connect with the candidate. But what many otherwise savvy businesspeople often forget is that one of the keys to effective interviewing is effectively evaluating *who* should be interviewed in the first place.

By engaging the *right* candidates in the hiring process, you are in the best position to maximize the interview phase. If you don't have an efficient evaluation process in place, two things are likely to happen, neither of them good for you nor your business. First, you may inadvertently weed out candidates who clearly deserve a second look. Just as unfortunate, your evaluation process may fail to accomplish its fundamental purpose: making sure that you're not wasting your time and effort on candidates who are clearly unqualified for the position you're seeking to fill. This chapter can help you avoid this common — but avoidable — hiring pitfall.

Reviewing the Résumé

As I discuss in Chapter 6, your first contact with candidates is most likely to be through an online sourcing tool where the candidates upload their résumés. When you're hiring, don't be surprised to see some of the following in addition to the traditional résumé as candidates attempt to stand out from the crowd:

>> **Video résumés:** A video résumé is a one- to two-minute video that allows the candidate to discuss their achievements and credentials while also giving potential employers a sense of who they are and how they present themself. Video résumés can convey a candidate's personality and enthusiasm better than a paper or electronic résumé, and job seekers are able to show off communication skills and creativity in a way that is more challenging to do in a traditional résumé.

>> **Infographic résumés:** An infographic résumé is based on visual representations of the candidate's skills and experience, such as timelines, graphs, icons, or bar charts. Unlike a traditional résumé style, which just uses text, an infographic résumé uses graphic design elements.

>> **Twitter résumés:** The rise of Twitter has led some applicants to promote themselves in 140 characters or less. As you can imagine, this doesn't allow a lot of room for exposition. So, a Twitter résumé is a concise summary of the person's professional biography and objective. For example: "Marketing whiz with ten years of experience seeks boundary-pushing firm. Offering enthusiasm and a long list of happy clients." Twitter résumés also typically include a link to the candidate's online résumé or networking site profile page, as well as the hashtag #twesume, making it easy for employers to search for these tweets.

>> **Online portfolios:** An online portfolio is a collection of the candidate's professional documents including their résumé, cover letter, a brief biography, and references.

Although the traditional résumé still dominates the recruiting space, it pays to be aware of these trends. Throughout the book, when I talk about a résumé, you can assume this refers to the entire gamut mentioned here. By and large, the same advice applies.

Based on résumés alone, you'd think all your candidates are such outstanding prospects that you could hire them sight unseen. And no wonder. Anyone who does any research at all into how to look for a job knows how to write a résumé that puts them in the best light. And those who don't know how to write a great résumé can now hire people who do know.

Why, then, take résumés seriously? Because résumés, regardless of how perfect or imperfect they are, can still reveal a wealth of information about the candidate — after you crack the code.

Mastering the basics

Here's what you probably know already: Basically, job candidates submit only two types of résumés:

>> **Chronological,** where all work-related information appears in a timeline sequence

>> **Functional,** where the information appears in various categories (skills, achievements, qualifications, and so on)

REMEMBER

Some applicants use a combination of the two formats, presenting a capsule of what they believe are their most important qualifications and accomplishments, together with a chronological work history.

Before diving into that pile of résumés, consider the following observations:

>> No job applicant intentionally includes unflattering information in their own résumé.

>> Many résumés are professionally prepared, designed to create a winning impression.

>> Résumé evaluation is tedious, no matter what. You may need to sift through the stack several times.

>> If you don't do any résumé evaluation at all (or delegate it to the wrong person), you're likely to miss that diamond in the rough — that ideal employee who unfortunately has poor résumé-drafting skills.

Reading between the lines

Now that more and more people are using outside specialists or software applications to prepare their résumés, getting an accurate picture of a candidate's strengths simply by reading their résumé is more difficult than ever. Even so, here are some of the résumé characteristics that generally (although not always) describe a candidate worth interviewing:

>> **Outcomes:** The more detailed the candidate is in their description of what they accomplished in previous jobs, the more reliable (as a rule) the information is.

>> **A history of growth:** The applicant's work history should show a progression and growth. But don't go by job titles alone; look at what the candidate actually did and what skills they acquired. Assess how important the work was to the company involved.

>> **A strong, well-written cover letter:** Some applicants don't send cover letters with their résumés. A savvy job seeker (in other words, someone you may want to have on your team) will still manage to prepare and send the modern equivalent of a cover letter, perhaps in the body of an email message. Someone who takes the time and effort to do this shows a sincere interest in your firm.

Watching out for red flags

Résumé writing is a good example of the law of unintended consequences. Sometimes what's not in a résumé or what's done through carelessness or a mistake can reveal quite a bit about a candidate. Here are some things to watch out for:

>> **Sloppy overall appearance:** This is a fairly reliable sign that the candidate is lacking in professionalism and/or business experience.

>> **Cookie cutter résumé:** A résumé that looks like it's not specific to the position can be considered a red flag. This may mean that the person isn't necessarily interested in working for your company, but rather just wants a job. If you're looking to hire people who are passionate about what they do, considering a résumé that hasn't been adapted for the specific position may be the wrong way to go.

>> **Static career pattern:** A sequence of jobs that doesn't include increasing responsibility may indicate a problem — the person wasn't deemed fit for a promotion or demonstrated a lack of ambition. That said, sometimes solid performers who enjoy just doing their job and don't necessarily have a career progression history still can add tremendous value as part of your team. Don't reject a résumé on this criterion alone. It's something to review and assess but not judge.

>> **Typos and misspellings:** Generally speaking, typos in cover letters and résumés may signify carelessness or a cavalier attitude. Although not all jobs require candidates to have strong spelling skills, most do call for attention to detail. Not proofreading a résumé (or not having someone else do it) may be a sign that a candidate isn't conscientious.

>> **Vaguely worded job summaries:** Perhaps the applicant didn't quite understand what their job was. Or perhaps the job responsibilities didn't match the title. Before you go any further, you probably want to find out what a

"coordinator of special projects" actually does. You want to see job summaries that indicate how crucial the job is to the company's success.

>> **Failure to quantify accomplishments:** Sometimes candidates give you a huge list of skills but don't describe how they used them in their previous positions. This is an issue because it may mean they have never actually demonstrated this skill in a professional setting, which doesn't answer the question of why they would be a good fit for this job. A good rule of thumb is that the more descriptive someone is in their résumé, the more likely it is that they are telling the truth about their accomplishments. Plus, this detail gives you something to talk about when you connect with the candidate.

Historically, unexplained chronological gaps in the resume have been considered a red flag, but they're increasingly considered acceptable and can be a source of unintended bias. Breaks in employment history occur for a variety of reasons. Before jumping to conclusions, seek to understand.

Considering a candidate's online persona

Résumés aren't your only source of insight into prospective job candidates. Social media profiles are another tool you can use in the pre-screening process. In the world of social media, many organizations use information they discover online about candidates in the recruiting process. All candidates should assume that their online persona can be seen by anybody, including prospective employers. If someone has a social media account containing a lot of vulgarity or inappropriate content, they may not be a fit for your culture. It's not unreasonable to search candidates online when looking for a new employee, so if you see anything that makes you feel uncomfortable, particularly if it isn't aligned with your organization's values, consider that as part of your search process, but it's important to exercise caution when doing so. Using information discovered on social media can introduce legal risk and unintended bias.

Employers have increasingly turned to general online searches to find out about an applicant's digital persona and interests. Although that can be as straightforward as a general search, employers also can see who applicants' Facebook friends are or the content that candidates are engaged in on Instagram, TikTok, and other social media.

REMEMBER

That may seem like a fertile way to discover more about potential candidates, but there are serious caveats for the companies and HR personnel doing this sleuthing. For one thing, the anonymity of the Internet can prove anything but reliable — anyone can post pretty much anything about you, regardless of whether it's accurate or completely contrived. There's no guarantee that the information you uncover is accurate or insightful.

Separately, legal risks abound. When you start exploring a candidate beyond the information contained in their résumé or professional profile or bio, you risk legal claims like invasion of privacy and discrimination, or even Fair Credit Reporting Act and similar state law violations. If you want to incorporate web-based searches of applicants into your overall evaluation procedures, work with a lawyer to develop lawful policies, procedures, and guidelines for the gathering and use of Internet-based information. Weigh the benefits and disadvantages as follows.

Following are some benefits of searching for applicants online:

>> You may get a sense of their professionalism and/or maturity.

>> The information you find may help you get an interview together and ask relevant and specific questions instead of general ones.

>> You may encounter extensive information about their background, experience, and personal life.

On the flip side, disadvantages include the following:

>> It can be considered an invasion of privacy, which can bring about legal issues for the company.

>> If the candidate is part of a protected class such as a certain religion or disabled, you might run into issues should you choose not to hire them, even if the choice is based only on lack of experience, skill, or education.

>> The information gained may not be reliable, considering it's public and anyone can add photos or data about the candidate to their social media profile.

>> There are people in the world with the same name. Information found may be about someone else with the same name.

>> There are various states within the United States that can prosecute those who Google candidates without their consent.

If you do choose to search online for candidate information, it's a good idea to enlighten the applicants on your intentions. That way, if you discover anything online that's considered questionable or you're in a state where this act could be punishable by law, you won't have any issues and they have the opportunity to be forthcoming with the data, in person, rather than allow you to find it online.

FIND
ONLINE

The online tools include a Sample Résumés document. You can see an example of a well-written résumé, as well as one that should give you reason to pause.

Simplifying the Online Job Application Process

For organizations using an applicant tracking system (ATS) (see Chapter 3 for more information), the application process is as simple as pressing the Apply button on the company's website or online job board, and the candidate is presented with the login page for an ATS. While this may sound easy, if the process is challenging, the likelihood that the candidate will complete the application process is low. According to a 2022 study by Appcast, the candidate drop-off rate for people who click Apply but never complete an application is a whopping 92 percent.

Barriers in the online job application process have always been a problem, and when there are too many steps involved in getting applicants to the finish line, candidates will abandon the process. Candidates are consumers, and they want quick, easy, and informative processes. Without them, they'll move on. A strong talent attraction strategy and a great employer brand, combined with an engaging and authentic careers site and an easy application process, is mission critical.

To get a sense of where your application process needs improvement, ask several members on your team to apply for an open role. Their feedback will give you a good sense of where in the process applicants become frustrated or confused, causing them to leave the application uncompleted. From there, consider the following tips for ways to improve and simplify your application process:

» Ensure your online application process takes less than 15 minutes total. According to a Built In study, 60 percent of Gen Z job seekers won't spend longer than 15 minutes on a job application.

» Include only the mission-critical information. At such an early stage in the process, limit the candidate information you collect to the following:

- First name
- Last name
- Email
- Phone
- Résumé
- Cover letter
- Where to find out more about the candidate (LinkedIn, website)
- A question for the candidate (for example, Which of our core values most resonates with you?)
- Compensation expectations

Note: If you aren't planning to review a cover letter for every application you receive, don't require it. If you need that information from candidates who make it past the initial review stage, you can ask for a cover letter or references at a later point.

In addition, you want to make absolutely sure that the questions you ask aren't discriminatory and are in line with federal and state laws. Don't shoot yourself in the foot by including questions in the application that relate to any of the following areas protected under federal law — and be sure to check whether state or local laws governing your operations protect additional characteristics (for example, marital or familial status):

>> Race

>> Color

>> Ancestry or national origin (although you can ask whether a candidate is eligible to work in the United States)

>> Sex/Gender identity

>> Religion

>> Age

>> Physical or mental disability (although you can ask whether the applicant can perform essential job duties, such as lifting certain amounts, either with or without a reasonable accommodation)

>> Genetic information

>> Sexual orientation

>> Veteran status or military service

>> Height or weight (unless directly related to job performance)

The following list describes other things you shouldn't ask for during the preliminary stages of the hiring process:

>> You can't ask the applicant to provide a photograph before employment.

>> You can ask an applicant's name but not a maiden name or a spouse's maiden name. Why? Such a question may be interpreted as another way of asking about marital status.

>> You can ask an applicant's address but not whether they own or rent or how long they've lived there.

>> Most education qualifications are fair game, but don't ask for high school or college graduation dates or dates of attendance. It's a dead tip-off for age.

Final rule: If you don't need it, don't ask for it.

Setting Up a System for Evaluating

No set rules exist for evaluating job applicants — other than common sense (and the legal considerations noted earlier). The important thing is to have some kind of system or protocol in place before résumés begin to arrive. While many of the principles in this section are built into recruiting systems and applicant tracking systems, for smaller organizations, these processes may be managed manually. The key is that these principles are built into your process, whether automated or done manually.

Using some criteria to make decisions

No matter who does the evaluating — an HR specialist, a line manager, or a business owner — the process should include a set of hard criteria to use as the basis for decisions. Otherwise, there's a good chance you'll end up making choices based on factors that may have no bearing on desired work performance, such as courses taken at a university you admire or a particularly impressive skill that would be virtually useless in tackling the responsibilities of your job opening.

TIP

You need to keep in mind the following three questions at all times:

>> **What are the outcomes for success in this position?** These should track with the outcomes noted in the position success profile, as long as it's current, targeted, and carefully thought through (see Chapter 5).

>> **What are the special requirements of your organization, such as certifications or special education?** If you own a public accounting firm, for example, you would most likely only consider applicants with a valid certified public accountant (CPA) credential.

>> **What qualifications and attributes are critical to success in this particular position?** Think of the key qualities of your best people (see Chapter 5). If your business depends on a high level of innovation and creativity, for instance, some people will possess greater strengths in this area than others. Identify those attributes, competencies, and/or values that you feel will best support success in this position. Look for these attributes in prospective employees.

If you haven't answered these three questions, you're not ready to start the candidate evaluation process.

Evaluating résumés, step-by-step

Here's an overview of the candidate evaluation process:

1. **Scan applications or résumés first for basic qualifications.**

   If you do a good job of communicating the job's qualifications to your recruiter or in the posting (based on the position success profile), you shouldn't get too many replies or résumés from unqualified candidates. Keep in mind, however, that some applicants apply to virtually any job opening, regardless of whether they're qualified. Their attitude is, "Hey, you never know." For example, if you're seeking to hire a medical technician who will be working on equipment that requires a license, and your job posting expressly says that such a license is required, eliminate applicants whose applications or résumés don't indicate they have that license.

2. **Evaluate résumés based on your hiring criteria.**

   After you eliminate unqualified candidates, you can focus on more specific hiring criteria, such as solid organizational skills, leadership experience, or a good driving record. Here again, your task is considerably easier if you do a thorough job of identifying these requirements at the time you put together the job description. But no matter how much time you spent identifying criteria, don't rush this step. Some résumés clearly reflect the skills and experience you're looking for; others may come close but just don't do the trick.

   TIP

   Begin the résumé evaluation process by setting a high standard (for example, the résumé must meet a certain high percentage of the criteria). But if your reject pile is growing, and you haven't cleared anyone, you may need to review your criteria to see where you may be able to be more flexible.

3. **Set up a process to flag and identify top candidates.**

   At this point, you probably want to separate the wheat from the chaff, which means establishing a separate file for every applicant who passes the initial evaluation process. If you're using an ATS, the system will automatically do this for you, but if not, create a simple manual process to identify top candidates.

4. **Extend an invitation.**

   Your next move depends on how many applicants remain. If you have only a few, you may want to invite them to participate in a video interview (which is becoming much more the norm versus in-person interviews). (See the section "Pre-Screening: Narrowing Your List," later in this chapter.)

I discuss the importance of simplifying the online application (refer to the section, "Simplifying the Online Job Application Process," earlier in this chapter). While focused, the online application still can be effective as an evaluation tool. Some application forms are *weighted*, meaning that you give each element in the form a certain value, putting more emphasis or weight on qualifications you feel may more heavily influence later performance on the job. In other words, weighting the application questions can help you figure out how likely a person with a certain type of experience or skill is to be the right employee for this particular job.

Weighing the evaluation criteria

The trick, of course, is figuring out how to weigh the criteria. The basic idea is to determine how accurately a specific criterion may predict superior job performance. The problem, however, is that no one has developed any sort of weighting scale flexible enough to cover everything that can affect job performance. Educational levels, for example, may closely link to success in a certain job in a company filled with people with advanced degrees. In that case, you would assign it a higher weighting value relative to other criteria. But education credentials may not be as important in a company focused on tasks that don't require advanced degrees. And if you assign values to work experience, licenses held, and so on, you have to be careful that the criteria you're using relate to actual job performance. Again, if you don't really need the skill, you shouldn't list it as a criterion.

Is the entire process scientific? Hardly. But a weighted system can weed out obviously unqualified employees and give you at least a preliminary idea of who the top candidates are for the job.

TIP

One way to add validity to a weighted application is to do your own tracking. Score applicants for a while and then recheck the scores of those you hire. You're looking for relationships between good performance and objective qualifications. The criteria used in an interview to assess how well an applicant may fit a job should be the same criteria used for the performance evaluation of the person in that job. If you can determine the attributes and qualifications that make successful employees, you may find that you can structure a weighted application form that indicates when these qualities are present in a candidate. This procedure is useful if you do a lot of hiring; if you hire only a few people a year, on the other hand, you may just create more work for yourself.

FIND
ONLINE

For those candidates who don't make it past your initial evaluation, the online tools include respectful language for rejecting candidates.

Assessment: Knowing What Works and Mitigating the Challenges

Pre-employment assessment is an important part of the hiring process, as assessment/testing aims to remove unqualified candidates from the pool *and* identify candidates who are the best fit for the position. However, like any other tool, pre-employment tests have their downsides. So, why test? There are three primary reasons why employers use pre-employment testing:

>> **To accelerate the hiring process:** Employers may use these tests to quickly narrow down the number of applicants they're trying to hire, especially if they have a lot of résumés to sort through.

>> **To test an applicant's skills:** Employers give pre-employment tests to see whether a candidate's skills match the requirements within the job description. For example, if an employer is hiring for a copywriter position, they might administer a writing test to find out whether the candidate's skills match their expectations. An employer may decrease their company's turnover rate if they hire someone who passes a skills test because it shows how an applicant can apply their knowledge.

>> **To increase the quality of interviews:** By gathering sufficient data on applicants, employers can use the results from the test to ask specific questions related to candidates' skills and work experience.

Pre-employment testing raises myriad legal issues that can be extremely complicated to work through. If you do test candidates, keep in mind that individuals can't be singled out to be tested. Tests must be applied consistently to all candidates for a position or, in some cases, for all positions within a particular department or business unit. For example, if you require a forklift ability test for a forklift operator, all applicants for this job must take the same test. Bottom line: Any testing policy for a specific situation (and not company-wide) should be clear, documented, and consistently practiced — as well as directly related to the job in question.

In general, employee hiring or selection tests must have a direct relationship to the employment in question. If a hiring test results in an adverse impact on a protected group (for example, women, African Americans, and so on), it's the employer's burden to show that the test is job related and consistent with business needs. (See Chapter 17 for a discussion of employment-related legal issues.) One way to make this clear, especially with scored tests, is to show that the testing procedures have been validated by scientifically acceptable methodology.

Finding the right test for your situation

Assessments and tests are tools meant to measure specific aspects or qualities of applicants' skills, knowledge, experience, intellect, or — more controversially — personality or natural style. Identify what you want to know about a candidate and then choose the appropriate assessment.

Selecting the right test for your situation probably won't be a problem because choices abound. Dozens of commercial test publishers collectively produce thousands of tests. Employment tests come in all shapes and sizes. The following sections provide a rundown of what they are, what they do, and how to use them.

Skills assessment tests

Skills assessment tests provide an overview of a candidate's soft and hard skills. Employers typically test for these skills after they're in the later stage of the hiring process to hone-in on candidates' specific expertise. For example, if an employer wants to hire for a public relations coordinator position, they might administer a writing test to gauge the candidate's ability to write content within a given timeline and determine how well the candidate proofreads content before submission. Additional skills assessment tests may require candidates to demonstrate research, presentation, or leadership skills to advance in the hiring process.

Cognitive ability tests

Cognitive ability tests ask questions to measure a candidate's cognitive performances. The answers provided help employers predict job performance because they'll then know more about how the candidate handles complexity. One of the common cognitive ability tests is the General Aptitude Test (GAT), which highlights the candidate's ability to use logical, verbal, and numeric reasoning to approach tasks.

Physical ability tests

Physical ability tests measure a candidate's health and physical condition or ability to perform certain tasks. They reveal whether the candidate is capable of performing in roles that require physical work, like that of a firefighter or police officer, or the ability to lift packages of a certain weight if this is vital to job performance. Testing for physical competencies adds another step to the hiring process for employers so they reduce the chances of workplace accidents in addition to finding a qualified candidate.

WARNING

Requiring a physical or medical examination before employment is illegal under federal law. Employers may test for physical agility or ability if it's a legitimate job requirement under federal law, but they may do so only after they have extended a conditional offer of employment to the candidate. Also, you must consistently administer the same test to other successful candidates conditionally offered employment for the same position. Before you decide that some physical attribute or ability is necessary for the job, however, keep in mind that a number of fire departments around the country have been successfully sued because of their physical tests. Likewise, physical or medical examinations may be unlawful under applicable state law.

Personality/Style assessment

Personality or Style assessments provide insight on a candidate's motivators and preferences. The results can indicate to employers whether the candidate fits within the company's culture. Assessment results may help employers evaluate a candidate's ability to demonstrate specific characteristics desired in certain position (such as a sense of urgency or detail orientation). The assessment results may also indicate whether the candidate's natural style will add diversity of preference to a work team. Review the different types of personality assessments to understand the format and the outcomes to determine the best fit for your needs.

Some common pre-employment personality/style assessments include the following:

>> Predictive Index

>> Myers-Briggs Type Indicator

>> Hogan Personality Inventory (HPI)

>> DiSC Behavioral Inventory

Personality/style assessments measure certain personality characteristics and preferences, such as assertiveness, resiliency, temperament, or stability. This group of assessments also includes interest inventories, which claim to show how close an individual's interests match those of a particular occupational group.

The greatest benefit of personality/style assessment is getting a sense of the candidate's natural preferences and motivators. Knowing this information not only helps you determine how the applicant most naturally communicates and works with others, but it also gives you a sense of the candidate's potential to fit with the culture, team, and leader that they'd be working with.

A primary challenge with personality assessments is that the results aren't crystal clear and sometimes need professional interpretation. If this kind of information is necessary to your evaluation process — for example, you're looking for people who can fit into a certain work team or have certain personality traits that are important to the job — you may feel compelled to use personality assessments. Be aware, however, that the subjective nature of the evaluation process creates a legal risk for any company that chooses to use them in the selection process.

Integrity tests

An *integrity test* measures an individual's personal honesty and sense of integrity. These tests generally include questions on situations of ethical choice. For instance, what should an employee do if they see a coworker stealing? Or the tests include questions that can reveal personal standards of behavior — whether the candidate can follow simple procedures and keep company information confidential. Typical questions include

» Do you have the same core values inside and outside of the workplace?

» How would you act if a manager or a coworker gave you a task that violates company policy?

» Is it ethical to publish work samples on your website?

» Have you lied to your manager in a previous role?

» If a client asks you to do something illegal, do you do it?

An integrity test is used when an employer needs to determine how an applicant may behave in a position of trust — handling cash or safeguarding property, for example. A test of this nature is designed to identify people who may be too unreliable to trust with the company cookie jar. Most employers understand that honest people make the best employees. Keep in mind, however, that integrity tests must be job related. You can't ask questions about an applicant's level of debt or credit rating (a violation of the Fair Credit Reporting Act). Tests must remain free of bias based on race, sex, age, or any other protected trait.

WARNING

As is the case with personality and psychological testing, these tests are risky legally, with many privacy issues to consider. Talk to a lawyer before using this form of testing.

Avoiding the common challenges with pre-employment assessment

When considering the use of pre-employment assessment, consider the following:

» Before adopting or implementing any employee selection testing, get legal advice. As mentioned earlier, pre-employment testing implicates numerous federal and state law regulations.

» Establish what traits or information the test is designed to evaluate and make sure that a relationship exists between these traits and the hiring criteria.

» Carefully check the credentials and reputation of any test vendor. Ask to see validation data.

» If you use a test, double-check that the test isn't biased either in its objective criteria or unintentionally by disproportionately impacting a protected group.

>> Verify that the test is certified by an established, reputable group and validated in accordance with the Uniform Guidelines on Employee Selection Procedures from the EEOC.

>> Talk to colleagues, associates, and people in other companies who use testing. Ask whether their testing has been successful.

WARNING

A final word of advice on testing: Remember that your company is ultimately responsible for any testing/assessment that you conduct. Given that this is a legally complex area, consult with an attorney before implementing a hiring test of any kind. Also, be sure to carefully manage the data you collect through these tests. Limit the number of people with access to this information to the fewest possible in order to protect the confidentiality of the candidates you test.

For more on pre-employment evaluation measures, see Chapter 9.

Pre-Screening: Narrowing Your List

Pre-screening refers to the process of narrowing down many job candidates based on their qualifications and abilities. The purpose of pre-screening candidates is to make the hiring process faster and more simplified. Pre-screening makes the hiring process easier by narrowing down the top candidates for the posted position.

Recognizing where to pre-screen

The most common technique is a pre-screening interview that typically takes place over the phone or through a video conference. This technique provides an easy way to break the ice and get to know the candidate without the time and challenge of getting to the workplace. It helps to save time for both the employer and the candidate. A pre-screening interview is conducted to understand the candidate's qualifications in more detail. These interviews are generally short and are meant to determine whether the candidate is to go further in the hiring process.

A pre-screening interview should answer some of the questions recruiters may have about the candidate's experience and education. Some of the questions may address previous experience in a job, why they are interested in this job, and how their skills fit with the job responsibilities. You may want to ask about how the candidate would handle scenarios specific to the job.

When thinking about whether to do a phone or a video interview, consider the following.

Interviewing over the phone

The phone interview has traditionally been the go-to format for first round interviews. Many aspiring job seekers expect a phone call interview as part of the first-step process to get a new job.

Here are the advantages of phone interviews:

>> Phone interviews are accessible to every candidate and have been used for hiring purposes for decades. Less tech-savvy candidates in traditional industries are more likely to feel comfortable with this tried-and-true interview method. Candidates pick up a call from the recruiter on their mobile phone, and they are good to go.

>> The phone interview is a great introductory call — usually with a recruiter prior to speaking with a member of the team the candidate would be working with. It is more relaxed and a great, no-pressure introduction for a company-to-candidate rapport.

>> Neither recruiter nor candidate can see one another, allowing for both parties to reference their notes during the interview and create a safe environment to explore the position.

Meanwhile, the primary disadvantage to pre-screening on the phone is sensing the nonverbal cues at this stage also can be challenging, further blurring the lines of how well you and the candidate can assess job skills and fit.

Pre-screening with video

The video screen has become a common technique as organizations are doing more remote hiring and engaging a virtual workforce. Here are the advantages of going this route:

>> During a video interview, both the candidate and the recruiter can visually see each other and interact with each other live. This method allows recruiters to assess candidate reactions to interview questions and can lead to more natural ease and flow of conversation.

>> Recruiters can get more of an inside look into how a candidate presents themselves during a video interview compared to the phone interview. It is also easier to see how prepared the candidate is without notes available to them.

Meanwhile, here are the disadvantages:

» Technical difficulties can disrupt the flow of the video interview and throw both the interviewer and interviewee off and take away the possibility for the best assessment of each party.

» The video platform and constant visibility may intimidate both the interviewer and the interviewee and cause them to misrepresent themselves.

Figuring out which method is better

Consider leveraging both the phone *and* video interview methods during your recruitment process. One strategy could be to use the phone interview for an initial 15- to 30-minute phone screen between a recruiter and a candidate. Next would be a video interview with the hiring manager and the candidate. Finally, you could opt to bring the candidate into the workplace (if possible) to meet the rest of the team, take them on a tour for an inside look, or finish the hiring process with one last video interview.

However, I recommend shortening your hiring process as much as you can to streamline it. The longer your process is, the more likely you are to lose candidates. Choosing between phone and video interviews, or a combination of both, may depend on the amount of time and resources that are available to you and your recruiting team.

FIND ONLINE

See the Sample Pre-Screening Questions for Hiring Managers online for a list of questions to ask.

Estimate how long you'll need to effectively conduct a telephone interview with job applicants. It typically can take from 15 to 30 minutes — 15 minutes for a basic preliminary evaluation, 30 minutes if you want to ask deeper questions for a more comprehensive evaluation and assessment. The key is to be consistent with your questions so you can fairly compare job hopefuls.

TIP

If the candidate isn't available and you need to leave a message or you're texting or emailing them, suggest a time frame (such as in the morning or between 2 p.m. and 5 p.m.) when they should return your call the next day. This request can be a good test of initiative — candidates who fail to return the call or who don't make a reasonable effort to contact you to make alternative arrangements demonstrate either a lack of interest or halfhearted commitment.

IN THIS CHAPTER

» **Looking at the basics and potential pitfalls of interviewing**

» **Preparing for an interview**

» **Beginning the interview**

» **Knowing the right questions to ask — and avoid**

» **Asking hard-hitting questions (and interpreting the answers)**

» **Ending the interview gracefully**

Chapter **8**

Maximizing the Interviewing Process

nterviewing is an important step in the employee selection process. If done effectively, the interview enables the employer to determine whether an applicant's skills, experience, and personality meet the job's requirements. By the time a candidate is brought in for an interview, the organization should be relatively confident about the candidate's ability to succeed in the position, and the interview can increase the level of confidence.

The interview's function is to confirm two important things, both for the organization and for the candidate:

» Can the candidate successfully accomplish the outcomes identified in the position success profile?

» From a values and motivational fit standpoint, does the candidate align with the organization and the job?

To answer these questions as accurately as possible, your interview process should be structured and consistent, and yet interviews are arguably the most subjective part of any selection system. As humans with natural bias and perspective based on our own experiences, we have to fight the tendency to judge people according to whether we simply like them or not, as opposed to making sure that the candidates we're interviewing are being graded on job-relevant characteristics. For this reason, interviews should come later in the hiring process, after objective components of the process have been completed.

Interviews are only as effective as how and when they're conducted. When they're held at the right time in the process and are conducted consistently, interviews can provide you with the confidence to move forward in your selection decision. In this chapter, I take an in-depth look at interviewing, with a focus on the things you need to know and do to get the most out of the interviewing process.

Grasping the Basics of Interviewing

Interviewing for a job is stressful, no matter what side of the table you're on. But when you're a new hiring manager faced with the challenge of trying to hire the perfect employee or a seasoned recruiter working hard to deliver a great candidate, the stress is amplified, so it's helpful to be super clear on the goals of the interview.

A well-done interview enables you to perform the following three tasks, which are essential to making a sound hiring decision:

>> Obtain firsthand information about the candidate's background, work experience, and skill level. This helps clarify what you discovered from the candidate's application, résumé, candidate profile, or previous screens.

>> Get a general sense of the candidate's overall intelligence, aptitude, enthusiasm, and attitudes, with particular respect to how those attributes match up to the requirements of the job.

>> Gain insight into the candidate's basic personality traits, values, motivation to accomplish the outcomes of the job, desire to become a part of the company, and ability to integrate into the organization's culture and the current work team.

The best interviews are interactive conversations with a purpose. They're focused and structured while allowing for an opportunity to get to know each other.

The people you'll be interviewing today are savvier than ever about interviews. Here are two things today's candidates know:

- **They know how to excel in an interview.** Candidates are well schooled in the art of making you believe, by virtue of their interview performance, that they're the answer to all your hiring prayers. Unless you're disciplined and vigilant, you may fall in love with the wrong candidate who has all the right answers.

- **They know about antidiscrimination laws.** Most candidates are well versed in antidiscrimination legislation, and candidates who don't get the job are more likely than ever to claim, justifiably or not, that your company's interviewing practices are discriminatory. Your best protection is to make sure that you and everybody else conducting job interviews steer clear of any subject or any line of questioning that may leave your company open to a discrimination claim.

Recognizing What Gets in the Way When Interviewing

Understanding common interviewer mistakes can help you improve your technique and make well-informed hiring decisions. Not only does a well-run interview provide you with great insight into the candidate's experience and ways of working, but good interview techniques can also help you make a positive impression on candidates. A job candidate is likely to feel more motivated and enthusiastic about accepting a role at your company after a positive interview experience.

This section takes a look at some of the all-too-common practices that get in the way of a successful interview and ultimately hinder the candidate experience.

Failing to be prepared and to allot the required time

Preparation is key for conducting a successful job interview. By being prepared, you can feel confident when greeting candidates and leading them through the interview process. To help you prepare for an upcoming interview, review the position success profile and the candidate's application materials. Be clear on the ideal candidate for the position and the list of questions to best assess the candidate's ability to achieve the outcomes of the position. If it's an in-person interview, you can also prepare by organizing the interview space and ensuring you have the materials you need before the candidate arrives so that you aren't taking valuable interview time to prepare the space.

Failing to give the interviewing process the time and effort it deserves is, by far, the main reason interviews fail to reveal useful information about a person. You can probably understand why managers frequently neglect to take the necessary steps to prepare for interviews, conduct them diligently, and evaluate the results in a thoughtful manner: They're busy. Everybody's busy. Time is at a premium. But your job is to make every interview you conduct count. Encourage line managers who make their own hiring decisions to do the same.

Mismanaging your time

The more prepared the interviewer is, the more likely they'll manage the time well and maximize the process. Most leaders are moving at a very fast pace, and it takes discipline to allow focused time before and during the job interview. Managing your time effectively before an interview allows you to prepare thoroughly and arrive on time to meet the job candidate. Being on time for the interview shows professionalism and your consideration for the candidate's time.

During an interview, structuring the time well allows you to ask the questions needed to gain a comprehensive understanding of the candidate's abilities. Finishing the interview within a reasonable period demonstrates your time management abilities and your respect for the candidate's schedule. Overall, managing the time well creates a positive experience for the candidate and reflects positively on the organization.

Lacking consistency in the process

Skillful interviewers think through the process and tend to follow the same method every time — albeit with variations that they tailor to individual situations. Unsuccessful interviewers tend to wing it, creating a different routine for each interview and entering unprepared. The hidden danger of a lack of planning: You deprive yourself of the one thing you need the most as you're comparing candidates — an objective standard on which to base your conclusions. Without structure, you have no way of knowing whether the impressions you gather from the interview would be different if your approach and other aspects of the interview were consistent for each candidate. If you wing it, you're also not creating a great experience for the candidate, which negatively reflects on the business as a whole.

Talking more than listening

An effective interview provides both the interviewer and the candidate opportunities to find out about each other so they can each make good employment decisions. The interviewer's time speaking should be focused on answering a candidate's questions and helping them assess whether this is the right opportunity for them.

Interviewers typically lead these conversations by prompting interview subjects to address various aspects of their candidacy. Allowing the candidate to speak about their experiences, credentials, values, and career goals is essential to recognizing the value they can bring to your company. Asking questions and providing ample time for the candidate to express their answers shows your interest in them while discovering important details about their qualifications. Probing through active listening (for example, letting the candidate's comments spark related questions) is a critical interviewing skill because it allows you to gain valuable information you'd miss if you did most of the talking. You can — and should — react to, comment on, and build on the answers that candidates give in job interviews.

Focusing on one positive attribute of a candidate and ignoring everything else

This situation describes the halo effect, a type of cognitive bias in which your overall impression of a person influences how you feel and think about their character. Essentially, your overall impression of a person ("She is nice!") impacts your evaluations of that person's specific traits ("She is also smart!"). For example, some interviewers may feel an instant positive connection to a candidate and assume that this interaction will translate into a dedicated, hardworking, innovative hire.

Speaking negatively about the business or the role

Undoubtedly, candidates will ask questions about you, your position in the organization, and the business's operations. When answering these questions, be professional by using positive or constructive statements. While it's important to provide an honest overview of the challenges within the role and organization, emphasize how you and the business plan to meet and lead through the challenges. This shows a solution-focused and positive outlook on how you and the business navigate challenges. It also demonstrates transparency, which many candidates value when making decisions about their careers.

Setting the Stage for the Interview

Your ability to get the most out of the interviews you conduct invariably depends on how well prepared you are. Here's a checklist of things you should do prior to any interviewing:

» **Thoroughly familiarize yourself with the position success profile, especially the outcomes expected of the position.** Remember, one of the primary goals of the interview is to determine with confidence whether the candidate is able to accomplish the outcomes of the position, so it's important that the interview is clear on the expected outcomes.

» **Review everything the candidate has submitted to date.** That includes their online application, résumé, cover letter, online profile, and so on. Note any areas needing clarification or explanation, such as quirky job titles, gaps in work history, or hobbies that may reveal aspects of the candidate's personality that can have a bearing on job performance.

» **Set up a general structure for the interview.** Create a basic schedule for the interview so that, as the meeting progresses, you reserve enough time to cover all the key areas you want to address, while also providing the candidate plenty of time to get the answers to the questions they have. Having a rough schedule to adhere to will help you begin and end the session on time, allowing you to be more efficient and showing that you respect the candidate's time.

A phone or video interview/pre-screen is a great use of time to provide the candidate an opportunity to ask and answer general questions and also determine whether both you and the candidate feel there is enough mutual interest to move on to the next step. (See Chapter 7 for more on pre-screens.)

» **Write down the questions you intend to ask.** Base your questions on the areas of the candidate's background that deserve the most attention (based on the position success profile and your hiring criteria). Keep the list in front of you throughout the interview.

» **If the interview is in person, hold the interview in a room that's private and reasonably comfortable.** Clear your desk, close the door, and set your phone to silent so that you can be free from distractions throughout the conversation.

WARNING

Try not to schedule job interviews in the middle of the day or at the end of the day. Why? You're not likely to be as relaxed and as focused as you need to be, and you may have a tough time fighting off interruptions and distractions. The ideal time to interview candidates is early morning before the workday starts. You're fresher then, and so is the candidate. If you have no choice, give yourself a buffer of at least half an hour before the interview so that you can switch gears and prepare for the interview in the right manner.

The Pre-Interview Checklist for Hiring Managers, found online, can serve as a handy reference when preparing for an upcoming interview.

FIND ONLINE

The Introduction: Warming Up

Your priority in meeting candidates face-to-face (in person or virtually) for the first time is to put them at ease. It's important to create an environment where the candidate feels safe and comfortable to share and connect. Disregard any advice anyone has given you about doing things to create stress just to see how the individual responds. Those techniques are rarely productive, and they put both you and your company in a bad light. Instead, view the first minutes of the meeting as an opportunity to build rapport with the candidate. The more comfortable they are, the more engaging the interview will be, and the more you'll find out about them.

If you're in person and seated at your desk as the candidate walks in, a common courtesy is to stand and meet the individual halfway, shake hands, and let them know that you're happy to meet them (basic stuff but easy to forget). You don't need to cut to the chase right away with penetrating questions. Skilled job interviewers usually begin with small talk — a general comment about the weather, transportation difficulties, and so on — but they keep it to a minimum.

MULTIPLE, PANEL, AND VIDEO INTERVIEWS

It's a common practice for organizations to engage multiple leaders within the business in the interview process, especially if the candidate will play a key role in the organization. In fact, sometimes these meetings are carried out simultaneously through the use of an interviewing panel made up of the hiring manager plus other members of the management team or work group, usually no more than three to five people.

Panel interviews are beneficial when you want to quickly get a promising candidate through multiple interviews in a timely manner. It's best for the hiring manager to conduct one-on-one preliminary interviews with applicants first, choosing only a few finalists for panel interviews. This saves panelists time and ensures that the hiring manager is presenting only those candidates they may ultimately hire. Panel interviews are most successful when the hiring manager distributes job criteria to the interview team in

(continued)

(continued)

advance, along with some suggested questions to ask the candidate. This ensures that panel members will be able to compare candidates in a consistent fashion, using like criteria.

For the most part, panel interviews are the exception to the norm because candidates can feel overwhelmed by a panel approach. If the interview is intimidating, the job seeker may not provide candid information and may even decide the position isn't right for them.

Given the increasing virtual nature of work and the expense of bringing remote candidates in for face-to-face interviews, video interviews are also a common practice. Approach a video interview with the same level of professionalism as you would any other. Conduct the interview from an uncluttered setting. Additionally, make sure that you're comfortable with the technology. If you're new to the system, try it out first with your company colleagues or friends. Any technical problems that crop up during the interview will reflect badly on both you and your business.

Leading a Successful Panel Interview

The foundation of a successful panel interview is thoughtful planning. This includes selecting which team members will participate in the interview, preparing your team, and deciding which questions each interviewer will ask the candidate. At their best, panel interviews allow interviewers to combine their strengths, perspectives, and experiences, leading to effective and comprehensive questions, but it's important that all of the panelists are aligned. Following are some considerations to maximize the panel interview:

>> **Be thoughtful in selecting the right panelists.** When selecting who will interview candidates, keep in mind who the primary stakeholders for the position are, who the candidate may interact with regularly once in the position, and who may be able to offer the candidate a sense of inclusion within the organization. Representation matters, and for this reason, it's important to make sure your interview panel include people from underrepresented groups. Underrepresented groups include a variety of diverse identities, such as race and ethnicity, religious affiliation, women, veterans, people with disabilities, and members of the LGBTQIA+ (lesbian, gay, bisexual, transgender, queer or questioning, intersex, asexual, and more) community.

Interview panels often consist of four to six people and may include

- A representative from human resources or the recruiting team

- The hiring manager

- One or two people from an internal client group that the new hire may interact with regularly

» **Be clear on roles in the panel interview.** The hiring manager generally acts as the leader for the interview, setting the tone and asking basic questions. The other members of the panel may act as the subject matter experts (SMEs) for areas specific to their skills base, but they mostly help the primary interviewer by asking clarifying questions.

» **Prepare the interviewers who are serving on the panel.** Interviewing can be stressful — not only for the candidate, but also for the interviewers. Before you schedule a group panel interview, properly prepare your team by doing the following:

- Share the position success profile with each of the interviewers, so they become familiar with the requirements of the position before interviewing candidates.

- Encourage panelists to review the candidate's résumé to become familiar with their background so they can ask appropriate questions for the role.

- Prep each panelist regarding which areas of the business they should focus on and, ideally, give them standardized interview questions to reduce bias.

» **Schedule the panel interview.** Determine whether to hold an in-person interview or a virtual interview. Traditional face-to-face interviews are best for companies that require employees to show up on-site, whereas virtual interviews are best for filling remote roles or interviewing executive talent that may be located in faraway areas. Because panel interviews involve multiple people with multiple schedules, an effort must be made to synchronize calendars.

» **Determine the best location/room for the interview.** If you're holding the group panel interview in person at your office, it's best to choose an effective location. These interviews work best when participants are able to hear and see each other comfortably. Therefore, avoid very large rooms or incredibly long tables for a small number of participants.

» **Make introductions at the beginning of the interview.** It's mission critical to create an environment that's welcoming and comfortable for the candidate. Introductions set a tone, establish trust, and are a great way to reinforce your organization's commitment to diversity and inclusion. Each panelist should introduce themselves including their name and title, at a minimum. A brief explanation of how their role or department would interface with the open role is helpful to add context for the candidate.

>> **Take turns asking interview questions.** Because one of the advantages of interviewing in a group panel format is immediate access to varying perspectives and experiences, you should leverage the people in the room. The hiring manager often acts as the "lead" during a panel interview, facilitating the conversational flow and line of questioning, but other panelists should ask appropriate clarifying questions as well. For instance, if the panelist is a subject matter expert, they should use their expertise to ask questions about the candidate's experience.

>> **Collaborate following the interview.** The final step in conducting a group panel interview is to discuss the notes taken during the interview and collaborate to decide. Using an evaluation and scorecard during the interview process can help put together all thoughts on the candidate. Each individual panelist should take their own notes during the interview, citing the strengths and weaknesses of the candidate. Once the interview has concluded, the panelists should gather to discuss the candidate and compare notes. The hiring manager can then use those notes to make the final hiring decision.

REMEMBER

The same guidelines for appropriate questioning and comments that apply to the formal interview apply to casual discussions and chitchat. (See "Recognizing What to Ask (and Not to Ask)" later in this chapter.)

After the small talk is out of the way, your next step is to give the candidate a very basic overview of what you're expecting to get from the interview and how long you estimate it to last. Be careful not to give too much information, though. Saying too much about the skills and characteristics you're looking for turns a savvy interviewee into a "parrot" who can repeat the same key words they just heard.

Mastering the Art of Q&A

The Q&A is the main part of the interview. How you phrase questions, when you ask them, how you follow up — each of these aspects of interviewing can go a long way toward affecting the quality and value of the answers you get. The following sections describe the key practices that differentiate people who've mastered the art of questioning from those who haven't.

FIND
ONLINE

For an Interview Q&A Form, see the online tools.

Have a focus

Even before you start to ask questions, you want to have a reasonably specific idea of what information or insights you're expecting to gain from the interview based on your research and the hiring criteria you develop in your position success profile. You may uncover two or three items on the candidate's résumé that warrant clarification. Or you may have a specific question, based on the notes you take during earlier candidate evaluation, about one particular aspect of the candidate's personality. Whatever the need, decide ahead of time what you want to know more about and build your interview strategy around that goal.

Make every question count

Every question you ask during a job interview must have a specific purpose. That purpose may be to elicit specific information, produce some insight into the candidate's personality or past performance, or simply put the candidate at ease. The general rule is this: If the question has no strategic significance, think twice before asking it. Again, tie questions to the criteria defined in the job description.

Pay attention

Listening attentively is difficult under the best of circumstances, but it's often an even tougher challenge during a job interview. That's because it's tempting to draw conclusions before the candidate has completed the answer. Yet another habit is to begin rehearsing in your mind the next question you intend to ask while the candidate is still answering the earlier question. Fight these tendencies. Consider writing down your questions before the interview begins and then direct the full measure of your concentration to the candidate and what that person is saying.

Don't hesitate to probe

Whenever a candidate offers an answer that doesn't address the specific information you're seeking, nothing's wrong with asking additional questions to draw out more specific answers. For example, if a candidate talks about the money they saved their department, ask how much they saved and what, specifically, they did to accomplish that. Too many interviewers let candidates off the hook in the interest of being nice. That practice, however, can prove counterproductive — the interviewee may give you valuable background on specific abilities if your questions are more penetrating.

Give candidates ample time to respond

The fact that a candidate doesn't respond immediately to a question you ask doesn't mean that you need to rush in with another question to fill the silence. Give the candidate time to come up with a thoughtful answer. If the silence persists for more than, say, ten seconds, ask the candidate whether they want you to clarify the question. Otherwise, don't rush things. Use the silence to observe the candidate and to take stock of where you are in the interview. Remember that the interview is a time for you to listen, and some candidates may need time to process your question before providing a thoughtful answer.

Tread carefully whenever you come across a candidate who seems flat and disinterested during the job interview. If a candidate can't demonstrate any real enthusiasm during the interview, don't expect them to muster any fire in the belly after you hire them.

Suspend judgments

A study from the University of Toledo found that judgments made in the first ten seconds of an interview can predict the outcome of the interview. The problem with these types of snap judgments? They're usually useless. Making a snap judgment in the first ten seconds creates a situation where the interview is spent trying to confirm what we think of someone — this is called *confirmation bias,* and it completely leaves out time for accurate assessment. In essence, by making a snap judgment, you render the interview unusable. Reserving judgment isn't easy but try to keep your attention on the answers you're getting instead of making interpretations or judgments. You'll have plenty of time after the interview to evaluate what you see and hear.

Take notes

Memories can do tricky things, leading people to ignore what actually happens during an interview and to rely instead on general impressions. Taking notes helps you avoid this common pitfall. Just make sure that you do so unobtrusively so the candidate doesn't feel like they have to pause for you to keep pace. Keep all notes factual and within ethical and nondiscriminatory boundaries. Also, give yourself a few moments after the interview to review your notes and clarify them or put them into some kind of order.

Vary the style of questions

You can usually divide questions into five categories, based on the kinds of answers you're trying to elicit.

Closed-ended

Definition: Questions that call for a simple, informational answer — often a yes or no.

Examples: "How many years did you work for the circus?" "Did you enjoy it?" "What cities did you tour?"

When to use them: Closed-ended questions work best if you're trying to elicit specific information or set the stage for more complex questions.

Pitfalls to avoid: Asking too many of them in rapid-fire succession and failing to tie them back to the job criteria can make candidates feel as though they're being interrogated.

Open-ended

Definition: Questions that require thought and oblige the candidate to reveal attitudes or opinions. One type of open-ended question is the behavioral interview question. With a behavioral question, candidates are asked to relate past on-the-job experiences to situations they are likely to encounter in the position being discussed.

Examples: "Can you describe how you handle tight deadlines on the job?" "Can you give me an illustration of how you improved productivity at your last job?"

When to use them: Most of the time but interspersed with closed-ended questions.

Pitfalls to avoid: Not being specific enough as you phrase the question and not interceding if the candidate's answer starts to veer off track.

Hypothetical

Definition: Questions that invite the candidate to resolve an imaginary situation or react to a given situation.

Examples: "If you were the purchasing manager, how would you go about selecting a new automated purchase order system for the company?" "If you were to take over this department, what's the first thing you'd do to improve productivity?"

When to use them: Use them when you can frame them in the context of actual job situations.

Pitfall to avoid: Putting too much stock in the candidate's hypothetical answer. You're usually better off asking questions that force a candidate to use an actual experience as the basis for an answer.

Leading

Definition: Questions asked in such a way that the answer you're looking for is obvious.

Examples: "You know a lot about team building, don't you?" "You wouldn't dream of falsifying your expense accounts, would you?"

When to use them: Rarely, if ever. You're not likely to get an honest answer — just the answer you want to hear. And you run the risk of appearing unprofessional.

Off-the-wall

Definition: Questions that, on the surface, may seem bizarre but may actually be revealing in the answers they elicit.

Examples: "What literary character do you most closely identify with?" "If you could be reincarnated as a car, which one would you choose?"

When to use them: Some businesses have used these kinds of questions to determine whether a candidate is a fit for the company culture or to see whether the interviewee can think outside the box, but most firms should approach them with a good deal of caution. A candidate's response to an off-the-wall challenge may highlight their creativity and offer insight into their thought process. The key is not to overuse, but recognize that for some candidates and cultures, these types of questions are incredibly helpful in assessing the candidate's open mindedness and creativity. This can also be helpful to express quirkiness and personality during the interview process.

WARNING

New technologies are emerging that record interviews specifically to reduce bias in the hiring process and also create a better candidate experience (for example, creating a highlight reel for other stakeholders to review so that hiring *process* is faster and candidate is not asked the same question multiple times). There are pros and cons here, so be thoughtful in recording interviews because it can be risky. In fact, some states make this practice illegal without mutual consent. If you plan to record an interview or use technology that does so, check first with a knowledgeable and experienced lawyer for any legal restrictions.

Recognizing What to Ask (and Not to Ask)

The questions you or others in your organization ask during a job interview can result in legal problems for the company if you fail to follow certain guidelines. Even the most innocent of questions can result in a discrimination suit at some point.

Antidiscrimination and consumer protection legislation restricts the type and scope of pre-employment questions that you can ask. Moreover, court decisions and administrative rulings have refined what you can and can't ask, and, to make matters even more confusing, standards can vary from state to state — and even from city to city.

Here are some current pitfalls:

>> **Be sensitive to age discrimination issues.** Remember that any question that may indicate the candidate's age may be interpreted as discriminatory. In other words, don't ask a question such as "When did you graduate from high school?"

>> **Beware of double-edged questions.** Caution all the interviewers in your company to keep their innocent curiosity (as evidenced in a question such as "What kind of a name is that?") from exposing your company to charges of discrimination.

>> **Don't confuse before and after.** Questions considered illegal before hiring may be acceptable after the individual is on the payroll. Age is a good example. You can't ask a person's age before hiring, but after hiring, the information may be needed for health insurance or pension forms.

FIND ONLINE

For more detailed information on how to avoid discrimination when you're asking interview questions, see the Employment Inquiries Fact Sheet in the online tools.

The following sections provide a rundown of which questions are permitted before hiring and which are not. Check with your attorney for any local restrictions or new rulings and keep in mind that all questions must directly relate to a bona fide job requirement.

Even questions that seem okay to ask under the following guidelines may be discriminatory if they're asked in circumstances that suggest a discriminatory intent — for example, asking only female employees who reveal that they have children whether they have any reason they couldn't work overtime or on the weekend.

REMEMBER

Keep your questions focused on the expected outcomes of the position and away from the candidate's personal life.

FIND ONLINE

During the interview, you can use the Nondiscriminatory Interview Question Reference Sheet in the online tools to help you avoid potentially problematic questions.

National origin

Questions okay to ask: None.

Risky ground: Questions related to the candidate's national origin, ancestry, or native language or that of family members. That also applies to the applicant's and the applicant's parents' places of birth.

Discriminatory: "What sort of an accent is that?" "Where were you born?" "Where were your parents born?"

Citizenship status

Questions okay to ask: "If hired, will you be able to prove that you have the right to remain and work in the United States?"

Risky ground: Questions that may oblige a candidate to indicate national origin.

Discriminatory: "Are you a U.S. citizen?"

Address

Questions okay to ask: "Where do you live?" "How long have you lived here?"

Risky ground: Questions about housing aimed at revealing financial status. (These may be considered discriminatory against minorities.)

Discriminatory: "Are you renting, or do you own your home?"

Age

Questions okay to ask: "If hired, can you provide proof that you are at least 18 years of age?" (Asking this question is okay to ensure that the candidate is old enough to work in a specific job that has a minimum age requirement.)

Risky ground: Questions regarding age when age is not a bona fide job requirement.

Discriminatory: "How old are you?" "In what year were you born?" "When did you graduate from high school?"

Family status

Questions okay to ask: "Can you relocate?" (only if it's relevant to the job).

Risky ground: All questions regarding marital or family status.

Discriminatory: "Are you pregnant?" "When are you due?" (even if the candidate is obviously pregnant).

Religion

Questions okay to ask: "Can you work overtime on days other than Monday through Friday?"

Risky ground: Any question whose answers may indicate religious beliefs or affiliation.

Discriminatory: "What religious holidays do you observe?"

Health and physical condition

Questions okay to ask: "Can you perform the expected job functions with or without reasonable accommodation?"

Risky ground: Questions that aren't directly related to a bona fide job requirement and, in addition, aren't being asked of all candidates.

Discriminatory: "Do you have a hearing impairment?" "Have you ever filed a workers' compensation claim?"

Name

Questions okay to ask: "Have you ever used another name or nickname?"

Risky ground: Questions about whether the applicant has ever changed their name or about the candidate's maiden name.

Discriminatory: "What kind of name is that?"

Language

Questions okay to ask: "What language do you speak, read, and/or write?" (permissible if relevant to the job).

Risky ground: Questions that reveal the applicant's national origin or ancestry.

Discriminatory: "What language do you speak at home?" "Is English your first language?"

Asking Solid Questions and Knowing How to Interpret the Answers

What makes an interview question "good"? A good question does two things:

>> It gives you the specific information you need to make a sound hiring decision.

>> It helps you gain insight into the candidate's values and their experience and style.

TIP

Avoid timeworn, clichéd questions, such as "What are your strengths and weaknesses?" or "Where do you see yourself in the next five years?" Instead, develop a list of questions designed to elicit responses that will be most helpful in evaluating a candidate's suitability for your position and organization.

You can ask hundreds of such questions, but here are some to get you started, along with ideas on what to look for in the answers:

>> **"What interests you about this job, and what skills and strengths can you bring to it?"** Nothing tricky here, but it's a solid question all the same. Note that the question is not "What are your skills and strengths?" but "What skills and strengths can you bring to the job?" The answer is yet another way to gauge how much interest the applicant has in the job and how well prepared they are for the interview. Stronger candidates should be able to correlate their skills with specific job requirements: "I think my experience as a foreign correspondent will be of great help in marketing products to overseas customers." They will answer the question in the context of contributions they can make to the company.

>> **"Can you tell me a little about your current job?"** Strong candidates should be able to give you a short and precise summary of duties and responsibilities. How they answer this question can help you determine their passion and enthusiasm for their work and their sense of personal accountability. Be wary of applicants who bad-mouth or blame their employers.

>> **"In a way that anyone could understand, can you describe a professional achievement that you're proud of?"** This question is especially good when you're interviewing someone for a technical position, such as a systems analyst or tax accountant. The answer shows the applicant's ability to explain

what they do so that anyone can understand it. Do they avoid jargon in the description? Do they get points across clearly? Failure to do so may be a sign that the candidate can't step out of their world sufficiently to work with people in other departments, which is a growing necessity in many organizations today.

» **"How have you changed the nature of your current job?"** A convincing answer here shows adaptability and a willingness to take the bull by the horns, if necessary. An individual who chose to do a job differently from other people also may show creativity and resourcefulness. The question gives candidates a chance to talk about such contributions as greater efficiencies or cost savings. If a candidate says they didn't change the nature of the job, that response can tell you something as well.

» **"What was the most difficult decision you ever had to make on the job?"** Notice the intentionally vague aspect of this question. It's not hypothetical; it's real. What you're looking for is the person's decision-making style and how it fits into your company culture. Someone who admits that firing a subordinate was difficult demonstrates compassion. Those who successfully decided to approach a coworker over a conflict may turn out to be great team players. Individuals who admit to a mistake exhibit honesty and open-mindedness.

Also, note how people went about making the decision. Seeking the advice of others, for example, may mean that they're team centered. This question is an especially important one if you're interviewing a candidate for a middle- or senior-level management position.

» **"Why did you decide to pursue a new job?"** This question is just a different way of asking, "What are you looking for in a job?" Some candidates come so well-rehearsed that they're never at a loss for an answer. Sometimes by phrasing the question in a different way, you can cause them to go off script.

» **"I see that you've been unemployed for the past few months. Why did you leave your last job, and what have you been doing since then?"** This question is important, but don't let it seem accusatory. Especially in challenging economic times, it's not unusual for highly competent people to find themselves unemployed through no fault of their own and unable to prevent gaps in their employment history. Pursuing the issue in a neutral, diplomatic way is important. Try to get specific, factual answers that you can verify later.

At the same time — and as noted in Chapter 7 — the reasons for employment gaps may pertain to legally protected information that you, the employer, may not consider in making hiring or any other employment-related decision. For example, an applicant who was unemployed due to cancer very likely has a protected disability under the Americans with Disabilities Act and similar state laws. Probing into the reasons underlying employment gaps can unearth information that you, the employer, may not want to be injected into the application/hiring process. You must be careful when approaching this issue.

>> **"Who was your best boss ever and why? Who was the worst, and, looking back, what could you have done to make that relationship better?"** These two questions are more penetrating than you may think. Among other things, the answers give you insight into how the candidate views and responds to supervision. A reflective, responsive answer to the second part of the question may indicate a loyal employee capable of rising above an unpleasant supervisory situation and/or learning from past mistakes, both highly desirable qualities. A bitter, critical answer may indicate someone who holds grudges or simply can't get along with certain kinds of people. Yes, personality clashes occur all the time, but in today's team-oriented workplace, you want employees who try to minimize these clashes and not use them as excuses.

>> **"Are you more comfortable and successful working alone with information or working with other people?"** The ideal answer here is "both." People who say they like working with information are obviously a good choice for technical positions, but it may be a red flag if they don't also enjoy communicating and collaborating with other individuals — increasingly a function of even highly technical jobs. An excellent candidate may say that the different perspectives within a group produce more innovative ideas than one person working alone can, but without information a team can't get very far.

>> **"What sorts of things do you think your current/past company could do to be more successful?"** This one is a great big-picture question. You're probing to find out whether the candidate has a clear understanding of their current or past employer's missions and goals and whether they have worked with those goals in mind. Candidates who can't answer this question well are demonstrating a lack of depth and interest, which can quite likely carry over into your organization. Sometimes the answer to this question also reveals hidden bitterness or anger at an employer. But make clear to the candidate that you're not looking for proprietary or confidential information.

>> **"Can you describe a typical day at work in your last job?"** Strong candidates can give you specific details that you can verify later, but the main point of this question is to see how the applicant's current (or most recent) routine compares with the requirements of the job in question. How interviewees describe their duties can prove highly revealing. Do you sense any real enthusiasm or interest? Do the details match the information you already have? You're looking for enthusiasm and some indication that the applicant connects their current duties with company goals.

>> **"What sort of work environment do you prefer? What brings out your best performance?"** Probe for specifics. You want to find out whether this person is going to be successful and fulfilled in the role and at your company. If your corporate culture is collegial and team centered, you don't want someone who answers, "I like to be left alone to do my work." You also may uncover unrealistic expectations or potential future clashes ("My plan is to spend a couple months in

the mailroom and then apply for the presidency of the company"). People rarely, if ever, work at their best in all situations. Candidates who say otherwise aren't being honest with themselves or with you.

>> **"How do you handle conflict? Can you give me an example of how you handled a workplace disagreement in the past?"** You want candidates who try to be reasonable but nonetheless stand up for what's right. Unfortunately, most candidates say the right things, which is why you want some specifics. Be suspicious if the answer is too predictable. Some people may be naturally easygoing, but candidates who say that they never get into conflict situations are either dishonest or delusional.

>> **"How would you respond if you were placed in a situation that you felt presented a conflict of interest or was unethical? Have you ever had this experience in previous positions?"** No rational candidate is going to say that sometimes it's okay to be unethical. But how individuals approach this question and any anecdotes they share can offer valuable insights as to how they may respond if faced with such a situation.

>> **"What are your compensation expectations?"** There's no "trick" to this question. You simply want to get a sense early on whether the candidate's desired pay is in line with what you've budgeted for the open position. This can prevent you from continuing to move through the hiring process a promising candidate whose salary expectations far exceed your own.

TIP

In addition to an opportunity to showcase their qualifications, savvy candidates use the interview to find out as much as they can about the position and company, so don't be surprised if they come prepared with questions of their own. Don't interpret questions as disruptive to your agenda. They're a show of interest and professionalism; remember that the interview process goes both ways. The candidate is interviewing you just as much as you're interviewing the candidate. In addition, you can proactively address many of their curiosities by proactively promoting your company during the interview. Just as candidates try to show how their skills are a match with the position, you also can point out programs and policies that fit the needs of promising applicants and highlight the aspects of the corporate culture that make your firm a great place to work.

End Game: Closing on the Right Note

With only a few minutes to go, you can bring the session to a graceful close by following these steps:

1. Offer the candidate a broad-brushstroke summary of the interview.

Sum up what the candidate has said about their fit for the position, reasons for wanting the job, and so on. This summary demonstrates that you were a sincere listener and that you care about the candidate as a person. That leaves a good impression. It also gives the candidate an opportunity to clarify any misunderstandings.

2. **Let the candidate ask questions.**

3. **Let the candidate know what comes next.**

Advise the candidate how and when you're going to contact them and whether any further steps need to be taken — for example, there may be additional assessments you want to include in the process. Being clear on next steps not only is a common courtesy but also creates a good impression and is an important part of a great candidate experience.

Also, let the candidate know you'll be in touch regardless of the hiring decision. Not all companies say, "Thanks, but no thanks" to rejected applicants, but it's a sign of respect and consideration.

4. **End the interview on a formal but sincere note.**

Thank the candidate for their time and repeat your commitment to follow up. If the interview is in person, either stand or shake hands again. This action formally ends the session and provides a signal for the candidate to leave. Walk the applicant out of the office to the elevator lobby or front door.

And one last suggestion: As soon as possible after the candidate's departure, take a moment to collect your thoughts and write down your impressions and a summary of your notes. You don't need to make any definitive decisions at this point, but recording your impressions while they're still fresh in your mind will help you immeasurably if the final choice boils down to several candidates, all of whose qualifications are comparable. Along these lines, collect all feedback from other interviewers who met with the candidate the same day that they met with the interviewee. This allows you to gather feedback while it's still fresh and when it's most relevant.

FIND ONLINE

The online tools contains a Candidate Interview Evaluation Form, which you can use to record your impressions of job candidates.

Completing the evaluation form will set you up for clarity as you're making hiring decisions.

Chapter **9**

Making the Hiring Decision

N ow comes the moment of truth in the hiring process: choosing who to extend an offer to. Because hiring mistakes can be costly, a lot is riding on your ability to select the best people for your available positions. If you find yourself constantly second-guessing your hiring decisions, you may want to take a close look at the process you're using to make your final choices. This chapter can help you get this process started.

Coming to Grips with the Decision-Making Process

Stripped to its essentials, the decision-making process in the final stages of hiring isn't really that different from selecting the right school for your child or deciding on a new home. You look at your options, weigh the pros and cons of each, and then make the best choice with the information available.

Of course, hiring involves people, not a school or home. Managers differ in their basic approaches to selecting new hires. Some rely entirely on their own judgment and assessments. Others are highly systematic and may also seek guidance from others.

You can never be absolutely certain that the decision you make is going to give you all that you expect. You can improve your chances significantly, however, if you manage the decision-making process in a reasonably disciplined way.

REMEMBER

Remain objective in evaluating candidates. Don't let your personal biases steer your focus away from your hiring criteria (the halo and cloning effects I describe later in this chapter). Consistently focus on the key hiring criteria you established at the outset of the process when you were identifying your needs and drawing up a job description that pinpoints the combination of skills, attributes, and credentials that a particular position requires.

Utilizing the Tools of the Trade

Here are some of the factors on which different leaders base their hiring decisions and what you need to keep in mind as you're considering each one. I discuss them in more detail later in this chapter.

Past experience

A long-time truism in successful hiring is the concept that the best indicator of a candidate's future potential is past performance — evidence that the candidate can successfully accomplish the outcomes of the position. If a candidate was hardworking, highly motivated, and team oriented in their last job, the same is likely to hold true in the new job. Similarly, the candidate who consistently lacked enthusiasm and drive in their last position isn't likely to turn things around in the next one.

WARNING

The only caveat to this usually reliable principle: The conditions that prevailed in the candidate's last job need to closely parallel the conditions in the job they're seeking. Otherwise, you have no real basis for comparison. No two business environments are identical, and environment has an impact on performance. For all you know, certain systems or people in place in the candidate's previous job may have been instrumental in their success (or lack thereof) — and you can rarely replicate such factors in your company (and may not even want to).

Interview impressions

Impressions you pick up during an interview almost always carry a great deal of weight in hiring decisions — and understandably so. Managers naturally place more trust in what they actually see and hear than in information from third-party sources. The problem with interview impressions is that they're just that — impressions. You're listening to answers and observing behavior, but your own preconceived perceptions and experiences almost always influence your judgment.

This doesn't mean that you should disregard your interview impressions — only that you should keep them in their proper perspective with test results, references, and other information you've collected to evaluate a prospective hire.

Test/assessment results

Some people regard test or assessment results as the only truly reliable predictor of future success. The argument goes as follows: Test results are quantifiable. In most tests, results aren't subject to personal interpretation. With a large enough sample, you can compare test scores to job performance ratings and, eventually, use test scores as a predictor of future performance.

The only problem is this: Some candidates simply don't test well. They freeze up, which affects their ultimate scores. Other candidates may be clever enough to figure out what most tests are actually testing for and tailor their responses accordingly. So, if you're going to use test results in your decision-making process, ensure the validity of the tests (whether they do, indeed, predict the quality of future job performance) and their legality (whether they comply with all state and federal laws and don't result in discrimination). (See "Discovering the Truth about Background Checks," later in this chapter.)

Firsthand observation

Call it the proof-in-the-pudding principle. Watching candidates actually perform some of the tasks for which you're considering hiring them is clearly the most reliable way to judge their competence. That's why more and more companies these days start out an applicant as a contingent, or temporary, worker, with the idea that if the person works out, they may eventually become a full-time employee.

Selecting Your Candidate: You Need a System

The easiest way to make a hiring decision is to weigh the options and simply go with what your intuition tells you to do. Easy — but risky. Gut decisions, whether they originate from one person or a group of people, are almost always biased in the following respect: Their roots tend to be firmly planted in wishful thinking. These decisions often reflect what you'd ideally like to see happen as opposed to what's most likely to happen based on the evidence. The following sections examine what you can do to make your own hiring decisions.

Knowing what to rely on

Decision-makers in organizations with good track records of making successful hires don't give themselves the luxury of relying solely on intuition. They use — and generally trust — their intuition, but they don't focus on intuition as the sole basis for their judgments. The following list describes what these decision-makers rely on (incorporate them into your process):

>> **They have some sort of system in place.** Their system is a well-thought-out protocol that assesses the strengths and weaknesses of candidates and applies those assessments to the outcomes expected in the job. They always make it a point, for example, to precede any face-to-face interview with a phone conversation. And they've established a set of steps that they routinely follow after they've interviewed a candidate.

>> **The system that they use, regardless of how simple or elaborate, is weighted.** The system presupposes that certain skills and attributes influence job performance more than others do, and it takes those differences into account. They know, for example, that the personal qualities that underlie effective performance in sales aren't necessarily the same ones that underlie effective performance in, say, administrative jobs.

>> **They constantly monitor and evaluate the effectiveness of the system.** They always have an eye toward sharpening their own ability and the ability of others to link any data they obtain during the recruiting and interviewing process to on-the-job performance. If a particular type of testing mechanism is used in the selection process, the validity of the test (how closely the test results correlate with successful on-the-job performance) is monitored on a regular basis.

Setting up your own protocol — creating a scorecard

Some organizations invest a great deal of money in developing elaborate selection procedures, the express purpose of which is to make the candidate evaluation process more objective and accurate. Whether you want to go that route is up to you; the following describes the fundamental steps you must go through with all such processes, regardless of cost, to create a scorecard.

1. **Isolate key hiring criteria.**

   By this point in the hiring process, you should know what combination of skills and attributes a candidate needs to perform the job well and fit your company's pace and culture. If you don't, refer to Chapters 4 and 5.

2. **Set priorities.**

   You can safely assume that some of your hiring criteria are more important than others. To take these differences into account, and, depending on the nature of the particular position at issue, some employers may want to set up a scale that reflects the relative importance of any particular skill or attribute. For example, to ensure reasonable accuracy in assigning these values ask the following question: If the candidate didn't have this skill or quality, how would it affect their job performance? The greater the effect, the higher the value of that skill or quality.

3. **Evaluate candidates on the basis of the weighted scale you established in Step 2.**

   This segment of the process is the tricky part. Instead of simply looking at the candidate as a whole, you examine each of the criteria you set up, and you rate the candidate on the basis of how they measure up in that particular category.

   This weighted system of evaluation considers the performance priorities unique to each of the key hiring criteria. It helps ensure that the requirements of the job reasonably align with the strengths and weaknesses of the candidate.

Say, for example, that one of the candidate's strengths is the ability to work as part of a team. The candidate's rating on that particular attribute may be a 5 on a 5-point scale, but the relative importance of teamwork to the task at hand may be anywhere from 1 to 5, which means that the overall ranking may end up as low as 5.

A weighted system gives you an opportunity to see how well candidates measure up against one another and how closely their skills and attributes match the job requirements. In other words, it allows you to create a scorecard. You must be careful, however. The effectiveness of this system depends on two crucial factors: the validity of your hiring criteria and the objectivity of the judgments that underlie any ratings you assign to various candidates.

Tables 9-1 and 9-2 demonstrate how a weighted evaluation system works. Notice that the candidate under evaluation in Table 9-1 is relatively weak in two hiring criteria — previous experience and computer skills — but is much stronger in the criteria that carry more weight. The candidate's aggregate score, therefore, is higher than that of a candidate who meets only the technical requirements of the job.

TABLE 9-1

How Candidate 1 Shapes Up

Performance Category	Weighted Importance (1–5)	Candidate Rating (1–5)	Score
Previous customer experience	3	1	3
Excel skills	2	2	4
Written communication skills	5	4	20
Reliability	5	4	20
Ability to work in a fast-paced environment	4	4	16
Empathy	4	4	16
Total			**79**

TABLE 9-2

How Candidate 2 Shapes Up

Performance Category	Weighted Importance (1–5)	Candidate Rating (1–5)	Score
Previous customer experience	3	5	15
Excel skills	2	5	10
Written communication skills	5	2	10
Reliability	5	3	15
Ability to work in a fast-paced environment	4	4	16
Empathy	4	1	4
Total			**70**

Factoring in the intangibles

The really tough part of any evaluation process is attaching numerical ratings to the intangibles: those attributes that are difficult to measure but are just as critical as the tangible ones. They may involve so-called *soft skills* such as communication or coaching skills. They may be character or personality traits that the company desires in its employees, or beneficial for a particular position. Intangibles are, by their very nature, more subjective and more difficult to define and identify. Yet, looking for and identifying these helps you select the best fit for the job and the company.

The following sections cover those intangible factors that you commonly find in the criteria for most jobs, along with suggestions on how to tell whether the candidate measures up.

Creative problem-solving and innovation

The work world is full of challenges. The last thing an employer or hiring manager wants is an employee who sees a challenging situation or a new task and says, "Wow, I don't know what to do here." Instead, they want to know that the candidate can think logically and creatively to develop solutions to problems or obstacles that naturally emerge.

They also hope the employee can help to come up with new ideas as well as address existing problems. And the more creative, the better; that kind of thinking leads to innovation and improvements within the company.

How to measure: Evidence of good decision-making and problem-solving in previous jobs. Evidence that the candidate has used creativity in the face of adversity, coming up with innovative solutions to problems that arose.

Time management

In the virtual world of work, without the natural structure that a day at the office provides, time management is a mission-critical skill that organizations look for in the hiring process. A candidate with strong time management skills knows how to organize their schedule, both daily and beyond, to get projects done on time and with efficiency.

How to measure: The best way to measure these criteria is to ask candidates during the interview how they manage their time and how they manage multiple priorities.

Growth mindset

When it comes to ensuring longevity in their career, candidates need to be able to grow and adapt to changes within their industry and the job market as a whole (you may want to take a look at TopResume's article, "5 Things You Should Do Right Now to Thrive in Your Career During a Pandemic" at www.topresume.com/career-advice/thriving-in-career-during-pandemic). With the mechanization of jobs and industries, having a growth mindset is essential. So, what is a growth mindset? Professionals with a growth mindset are motivated to reach higher levels of achievement by continuously learning new skills in order to move with a changing market. (Check out TopResume's "Will Robots Take My Job?" at www.topresume.com/career-advice/will-robots-and-automation-take-my-job). Essentially, it entails being adaptable and willing to go above and beyond the soft and hard skills candidates already have.

How to measure: Examples of showing initiative by learning a new skill in order to better do their job or keep up with industry changes.

Collaboration

Collaboration skills enable team members to successfully work toward a common goal with others. They routinely top the list of skills companies need most.

Collaborating with your coworkers isn't as easy as it seems. Those who believe that they know how to do the job and don't have faith in others to do their parts can create tension in the office and hurt overall efficiency. In a virtual environment, it's critical for employees to collaborate while not being in the same room as their coworkers. The ability to trust others, work together, and give and accept ideas is important to accomplishing tasks together.

How to measure: Previous work experience. (Did candidates work on their own or with groups?) Team successes mentioned during the interview. Evidence of ability to work within project team rules, protocols, and work practices. Support for coworkers. Willingness to ask for (and offer) help.

Emotional intelligence

Emotional intelligence is the ability to perceive, evaluate, and respond to individual emotions and the emotions of others. A candidate with a high level of emotional intelligence is able to think empathetically about others and the interpersonal relationships that develop in the workplace.

This is another soft skill that has taken on new meaning. Post-pandemic stress, grief, and frustration are abundant. From new work-from-home challenges to lost loved ones or other pandemic issues, having the ability to read the emotions of your coworkers and respond with compassion is essential. A 2022 CareerBuilder survey reported that 71 percent of employers value emotional intelligence (EQ) in an employee more than IQ (intelligence quotient), while 75 percent are more likely to promote an employee with a higher EQ over someone with a higher IQ.

How to measure: Look for evidence of EQ during the interview process through the following: active listening, showing genuine emotion, sharing stories about their growth, asking questions about company culture.

Dealing with Common Challenges in the Hiring Decision

Bad hiring decisions rarely happen by accident. In retrospect, you can usually discover that you didn't do something you should have. This section covers the key principles to follow in order to hire the right person.

Anchor yourself to the hiring criteria

The hiring criteria based on the outcomes of the job in the position success profile that you establish from the beginning should serve as your strict guide throughout the evaluation process. If, in looking ahead, you decide to change the criteria, fine. Just make sure that you aren't changing criteria simply because you're enamored with one particular prospect and decide to change the ground rules to accommodate that candidate.

Anchoring yourself to hiring criteria helps to prevent three of the most common pitfalls in hiring:

>> **The halo effect:** Becoming so enraptured by one particular aspect of the candidate — appearance, credentials, or interests, for instance — that you let that aspect influence all your other judgments

>> **The cloning effect:** Hiring someone in your image even though someone with your particular mix of skills and attributes clearly isn't qualified for that particular job

>> **How much you "like" the candidate:** Hiring someone because they're friendly and "likeable" versus evidence that they'll be successful

Take your time

The more pressure you're under, the greater the likelihood of rushing the decision and ending up with someone who not only isn't your best choice but whom you're also probably going to end up firing — with all the disruption that firing someone entails. Keep in mind the main pitfall of acting out of urgency: You overestimate the qualities of candidates who may be only marginally qualified to fill the job. If you're worried about finding someone right away, see whether you can bring in a temporary replacement to keep projects on track as you continue the search.

Cross-verify whenever possible

Whatever else they may disagree on, most hiring experts contend that you can never have enough information from enough different sources. So, try not to rely solely on any one source, whether interview impressions, résumé data, reference checks, or assessment data. Cast a wide net and pay careful attention to discrepancies.

Get help, but avoid the "too many cooks" syndrome

A smart practice — particularly when filling a key position — is to get input from others before you make a final choice. Involving too many people in the final decision, however, is a mistake. If too many people have a say, the likely outcome is a compromise choice. Instead of getting the best employee, you end up with the candidate who's the least objectionable to everyone.

TIP

Try to restrict your circle of decision-makers to three to five people who understand the job, your company's culture, and the personality and working style of the potential hire's manager. As I discuss in Chapter 8, you can gain these additional perspectives on candidates by holding multiple and panel interviews. When it comes time for the final decision, these same people can help you choose the best applicant.

Don't force the issue

The recruiting process sometimes uncovers a "dream" employee — except for one problem: The candidate's skills and attributes don't match the hiring criteria of a particular job. The best thing to do if you find yourself in this situation is to see whether you can find another job in the company that better suits this particular candidate. The worst thing that you can do is try to put a good worker in the wrong job.

Avoid the "top of mind" syndrome

Do your best to stay alert to any extraneous factors that may distort the selection process. Employers tend to choose some candidates over others, for example, not because those candidates are more qualified but because they're interviewed later in the hiring process and are fresher in the minds of the interviewer. The best way to avoid this pitfall is to keep your focus on the hiring criteria, no matter what.

Getting a Broader View: Employment Reference Checks

Employment reference checks have long been an important part of the hiring process. At the most basic level, they help you confirm that your candidate for a role has the experience and skill set that they say they do. The key is to connect with at least two candidate references to gather information about the candidate's qualities, qualifications, and work habits. Even though most references provided by an applicant are biased in their favor, asking the right questions can help you uncover some red flags or confirm your hiring choice.

Not taking these steps can increase your risk of making a hiring mistake and putting your organization at a disadvantage. If you succeed in matching the candidate and the credentials presented to you, however, there's a much better chance that the applicant will prove to be a productive and valuable member of your team. It's best if you conduct reference (or other) checks personally if you'll be the one working with the employee.

In this section, I provide guidance on how to gather valuable reference information that can be used to help make the best hiring decision.

Checking hard-to-check references

Getting a candid reference from an employer can be challenging because previous employers, who know that both saying too much and saying too little can have legal consequences, are increasingly wary of being specific about past employees and their work histories. Although companies have been sued for not disclosing enough information about former workers, others have paid enormous settlements because they provided negative references — whether true or false.

Because of these difficulties, rushing through the reference-checking process — or bypassing it altogether — to make a quick hire may be tempting. But getting reliable information from former supervisors and peers is an important task to complete before selecting someone as an employee of your company.

TIP

Here are some tips on approaching this often-difficult process. Like much of the advice in this book, these tips apply to you directly if you're the hiring manager; if you're not, they're for you to communicate to line managers who are spearheading the hiring process in your organization.

>> **Let the candidate know that you check references.** Be clear with candidates from the outset that your organization will be checking their references. Checking references is perfectly legal as long as the information being verified is job related and doesn't violate discrimination laws. Informing applicants that you're checking usually helps ensure that the answers they give you during the interview are truthful, especially when you start the interview by saying, "If we're interested in you, and you're interested in us, we'll be checking your references."

>> **Don't delegate it.** If the employee will report directly to you, *you* should check the references. No matter how thorough a delegate or deputy may be, the hiring manager will have corollary questions that may not occur to others. Also, calling someone at your same level may establish greater camaraderie that can prompt a more honest and detailed reference. Furthermore, checking references yourself is a great way to gain insight from a former supervisor on how best to manage the individual. If you lack the time to do the complete job, then compromise by assigning just part of the reference checking to capable coworkers in your group. Handle one — preferably, two — yourself.

>> **Use responses from the interview.** Asking candidates during the job interview what their former employers are likely to say about them can provide you with a good starting point for getting the former employer to talk openly. You can start out by saying something such as, "Joe tells me that you think he's the greatest thing since sliced bread," and have the employer take it from there. You may not get a totally frank answer, but you can get valuable comments and insights. After all, candidates must assume that you're going to check out their answers.

>> **For the best responses, pick up the phone.** The best way to communicate with references is via phone. Emailing companies is usually ineffective. Calling gives you an opportunity to ask spontaneous questions based upon what's said in response to one of your primary questions. You can often detect enthusiasm, or lack of it, if you pay attention to tone of voice.

FIND
ONLINE

The online tools include Sample Reference Check Questions you can use when contacting a candidate's references.

Using your own network for checking

You don't need to limit your search for reference information to only those people the applicant suggests. You may find people in your own circle of professional acquaintances or friends with firsthand knowledge of the candidate who probably aren't as reluctant as a former employer may be to level with you. Also, ask the candidate's references for names of other individuals you may contact for information.

Try to be fair, however, if you get information that puts the candidate in a bad light. Try to get verification from one or two other sources, just to make sure that what you're hearing isn't sour grapes from one specific individual.

Online reference checking: Proceed with caution

Advances in technology and more sophisticated online search capabilities have increased the popularity of reference checking via the internet. The practice will undoubtedly grow as more record holders create databases that employers can easily access. (See the next section.)

WARNING

Everyone knows about the practice of searching for a person's name online to see what comes up. Social media offer other means of accessing information online. Some employers also access blogs and personal websites. My recommendation here: Proceed carefully. Although this approach can reduce costs and sometimes yield faster results, you also must understand that much of the information on a candidate you discover can be either erroneous or irrelevant. A person's digital footprint also can reveal facts that are illegal to consider in a hiring decision, and your company's review of online information can raise privacy concerns. The same legal constraints that govern interviewing apply to reference checking. Online reference checking should be viewed as a complement to, not a replacement for, traditional methods. A web search is no substitute for personal assessments of the work quality and professionalism of candidates that carefully selected individuals can offer. Inaccuracies exist in many online data records, and some forms of investigation require written permission from the applicant and are subject to other legal limitations.

Discovering the Truth about Background Checks

Background checks take reference checks a step further, and businesses use them because they feel they're a way to protect the organization and gain assurance that the people they hire are what they represent themselves to be. In other words, whereas reference checks allow you to verify with former employers a potential hire's accomplishments and personal attributes (see the preceding section), background checks attempt to delve into additional aspects of a candidate's activities and behavior. Even though it's illegal to discriminate based on someone's race, color, national origin, sex, religion, or disability — and there are certain questions regarding medical conditions and age you should always avoid — conducting a background screening is legal; however, proceed with caution. California and many other states prohibit the use of credit reports in hiring decisions except in narrow circumstances. Other states have laws prohibiting checking criminal history before an offer of employment.

With the rise in technology, background checks have become more accessible. Background check providers now offer instant access to a person's criminal history, education history, employment history, driving records, and more. Applicant Tracking System (ATS)/ background check integrations are changing the world of employee background checks. Regardless of how you're administering background checks, the process starts with researching and collecting information about an individual's criminal history, education, employment, and credit history.

In this section, I provide insight on the variety of information that can be gathered in the background check process.

Understanding the basics: Background checks 101

Background checks are conducted by authorized parties such as the federal government or private companies and organizations. They should be conducted in compliance with all applicable laws that govern both the employer and the authorized party conducting the search.

The process typically includes the following:

>> A request for information from the applicant

>> A review of any documents submitted by the applicant

>> A search of government records and databases

The contents of a background check vary depending on the industry and the type of job an applicant is seeking, as well as the employer's preference. The most common background checks consist of criminal history, education, and previous employment verifications. These reports can also include results of pre-employment drug testing. The goal is for an employer to feel confident a new hire will not bring foreseeable trouble to the workplace.

Please note that this is an area in which to seek legal guidance, as California and many other states prohibit the use of credit reports in hiring decisions except in narrow circumstances.

Recognizing the different types of checks

Many different kinds of background checks can be run on job applicants. A check can include any combination of the following:

» **Social Security number trace and address history:** Doing a Social Security number trace and getting an address history comprise the starting point for any reliable background check. They allow you to confirm that your candidate is who they say they are. These checks reveal where a potential employee has lived and worked and provide other names or aliases connected with the candidate to check during the criminal screen.

» **National Criminal Records Database search:** This is useful for finding out whether applicants have committed a crime outside of the state or county where they live and work. Also known as the NCRD, the National Criminal Records Database includes hundreds of millions of records that can be searched quickly.

» **Federal criminal records database search:** A federal criminal database search pulls records from all U.S. federal courts and returns any violations of Federal laws. Federal violations include white-collar crimes, fraud, embezzlement, tax evasion, illegal sale of firearms, pornographic exploitation of children, and so on. Because of the nature of these crimes, federal criminal background checks are often performed on C-level executives, CPAs, financial and banking staff, and other employees with access to financial information.

» **County/statewide criminal records checks:** Most crimes are prosecuted at the state and county level, making the county/statewide criminal history checks a frequently used search. Statewide criminal checks search state criminal repositories (databases) for criminal records. These databases typically contain felonies and misdemeanors committed by an individual. All felony and misdemeanor crimes (which make up most crimes) are tried at local jurisdictions and filed in county courthouses. These records are housed in the 3,200+ counties in the United States and contain the most accurate and up-to-date information.

>> **Federal and state fingerprint-based checks:** A fingerprint background check can show Criminal History Record Information (CHRI) if a match is found. Fingerprint-based checks are frequently conducted as a part of the pre-employment background checking process and are mandatory for such employers as law enforcement agencies, fire departments, hospitals, airports, and public schools. Fingerprint-based checks are also required for certain types of professional licenses, including licenses for attorneys, realtors, physicians, brokers, pharmacists, and casino workers.

>> **Credit report check:** Credit report checks obviously check credit and cover a lot of personal information including present and past addresses, Social Security number, as well as any present or past debts, payments, and late payments. As noted previously, this is an area in which to seek legal guidance because California and many other states prohibit the use of credit reports in hiring decisions except in narrow circumstances.

>> **Education verification and credentials check:** You can also verify the educational background and professional credentials of applicants. With an education verification, you can confirm whether the applicant has received the diplomas, degrees, and certificates your positions require. An education verification allows you to see every educational institution the applicant has attended, attendance dates, and any diplomas, degrees, or certificates that were awarded. For positions requiring professional licenses, you can also request a professional license and credentials check. This type of check reveals whether the person has the required licensure and if their license is current, valid, and in good standing.

>> **Employment verification:** While a job candidate will likely disclose their past work experience on their résumé and job application, conducting a background check that includes employment verification allows you to be sure they have the experience they claim to have. This includes checking their past job titles, time frame of employment, salaries, and more.

>> **E-Verify:** E-Verify is an online system created and operated by the United States Department of Homeland Security. Employers use E-Verify to determine their employees' U.S. citizenship or right to work for a company in the United States. This ensures that employers uphold employment laws and refrain from receiving legal repercussions or loss of business.

While E-Verify technically isn't a background check, it's a system enrolled employers can use to verify the eligibility and identity of an employee. This check is performed online and compares information supplied on the I-9 form with government records. There are a few key differences between E-Verify and the I-9 form. Form I-9 is required for all employers, but E-Verify is voluntary for most.

Wading through the murkiness of background checks

Many factors contribute to the complexity of background checks:

>> **No central information source:** It may come as a surprise to you that no single, national source of information exists for most types of background checks. Criminal records, for example, are generally maintained by individual states or counties, many of which don't store them electronically.

>> **Possibility of flawed data:** Another issue is reliability. Even the most comprehensive checks yield flawed or incomplete records with greater frequency than some employers realize.

>> **Need for retesting:** The frequency with which you conduct background checks must also be a factor in deciding whether to use these methods for evaluating prospective new hires. Academic credentials must be verified only once, but a drug test or criminal background check can become out-of-date almost as soon as it's conducted.

>> **Legal restrictions:** Further adding to the complexity of conducting background checks on job candidates are federal laws governing them, as well as state laws that can vary considerably from one to another. For example, if your company uses an outside agency to furnish background information, you may be required, under federal law and the laws of some states, to provide applicants certain disclosures and get their permission before the background check can take place. As a result, you may want to consider seeking legal advice before you even request some types of checks.

>> **Technology not keeping up:** Although technology makes background checks easier to some degree, obtaining reliable information can be much more difficult than most people recognize. The apparent ease of accessing information online obscures the fact that the quality and completeness of the underlying information may not have kept pace with the technology. Many records simply aren't available electronically and are accessible via paper-based systems only. And many of the databases that do exist aren't updated frequently.

FIND ONLINE

The online tools include A Summary of Your Rights Under the Fair Credit Reporting Act that may be useful during the background-check process.

Conducting background checks: Yes or no?

Conducting background checks frequently isn't a simple matter. But that doesn't mean that they aren't useful tools when pursued appropriately. Whether to conduct a background check depends mostly on the nature of your business and the position for which you're hiring. In limited cases, you don't have a choice because federal and state laws require background checks for certain jobs. But for most positions, the employer determines the need for investigation.

You need to weigh many questions, including the following:

>> Is the job highly visible, such as a senior executive or someone who will be in the public spotlight?

>> Does the position involve working with children or the public?

>> Do you have a specific suspicion or concern about a candidate?

The list goes on, but the point is that no formulas or universal criteria dictate whether background checks are necessary or appropriate for a position or an organization. Unless the law requires a check, only you can determine what's right for your business.

Similarly, you shouldn't assume that staffing companies perform background checks. Most staffing firms don't routinely conduct background checks. If a background check is required, the staffing company will likely have you work directly with a firm that specializes in this area. Although staffing companies are very good at what they do, they don't specialize in this type of investigation. Given the complexities, you want a firm that *does* specialize in background checks.

REMEMBER

The logistical and legal complexities alone shouldn't determine whether you conduct a background check. Although risk is involved (in addition to the time and expense) when businesses conduct checks and obtain erroneous information, businesses also can invite problems if they fail to adequately evaluate candidates. The decision is yours to make, and the key is to understand the role and understand the risks.

Using outside expertise for background checks

Because of their complexity, background checks require unique expertise. If, after weighing all the factors, you decide to conduct a background check on a job applicant, employ the services of a third-party investigative agency. Not only is it difficult for a nonexpert to conduct a thorough search, but you'll also likely need assistance in navigating the legal restrictions, which aren't always obvious or commonly known. Laws, for example, govern how information obtained during a background check can and can't be used in your hiring decision — and whether certain information may be collected in the first place. The best choice is to retain a firm that specializes in performing these services.

Go in with your eyes open. If performed properly, background checks can be much more complex than many people realize. Conducting rudimentary searches on your own just to "cover all bases" is unlikely to yield accurate and useful information. That's why your decision to conduct a background check should be based on the unique needs of the position and your business, and a reliable firm should conduct the check. It also should be consistently applied to all positions that fall into this category.

Making Offers They Can't Refuse

After days, weeks, or even months of sourcing, shortlisting, and interviewing candidates, you've finally identified the right candidate for the role! The next step in your hiring process is to make them a job offer. At the offer stage, you need to move fast, proactively reach out to your chosen candidate, send them an offer letter, potentially consider a counteroffer, and carry out pre-employment checks (see the previous section for more detail). It's a lot to sort out, and it's important to handle the offer with care. If you fail to handle this phase of the hiring process carefully, one of two things can happen: You can lose the candidate, or, even if the candidate comes aboard, you can start the relationship off on the wrong foot. The following sections tell you what to keep in mind.

Don't delay

A slow recruiting process is one of the most prominent reasons why hiring organizations miss out on quality candidates. According to global talent services company Morgan McKinley, 48 percent of job applicants decline a job offer because the hiring process took too long. If you hesitate and delay making a hiring decision, your ideal candidate may have accepted another offer if they're engaged in conversations with multiple organizations.

If possible, contact the candidate you want to offer the job to shortly after their final interview (one to two days after the interview). That's a great way of showing that you're genuinely excited to have them on the team, while at the same time easing the candidate's stress and anxiety that naturally follows a job interview.

Make an offer over the phone

Before you write the official letter, call the candidate first to ensure they're still interested in the role. They may have accepted a different role or want to withdraw their application for other reasons. Not only is this your chance to confirm that they're still interested in joining your organization, but it's also a prime opportunity to discuss the offer in more detail and determine whether any negotiation is needed around the compensation you have outlined.

Calling a candidate and offering the job over the phone expresses your enthusiasm. After all, making a job offer is exciting to both sides and should be a memorable experience. It's hard to convey your excitement via an email. Remember, the professional relationship starts before the first day, and this is a great opportunity to further connect with the potential new team member!

REMEMBER

You should establish a salary range for the position even before you begin recruiting (see Chapter 5). This parameter can help you stay within your budget should you need to negotiate. (In Chapters 11 and 12, I discuss the details of salary and benefits and what constitutes an effective compensation structure.)

Prepare and send an official offer letter

Most companies make job offers verbally by phone and then follow up with an official letter or email. Making the offer by phone rather than waiting to get the candidate back into your office avoids having too much time elapse between the interview and the offer. Make sure that you have a standard job offer letter as a template that you can customize and that you clear the template with legal counsel.

Include the following in the offer letter:

>> The candidate's full name

>> What their official job title will be

>> The formal start date *(and the end date if it's a temporary position)*

>> Whether there are any conditions the offer is subject to

>> Any actions that the candidate needs to take prior to starting

Some organizations ask candidates to sign a duplicate copy of the job offer letter as an indication of acceptance. The signature confirms that the candidate understands the basic terms of the offer. If you're making a job offer contingent on reference checks, a physical examination, drug and alcohol testing, or background checks, make sure that the offer letter says as much and the candidate understands and accepts this restriction.

FIND ONLINE

See the Offer Letter to a Prospective Employee in the online tools.

Set a deadline

Set a time frame of when you expect to hear a decision from the candidate. Generally, a week is plenty of time for them to think about everything, but don't rush them; it's a big decision! If the candidate is happy with everything on the offer letter after checking that all details are correct, they should sign the letter, make a copy of it (so they have one for their personal reference), and send a signed copy back to you.

As an employer, you should keep their signed letter on file in case there are any disputes in the future. It's important to remember that this is not a binding contract of employment and that either side can still back out.

Stay connected

While a candidate is considering an offer, you or the hiring manager should stay in touch with or have individuals from the interview team contact the candidate if you're using multiple or panel interviews. The purpose is for you to reinforce your enthusiasm about the candidate potentially joining your team.

Know how to negotiate salary

You've found your ideal candidate, and you've made an offer. Depending on your candidate's response, you'll face one of three scenarios:

>> **Your candidate accepts your offer.** You finalize important details and mark the position as filled. You provide the candidate with the appropriate details and information needed to move forward.

>> **Your candidate declines your offer.** You have several options depending on your workload, preference, and company policies. You can cut your losses and move on to the next candidate. You can ask candidates for more information, or you can ask to match a competitor's offer.

>> **You begin the salary negotiation process.** Many recruiters and candidates see the negotiation process as a zero-sum affair (if you win, I lose). In reality, a successful negotiation is more closely related to adjusting the dials on your radio. You're looking for the right mix of salary, compensation, and benefits.

Candidates have more power than ever before with compensation, and they know it. They have access to an abundance of information on salary negotiation, so most enter the meeting knowledgeable on the topic. To reach a fair deal, you need to be equally prepared.

In addition, be prepared for the candidate to receive a counteroffer from their current employer. If the applicant is a highly skilled professional, chances are good that their current employer will do everything possible to hold onto them. The prospect of losing a key team member is not attractive; beyond the costs and length of time to replace an employee who resigns, a skills hole is left in their wake, and their departure may cause a feeling of instability across their team. With this in mind, the current employer may react to the news by promising your prospective new employee more money, more responsibilities, and/or more freedom in their day-to-day activities if they stay. This is known as a counteroffer.

Decide how far you're willing to go in negotiating salary

The first step is not unlike that in any other form of negotiating. If the candidate suggests a higher figure than you've offered, you can choose to raise the amount of your proposal or stick to your guns. If the candidate keeps pushing, whether you want to exceed the established range generally depends on two factors: how badly you want the person and the policies and precedents in your company.

Ask yourself three questions before you start promising the moon:

>> **Are other, equally qualified candidates available if the applicant says no?** If the answer is yes, the leverage to make accommodations rests with the organization.

>> **Has the job been particularly hard to fill, or are market conditions making finding and recruiting suitable candidates difficult?** If the answer is yes, the leverage rests with the candidate.

>> **Will a stronger offer be significantly out of line with existing pay levels for comparable positions in your company or hiring manager's department?** As I discuss in Chapter 11, the lack of a reasonable degree of internal equity in compensation levels diminishes the spirit of teamwork and fairness.

WARNING

Recognize that if you decide to go beyond the firm's pay scale to win a stellar candidate, you risk poor morale among existing staff should they find out that a new hire in the same role is being paid at a higher rate. You also risk internal equity issues. Paying above scale may create a legal issue if the pay isn't equitably distributed among the members of your workforce.

If you're not able to match a candidate's salary request, consider expanding other components of the total rewards package (see Chapter 11 for more detail). Applicants often are willing to compromise on base compensation if concessions are made in other areas.

Providing additional time off may be acceptable to a candidate in lieu of higher wages. Also, consider a signing bonus (see the nearby sidebar) or a performance-based bonus after a specified time period (see Chapter 11).

Know when to draw the line

Some HR experts insist that you shouldn't push too hard if a candidate isn't interested. Probing a bit in order to find out why they're being hesitant isn't a bad idea, though. Try to identify the source of the problem and make reasonable accommodations.

But don't get so caught up in negotiations that you lose sight of what's appropriate for your organization. Sometimes you just have to walk away. If your attempts to woo a reluctant candidate fall short, the best thing to do in many cases is to cut your losses and look somewhere else. It may well be that the candidate knows something about themselves that you don't know, so don't push too hard. The goal at this point should be to end the process so that the candidate leaves with a feeling of being treated fairly and with dignity.

Clarify acceptance details

If a promising candidate accepts your final offer, congratulate yourself! You're helping to build a strong team for your business. But before you break out the champagne, you still need to take care of some details. Make sure you clarify the acceptance details of the offer, including the following:

>> Position title

>> Hiring manager's name

>> Salary (including bonus or commission information) and benefits eligibility

>> Paid time off (and eligibility)

>> Start date

>> Schedule (expected start and end times)

Stay in touch

Even after a candidate accepts your offer and you agree on a starting date, keeping in touch with the new employee is a best practice to keep them engaged before the start date. The more you can stay connected through regular communication, the more excited the person will be about working for your organization and the more confident they'll be in their decision.

OFFERING SIGNING BONUSES — YAY OR NAY

A *signing bonus* — sometimes referred to as a *hiring* or *sign-on bonus* — is a financial award offered by an organization to a prospective employee as an incentive to join their company. A signing bonus may consist of one-time or lump-sum cash payments and/or stock options. Companies typically offer these types of bonuses to highly qualified job candidates.

There are several reasons why an organization may offer sign-on bonuses. They may want to snag high-quality talent for a position that is in high demand and is hard to fill (for example, nurses or engineers). Or perhaps a candidate is requesting a salary that is well above the set range for the role, and a signing bonus will make the company a more attractive option. Similarly, the organization may want to create a more attractive total compensation package for a candidate.

If you use signing bonuses, however, it's a good idea to make them contingent upon a specified period of employment. For example, you might specify that a new manager will receive a signing bonus of $10,000 as long as they are employed with your company for a period of at least one year. Make sure the offer specifies that the new hire must repay the signing bonus, on a prorated basis, if they leave the company before 12 months have passed.

Two to three weeks is the customary time between an acceptance and start date. Most people who are changing jobs give a standard two-week notice to their former employer. For those who want to take a few days off before starting their new job, a three-week interval is not unusual. Use the transition period to mail off all those informational brochures and employment forms and to schedule a lunch or two, if appropriate. You want to subtly help the new employee transfer loyalty from their old employer to you and to make dismissing any other offers that may surface from prior interviews easier for the person you now want on your team.

The onboarding process begins in the recruiting process as you're building a relationship with the candidate. It's important that there's no sense of wasted lag time between acceptance of a job offer and the candidate actually starting work. Take advantage of this time to get a head start on certain tasks and to begin cementing what you hope will be a positive and long-lasting relationship. Provide the new hire with a copy of an employee handbook and any other materials that are helpful to review in advance. Stay in touch and ask whether any additional questions or concerns have cropped up prior to the first day of work. The more you can accomplish during this time, the greater the sense of connection and involvement the new employee will have. That makes a solid start all the more likely.

At the same time, if you plan to have nonexempt employees perform any tasks to prepare for their first day of work, it's a good idea to check with a lawyer to see whether the tasks you're assigning are compensable.

EMPLOYMENT CONTRACTS: SHOULD YOU OR SHOULDN'T YOU?

FIND ONLINE

An *employment contract* or *contract of employment* is a legal agreement between an employer (you) and an employee that covers all the terms and conditions related to employment. Employment contracts are important because they protect you and your employees, set clear expectations about the work, and form a legal relationship between your business and its workers.

These contracts are usually (but not always) made for executive or senior-level positions. The following are some instances when an employment contract is most beneficial for the employer:

- **When the employee is difficult to replace:** A professional with specific skills or an employee who has knowledge of your market and your competition is one example of someone you may have a hard time replacing if they should suddenly leave your employ. In these cases, the employment contract limits the employee's ability to leave without giving you ample notice.

- **When the employee has knowledge of confidential information:** This may include trade secrets or knowledge of other sensitive materials. In this case, include a confidentiality clause in the contract to prevent the employee from divulging this information during and after the end of the contract.

- **When you want to avoid competition:** An employment contract can be a good idea when you don't want the employee leaving and competing against you for business. You may want the employee to sign a non-compete agreement as part of the employment contract, limiting their ability to compete with you within a certain time period and within a defined geographic area in a specific type of business. Please note that whether these are enforceable and the scope/length they can legally cover varies by state.

An employment contract doesn't need to be a 20-page legal document. You have to be careful, however, that you don't word the contract in such a way that guarantees employment.

(continued)

(continued)

A well-written employment contract generally includes the following:

- Job title and responsibilities of the role
- Benefits
- Work hours and place of work
- Holiday, sick, and paid leave
- Rate of pay (hourly, monthly, annually, overtime)
- Duration of contract
- Non-disclosure and non-compete clauses
- How disputes will be resolved

See the sample Employment Agreement in the online tools.

3

Retaining and Engaging Talent

Set new team members up for success through onboarding.

View compensation and benefits as a total rewards package that your business provides team members.

Determine your compensation philosophy as the foundation of all of your compensation decisions.

Provide benefits that support your team members both professionally and personally.

Create a meaningful and positive employee experience to engage and retain team members.

Chapter **10**

Onboarding: Setting Up New Team Members for Success

A new job is a big moment for anyone. You've been there yourself and no doubt can relate to the excitement around starting something new and the anxiety of the unknown. It's important for employers to remember and recognize that starting a new job comes with a flood of emotions. There's pressure to perform. There are expectations to achieve great things. There are new people to meet. It's a lot to take in, and the more employers acknowledge this, the more time and energy they'll spend supporting the transition and setting up the new employee for success. One thing is certain: New team members will feel more confident and grounded if their new employer is prepared and has a clear process in place for integrating them into the organization.

In this chapter, you discover ways to ensure that newcomers thoroughly grasp the part they play in the business, become productive and confident, and feel that they're an important part of the team. That way, you can do your part in helping them to integrate into the business most effectively.

Explaining What Onboarding Is

The initial weeks or months on the job are especially pivotal for newcomers in establishing attitudes about their role in the organization, their colleagues, and your business. The approach and activities planned for this early period must not only provide job-related information but also foster a clear understanding of your organization's philosophy and core values.

Onboarding refers to the processes by which new hires are integrated into the organization. You're likely familiar with many of the logistical aspects of helping a new hire adjust to a company, ranging from completing new hire paperwork to finding out about company technologies and ways of working, but the big-picture goal of this chapter is to help you onboard team members by creating a rigorous, ongoing process that truly helps new employees thrive and integrate into the organization.

REMEMBER

With a hybrid work environment being the norm and many employees working in a remote environment 100 percent of the time, traditional onboarding practices created for an in-person environment need to be adapted for a remote workforce. After all, remote employees have gone from being the exception to becoming a major part of the workforce. In fact, the number of people working remotely has increased by 159 percent since 2005. In recent years, this increase has been exacerbated by the shift to remote work throughout the pandemic. A 2021 American Community Survey reported that between 2019 and 2021, the number of people primarily working from home tripled from 5.7 percent (roughly 9 million people) to 17.9 percent (27.6 million people).

With a larger population working remotely, there's been a change in how companies onboard new employees, so I highlight specific challenges and opportunities for onboarding remote employees, as well.

Integrating New Team Members into the Organization

The onboarding process begins as soon as the new employee signs the offer letter, but the process of learning about your company and the opportunity begins well before that. When they join the business, you have an opportunity to build on the connection that has begun or repair any challenges that emerged in the recruiting process.

Now that they're officially part of your organization, you can do far more to ensure that new employees become productive and satisfied members of your staff. The onboarding process is also known by other names among HR professionals, such as alignment, assimilation, integration, and transition.

Onboarding goes beyond mere practicality and acknowledges that what new employees learn in their first few weeks has long-term effects on their ability to tackle the challenges of today's faster-paced business environment. In other words, starting out on the right foot is even more important than employers ever thought, and it sets up team members for long-term success. Research by Brandon Hall Group found that organizations with a strong onboarding process improve new hire retention by 82 percent and productivity by over 70 percent.

Depending on your organization's size and the complexity of the work, an onboarding program can last from several weeks to several months. It covers matters related to learning and development, scheduled milestones, mentoring programs, and interactive meetings where employees can ask questions about corporate or departmental initiatives.

Above all, onboarding is an opportunity. Virtually all new employees are enthralled by the experience they're about to have. This period is the time to capitalize on that excitement and begin building strong bonds between new hires and the organization.

REMEMBER

Although you set up overall onboarding events and policies, the line manager handles specific job-related parts of the process. But here, too, you're responsible for offering advice and guidance to supervisors, especially those who are new to people leadership. You play an important role as a resource for both the manager and the new employee. The policies and procedures you establish about how to onboard new employees greatly shape how managers and employees interact with one another. Your role is to ensure that managers understand these guidelines and the importance of adhering to them. And you also want to make yourself available throughout the new employee's early days to address any concerns or questions.

Recognizing Three Unproductive Approaches That Don't Work

The key to successful onboarding is to get the right results. No one formula works for everyone. Every company and every new employee is different. Some ways do exist, however, that are clearly *unproductive*. The following sections cover three examples that unfortunately occur all too often.

Osmosis

How the method works: No formal orientation or adjustment process exists for new employees. You leave each employee alone to learn the ropes simply by observing and asking questions on a spontaneous, as-needed basis.

Faulty rationale: If employees are smart enough to get hired, they can probably figure out for themselves what they need to know about the job, the company, and the facilities.

Why this method doesn't work: Relying on osmosis fails to consider how difficult it is for new employees to grasp the nuances of a company and simultaneously grasp what's expected in a new job. Worse yet, this method conveys a general attitude of indifference that can very easily carry over into employee performance. Another problem is that new employees are often shy about asking questions, which means that they don't get the answers or guidance they need until after they begin to make costly mistakes.

"Just follow Joe around"

How the method works: "Joe" can be "Jill," "Frank," "Javier," or anybody who has been with your company for more than a few years. The idea is to pair the newly hired employee with one of your tenured staff members — but without giving the experienced employee specific instructions on how to manage the process.

Faulty rationale: If you have the newcomers simply follow around more tenured employees for a couple days, they pick up the basics. This approach is simple and inexpensive.

Why this method doesn't work: Without giving Joe specific instructions on how to manage the process, he may have little or no insight into the new hire's role or the expectations of the person's manager.

Watch the video

How the method works: You hire a production company to produce slick video content that tells new employees everything they need to know about your company in a 12- to 15-minute session. You email new employees the link to the video, asking them to watch it whenever they have the time.

Faulty rationale: Everybody loves videos, right? Besides, you don't need to waste any time with person-to-person contact or training.

Why this method doesn't work: Videos, no matter how cutting edge the presentation, can't answer questions. You have no guarantee that the newcomer is actually paying attention and not daydreaming. Nor do videos offer concrete insights into that specific individual's job. By simply using a piece of technology with little or no input from you and other key managers, you also run the risk of employees assuming that you view helping new employees adapt to the company as little more than a formality, like getting your driver's license renewed. That's not a good message to send.

Doing It Right: A Little Empathy Goes a Long Way

The first few days and weeks on a new job are exciting — and often just as intimidating. As the new kid on the block, the most recent addition to your company encounters a host of firsts and unfamiliar people, policies, and procedures. Everything from your first-day welcome to the remainder of your onboarding process should address those concerns and help to alleviate the natural anxiety they are feeling.

Think about what *you* would want and need if you were going through the process of joining a new organization. Your concerns or areas of interest most likely include new employee anxieties (for example, how best to communicate and where to go for help), job tasks and goal setting, company operations and culture, as well as basic ways of working. Focus on the areas regardless of how formally or informally you want to approach the onboarding process. Encourage your line managers to pay attention to them as well.

After the number of new employees joining your company reaches a certain threshold — and you must determine when the organization gets to this point — you'll probably want to formalize your approach, creating a series of onboarding activities that you repeat whenever a new employee or group of new employees joins your company. The following sections should help ensure that any program you develop is as effective as possible.

TIP

Your onboarding program can be as elaborate as a weeks-long combination training and boot camp or as simple as a series of scheduled one-on-one conversations between the new employee and their internal key stakeholders — or something in between. Whatever form you take, you want to give it structure and document key activities and milestones. You need to provide a schedule, and everyone involved needs clearly defined roles. You want the individual elements of the program to be *weighted* — in other words, a logical and strategic connection must exist between the importance of a particular issue or topic and how much time you devote to that issue or topic.

The First Day: Easing Anxieties

Even though new employees may have been on your company premises (if the business has a physical presence) previously during the interview phase, their experiences on the first day of work leave a lasting impression. It begins from the very minute they walk into the building or onto the jobsite or log into their laptop (if they're working remotely). Regardless of where they are located, it's important to offer a first-day welcome to begin the process of making them feel like they belong.

Following are tips for you — or the individuals' manager if you're not supervising the new hires — to remember:

>> **Ensure that the new team member's workstation/office has everything they need to be successful.** Nothing is worse on your first day only to realize that your laptop isn't there or you don't have a designated place in which to work. Give your new hire a clean, stocked, and organized place to work right from the start. They'll appreciate it, and they'll feel like they can start being productive right out of the gate.

>> **Alert whomever will greet the new team member and escort them to their new workstation or office.** Provide that greeter with the information needed to give a warm welcome (name, role). Remember, the new employee is walking in with a lot of uncertainty, so those first few minutes can do a lot to ease the anxiety and set a positive tone for the rest of the day.

>> **Share the onboarding plan.** This can be outlined as a 30/60/90-day plan with specific activities for the first day and the first couple of weeks. The key is that the new team member knows what to expect. It may include, for example, meetings that have been set up for them, research they need to do, training

sessions they may need to attend, and even group lunches meant to help welcome them to the team. Give them a light workload the first week and run through a general plan for the first month or so.

>> **Personally introduce the newcomer to the other team members.** Everyone else already knows each other, so the sooner you can help them assimilate, the sooner they'll feel comfortable and start producing their best work. They're going to have a lot of new names and faces thrown at them, so create multiple opportunities to get to know everyone.

>> **At some point in the day, if the employee will be working in a physical office, give them an office tour.** During the tour, don't just point out the water cooler and the copy machine. Show the new team member where people get together during breaks, point out a good place to get some quiet thinking done, and give them a sense of what your office is all about. This helps them adjust to their new surroundings right away.

>> **Show the new team member where they can find company employees' names, job titles, phone numbers, and email addresses.** Keep this information in a folder on the server so all can access it.

>> **Encourage current employees who haven't formally met the new hire to introduce themselves and offer to help in any way they can.**

>> **At some point during the day, meet with the employee to take up where the last interview left off.** Let them know how glad you are to have them aboard and that you'll be providing a comprehensive introduction to the company and the job over the next few days.

>> **Create a small win opportunity.** Start small, but create an opportunity for your new team member to feel successful, to have a win right out of the gate. Your new hire wants to demonstrate their value to the company, so let them! When they go home that night, they'll not only feel like they accomplished something, but they'll have an opportunity to digest the next few days of work.

>> **Take the new team member out to lunch.** If remote, send them a gift card to order lunch and schedule time to eat and chat virtually. This is one of the best things you can do for a new hire on their first day of work, as it provides an opportunity to chat outside of the work environment. Let them know ahead of time so they don't waste time worrying about what or where they're going to eat.

>> **End the day with a friendly conversation.** Check in with your new hire before they head home or log off from their first day of work. Ask them how everything went, see if they have any questions or concerns, and thank them for their engagement. They'll leave the office knowing that you've got their back, and they'll come in the next day feeling like they belong.

With these simple steps, you can turn one of the most stressful days in a new hire's life into a positive experience. A happy employee is a productive employee, and starting your new hire off on the right foot will do wonders for the employee onboarding experience and your company's growth! The key is to determine what a meaningful first day experience should look like at your company and build a base plan.

The First Week: Revealing More about the Company and the Job

You probably gave the new employee plenty of information about your company while recruiting and interviewing. Even so, the first few days on the job are the best time to reinforce that information and build a sense of connection with the company and with the role.

At the very least, a new employee should know the following:

>> Your company's basic products or services

>> The size and general configuration of the organization

>> Where your company fits into the overall industry (including who the chief competition is)

>> Your organization's mission, vision, and values

>> Department goals (for the department in which the new team member will be working) and strategic objectives for the organization

Providing the rules of the road

If your company has an employee handbook and/or procedures manual, make sure that the employee gets copies on their first day and give them time to look over the materials, just to make sure that the new hire has no misunderstandings. If the handbook is online, provide appropriate access. (See "Employee Handbook and Separate Procedures Manual: Yes, You Need Both," near the end of this chapter.)

Make sure, in particular, that new employees are aware of policies regarding their immediate work areas. If your company has unusual rules in this regard, take the time to explain the rationale.

Don't take anything for granted, particularly about basic considerations such as where employees park, how they sign in, and, for nonexempt employees, how they clock in and out for work shifts and meal periods — and the importance of doing so properly. Make sure that the newcomer knows whom to contact — and how — for questions and emergencies. Provide keypad door codes and advise employees of any security procedures.

For employees working from a physical office, other locations that you should show new employees as soon as possible include the following:

>> Company bulletin boards or other display areas or walls on which important legal notices (like equal employment opportunity [EEO] posters) and employee information are posted

>> Restrooms, break rooms, lunch areas, and employee lounges

>> Fire exits, evacuation points, and emergency assembly areas

>> Immediate supervisor's workstation/office

>> Human resources representative's workstation/office

>> Departmental facilities (such as the copy room and supply cabinets)

>> Health facilities and first-aid kit

If your company has specific security procedures or policies regarding personal phone calls or email, make sure that you communicate these policies on the first day of work.

FIND
ONLINE

See the online tools for an example of an Onboarding Checklist.

Keeping onboarding practical

Because new employees join your company at varying intervals, scheduling formal onboarding sessions with business leaders can present a problem. On the one hand, an onboarding event should be conducted as soon as possible. But if you're frequently adding new employees, holding a formal session on each new hire's first or second day may be impractical. The best option is a combined approach — a formal event that takes place on a weekly or monthly basis (depending on how many employees you're hiring), preceded by an informal, first-day, personalized orientation that covers the mandatory administrative and operational aspects of the job. (See "The First Day: Easing Anxieties," earlier in this chapter.)

Involving senior leaders from across the business

Formal onboarding sessions should always include an appearance (and, ideally, a brief message of welcome) from some key senior leaders — the greater the influence in the business, the better. (If you're the business owner, this is you!) Some companies launch these sessions with a video message from the head of the company. Generally speaking, however, having key company leaders appear during a session gives more credibility and importance to the entire process.

Holding large-group sessions in a suitable location

If you're running large-group, in-person onboarding sessions with video or oral presentations, you need a room large enough to accommodate the audience comfortably. Unattractive, cramped surroundings sabotage your ability to communicate and send the wrong message to new employees. An attractive environment tells new employees that the company is organized and professional and cares about its workers. If you don't have suitable facilities for holding these sessions on the premises, consider renting a hotel conference room or off-site venue for this purpose.

Making group presentations user-friendly and engaging

Keep in mind that formal onboarding sessions with other new team members are often the first formally structured experience an employee has inside the company. With that in mind, you want everything that occurs during the session to be consistent with the message that you conveyed during the recruitment process. To put it simply, everything should reflect how the company presents itself to the business world.

You can convey information in several ways: verbally, in written form (such as in a workbook), or through audiovisual materials. Each does a different job. The following list gives you a look at which option works best with varying types of information:

>> **Verbal information:** This type of information is okay for the simple and most obvious stuff — the location of the lunchroom and restrooms, how to use the door keypad, the best places to eat lunch in the area, and so on.

>> **Audiovisual presentation:** This type of presentation is most effective if you're seeking to create an emotional effect, as in the case of the company mission and goals.

>> **Written documentation:** Use written documentation for anything complex or legally mandated, such as the company's compliance with equal employment opportunity legislation or the Americans with Disabilities Act. (See Chapter 17 for a complete discussion of these and other laws and the associated documentation.)

Deciding on the mix of oral, audiovisual, and written information to include in an onboarding event depends primarily on how often you need to conduct a session and how many employees you're working with at any given time. You don't need to go overboard. Unless you're typically hiring large groups of new employees at the same time, a company video is a luxury you can probably do without. Rely instead on a PowerPoint presentation or something similar, but don't bore new employees with lengthy one-way presentations. Create opportunities within the presentations for new employees to ask questions and engage with the content provided.

Also, ensure that you provide new employees with information on key policies and benefits in writing. If you contract out your benefits administration, vendors usually provide brochures, forms, and other materials that can be shared. One last point: Have everything ready before new employees walk in the door.

Providing an onboarding session agenda

A written agenda for onboarding sessions serves three main purposes:

>> It eases a new employee's anxiety by mapping out what's going to happen during the session.

>> It enables you to adhere to a formal structure.

>> It shows newcomers that you take the matter of onboarding quite seriously as opposed to feeling you can just wing it.

By creating a well-organized agenda, you also let employees see how your company likes to conduct business. The document doesn't have to be fancy. A single sheet of paper works fine.

Offering information in digestible chunks

One consistent criticism shared by new employees is that they have to take in so much new information at one time. So, try to space things out and provide content in digestible chunks. If possible, break up orientation sessions during the first week or move parts of them into the second or third week to give your new team members a chance to absorb what they're learning. Another benefit of this approach is that subsequent information is likely to make more sense to employees after they have several days of experience under their belts.

Here's a sample agenda for a one-day orientation program:

9:00 a.m.	Welcome by HR or business leader
9:15 a.m.	Remarks by company president or CEO
9:45 a.m.	Connection opportunity with business leaders and other new team members
10:00 a.m.	Company overview (mission, vision, values, culture) by HR or business leader
11:00 a.m.	Benefits overview and completion of forms
12:00 p.m.	Lunch
1:00 p.m.	Review the Employee Handbook and key policies: anti-harassment policy, pay periods, travel, personal vehicle use, training requests, and so forth
2:15 p.m.	Department overviews provided by a representative from each department about the purpose of and functions within their departments

Giving a clear sense of tasks and setting concrete goals

At some point during the first week of work, newly hired employees need to sit down with their supervisors for an in-depth discussion about job responsibilities and goal setting. The role of the HR leader is to ensure not only that this meeting happens but also that the manager is well prepared and understands its importance. The new employee should come away from this discussion with a crystal-clear understanding of expectations, tasks, and priorities. In the process, the employee and supervisor clarify the job's objectives and, most important, work together to set specific, concrete goals for the newcomer.

The following list provides several suggestions for this meeting:

>> Tell new employees about how the department operates, including expectations about quality standards.

>> Make sure that the employee understands the nature of the job, its importance, and how it fits into broader corporate objectives.

>> Define the factors that will shape the new employee's evaluation.

>> Together, set short- and long-term goals. Involving employees in defining their objectives makes it more likely that they'll work hard to achieve them. Goals should include not only specific job tasks and results but also learning and development activities.

>> Build a timetable for reaching goals over the next 30 to 60 days, as well as longer-range objectives.

>> Discuss a development plan for any learning that can address skills gaps pinpointed during the hiring process.

CASCADING GOALS: ALIGNING INDIVIDUAL GOALS WITH CORPORATE STRATEGY

In the most successful organizations, employees don't set their goals in a vacuum. HR professionals ensure that line managers fully understand the company's strategic goals and are properly prepared to help their employees create individual objectives that support this higher-level vision. Called cascading goals, this approach allows the broader perspectives of senior leadership to cascade, like falling water, into more specific goals at all levels of the company.

In the case of a food company, for example, senior leadership might share a new direction, such as "Connect more with the desires of local families." This vision, in turn, takes on several meanings as it cascades through the organization and to individuals in each department. For product development, the focus may be on creating more family-friendly food items. For marketing, it may mean researching the attitudes of local families toward eating. This method also allows employees to set their objectives in line with their managers' goals, all of which are part of the cascade throughout the organization. Simply stated, cascading goals put everyone on the same page.

The net result of cascading goals is improved company performance. When employees are aware of what they're being evaluated for and what's expected, they tend to do a better job. And when they're encouraged to create goals that are in sync with something larger, workers tend to feel more of a sense of purpose and importance, which leads to increased morale and productivity.

Employee objectives must be periodically revised as time goes on to ensure that they remain aligned with current company strategies and departmental priorities. It's counterproductive for an employee to be focused on a set of tasks that aren't quite in sync with a new overall company direction. You, line managers, and employees all need to keep goals cascading and attuned to the visions articulated by senior management.

Onboarding: A Process, Not an Event

Obviously, the structure and support you provide on the first day and in the first few weeks is critical to setting up the new team member for success, but it doesn't stop there. A 2022 report by Sapling suggests that new hires have a 25 percent productivity rate in their first month on the job after completing training to support their success in their new role. That number then increases to 50 percent in their second month of work and 75 percent in their third month on the job. In fact, Gallup finds that new team members typically take around 12 months to reach peak performance potential, so it's important to stay close to the new team member's productivity and confidence throughout their tenure.

The best employee onboarding programs extend throughout the employee's first 90 days — and may even extend for a full year — to ensure new hires are fully supported as they ramp up to full productivity. Employees are twice as likely to seek out another job if they have a bad onboarding experience, so starting out on the right foot saves your company time, money, and having to retrain new hires frequently.

A key part of the onboarding process is thorough follow-up. You or supervising line managers should meet with employees at predetermined points: two weeks after the first day on the job, a month after, two months after, or at intervals that work best for each job's complexity, taking into account any changes in responsibilities. These meetings allow you to check in with new team members to find out how things are going for them. How well do they understand the company and their roles? Do they have any questions that haven't been answered? How has communication been with their managers? Do they feel prepared for their new roles? In particular, ask about the value of job-specific training the company has provided. Is it helpful? Does it address the right areas? Is it worth the time spent? What future developmental experiences would they like to see?

These follow-up meetings also are good times to hear new team members' assessment of the onboarding process thus far. (See the section "Getting feedback: How good is your onboarding program?" later in this chapter.)

Here are some important considerations to maximize your onboarding experience.

Developing a checklist

To make sure that you're covering all bases during an employee's first 90 days and beyond on the job, create a checklist of everything the new team member needs to know — every place they need to see, the systems and technology needed to support their support, every form they need to complete, and everyone they need to meet. If possible, sort everything by time and priority. Make both the new team member and their manager responsible for completing all items, signing the checklist, and submitting the completed checklist.

TIP

When you get the signed checklist back, place a copy into the employee profile. It could prove invaluable in showing that the employee was informed right off the bat about key company requirements, policies, and procedures if they bring a later claim against the company, such as a breach of contract claim, wage and hour lawsuit, or discrimination claim.

Keeping the message alive

The company values and best practices you stressed during the onboarding process should come through loud and clear month after month — through the actions of role models such as supervisors and mentors, as well as through internal communications, such as employee publications and your company communications. In ongoing learning and development activities, continue to make it clear that values such as respect for colleagues, commitment to quality service, and doing what's right rather than what's easy or convenient aren't just first-day lip service but integral to your philosophy of doing business.

Using mentoring to build a solid foundation

Mentoring programs are a popular way for firms to assist new team members during the initial months on the job. By being paired with appropriate mentors (more experienced employees who act as a new hire's guide to your workplace), newcomers gain valuable, real-world experience and skills that are difficult to transmit in classroom settings or workshops.

Mentoring relationships are a key part of the onboarding process, although they often continue beyond an employee's initial period with the company as well. These pairings augment other elements of onboarding, helping to fill in the gaps that even the best-thought-out programs invariably overlook. After all, no matter how many steps you take to ensure a smooth adjustment to the company's culture, a few areas invariably require additional clarification. And a mentor and an employee can discuss certain "unofficial" topics in a way that isn't possible in a structured setting or with an immediate supervisor.

The one-on-one nature of the mentoring relationship can help a new hire integrate quickly into your firm's culture and become a productive member of the staff. Mentors can show new employees the ropes; introduce them to individuals in other work areas; and serve as a sounding board for thoughts, ideas, and concerns. Good mentor-mentee relationships also nurture an inviting culture, demonstrating to newcomers the benefits of an open environment where people are constantly sharing knowledge, generating ideas, and mutually committed to building a successful company.

But keep in mind that mentoring is not a one-way street. Individuals who become mentors stand to gain as well. For example, serving as a mentor can help even the most accomplished long-term team members engage more fully in the business and improve their leadership skills. In addition, new employees often bring with them fresh perspectives and enthusiasm that can benefit a tenured mentor in return.

Mentoring is also a valuable recruiting and retention tool. When evaluating a firm as a potential employer, many job candidates consider a formal mentoring program an attractive asset. It indicates that the company is committed to the professional development of all its employees.

REMEMBER

Mentors are different from supervisors, and it's important that everyone is clear on roles and responsibilities. Mentors don't typically oversee the new employee's day-to-day work performance. Their true function is to act as an additional source of support during an employee's early period with your company (although, again, these relationships can continue indefinitely).

TECHNICAL STUFF

Sometimes you'll hear the term coaching used in place of mentoring; however, coaching and mentoring have different, but related, meanings. In general, coaching is more performance oriented and focuses on changing particular behaviors through specific skill improvement. A coach, who can be either external or internal to the company, helps an employee improve in specific, targeted areas of growth. Mentoring, on the other hand, typically implies a more long-term relationship. It occurs most often between a senior or more experienced company representative who is quite familiar with an organization's overall structure, policies, and culture and a less experienced individual. Mentoring is often, but not always, a one-on-one relationship. (For an extended discussion of the distinction between the two and a broader discussion of mentoring as a career development tool, see Chapters 14 and 15.)

Getting feedback: How good is your onboarding program?

Whether through surveys or meetings, it's important to get feedback on your onboarding program so you can make improvements for future new hires. Here are some questions that can form the basis of any feedback mechanism you develop for new employees immediately after the initial onboarding session:

>> What elements of the session were most helpful in setting you up for success?

>> What elements were least helpful?

>> What information should be included in future programs?

But, of course, your work isn't done after you've received initial feedback. I also suggest you gather additional feedback from employees several months after they're hired. When they've been part of your organization for a while, they'll likely have a broader perspective about what helped them effectively adjust to the company and what was less valuable — and perhaps offer suggestions for improvement.

Here are additional questions you can ask employees several months into the job:

>> What were the things you most wanted to know when you first joined the company?

>> Has your experience so far been in line with the information about the firm that you received during the hiring process?

>> Were those issues and concerns adequately covered during your first month on the job?

>> Were you given enough time to acclimate yourself?

>> Were other employees helpful when you asked questions?

>> Were the materials you received useful? What could be improved?

>> What do you know about your job and this company now that you would have benefited from knowing during the first few days you were on the job?

Strategizing for a remote workforce

An important goal of the onboarding process is to create connection with the new employee, and sometimes challenges crop up when those connections are virtual. Smart organizations have changed the way they orient new employees by working together with remote employees to find out what they need. Many organizations host onboarding materials on a dedicated website including documentation and videos. Others set up calls between new hires and the company's executives to hear the company story. These remote onboarding processes have eased the transition of joining a new team and feeling like you have support and camaraderie, all from your home office with a sleeping two-year-old in another room.

Here are specific strategies for onboarding virtual new hires:

>> **Send them a welcome package.** Make a lasting first impression by sending a care package with helpful information and materials prior to the employee's

first day of work. This is a good way to familiarize the new hire with company culture, as you can include free company swag and branded items, and information about onboarding. It should also include a warm note welcoming the new employee to your organization. This eases their new-job jitters, making them feel confident and organized before starting their new role.

>> **Provide an individualized remote onboarding plan.** Show remote employees what their onboarding will look like. One way to do this is to create a 30/60/90-day plan with action items and goals for each milestone. This can be a living document that grows and changes with the employee.

>> **Establish clear expectations and create alignment.** Ensure that remote team members are clear on what success looks like. Building off their position success profile, describe their responsibilities, help them to prioritize their time, and reinforce the outcomes you're hoping to see during their first months on the job. Also, give your new hires a sense of purpose by showing them how their responsibilities fit into the larger mission and goals of the organization.

>> **Provide them with the right technology.** To ensure that new hires are immediately productive, provide them with access to email, online resources, and internal platforms. Ensure their laptops are set up in advance and equipped with specific applications they need to perform their work. Also, ensure they know how to use your virtual communication tools and have access to videoconferencing and chat tools so that they can easily connect and collaborate with others as they acclimate into the business.

>> **Schedule a virtual orientation session.** Just as you would for in-person team members, ensure that all remote team members get the same information in an online orientation session.

>> **Provide a digital employee handbook and easy access to new-hire paperwork.** Try to digitize all existing employee documentation. Consider using an e-signature tool, like HelloSign or DocuSign, so that employees can add their signatures digitally and share employee documents with you in a secure environment.

>> **Help them build connections.** Set up meetings with their team members and other key employees. These meetings can be one-on-one and/or group calls. This gives them an opportunity to virtually interact with your people, creating a relaxed work environment.

>> **Introduce them to the company.** Integrating the new team member into your collaboration tools (for example, Slack or Microsoft Teams) helps to create a sense of community among your remote employees.

>> **Initiate professional development and personal growth from the start.** Arrange for role-specific training and provide opportunities for new hires to access online courses. To effectively train remote workers, use interactive training

courses that are user-friendly and include games and quizzes to boost engagement. Be sure to follow up after each training session to answer questions.

>> **Set them up with a virtual buddy.** Creating connections quickly boosts engagement and creates a sense of belonging, so pair new hires with a virtual buddy or mentor to give them an opportunity to ask questions. This also helps them discover more about the company culture.

>> **Create opportunities for regular check-ins.** Set up ongoing one-on-one meetings with the new hire to stay connected, address any questions, and ensure they're on track.

>> **Arrange an in-person meeting.** If your new hire is based near your office, consider having them work from your offices during their first week. If that's not feasible, invite them on-site as soon as possible, so that they get to know coworkers in-person. If you have distributed teams and all employees work from home, try to schedule quarterly or annual events or retreats so that entire teams get the chance to meet.

>> **Gather feedback.** Survey your new hires at different intervals during their first few months on the job to understand what worked and what didn't during their onboarding experience. Consider making these surveys anonymous so that you obtain candid responses.

By developing a welcoming onboarding experience for virtual employees, you can establish high morale, productivity, and loyalty right from the start — helping you to successfully assimilate new talent into your company.

Employee Handbook and Separate Procedures Manual: Yes, You Need Both

Sometimes the terms "employee handbook" and "procedures manual" are used interchangeably; however, it's important to recognize that they're two different documents with different objectives and different content. An employee handbook is a document that introduces team members to the organization and familiarizes them with the policies, guidelines, and benefits that affect their employment. A procedures manual includes the step–by–step processes (often called standard operating procedures or SOPs) that team members follow to ensure consistency and compliance of company policies. These SOPs go hand–in–hand with the policies outlined in the employee handbook. For example, your employee handbook will likely include a policy for requesting time off, and the procedures manual would include the SOP for submitting time off requests.

Even if your company has only a handful of employees, keeping your basic policies and procedures well documented is always a good practice. Whatever effort may be required to get basic company information in print or online can save you time and headaches down the road.

The following list gives advice for creating an employee handbook and separate procedures manual:

>> **Separate company policies from job-specific procedures.** Your employee handbook should consist of policies that apply to everyone in the company (general hours, payroll, PTO (paid time off), and so on). Set forth in a separate manual or other format those procedures that relate specifically to how people do their individual jobs. Keep these distinctions separate.

>> **Keep it simple.** Employee manuals don't need to be literary works, but they do need to be clear and concise. Use plain English and try to avoid overly formal, bureaucratic wording and phrasing. You may want to consider hiring a professional writer to polish your final draft.

>> **Pay attention to legalities.** Anything that you put in writing about your company's policies or procedures automatically becomes a legal document. That means someone may use it against you in a wrongful dismissal suit. Numerous cases have occurred in which discharged employees received large settlements because they proved in court that either they were following procedures published in the company handbook or the company itself didn't comply with these procedures. Also, some laws require that if a company has a handbook or manual of policies, certain policies — with certain key elements addressed — must be included (for example, the federal Family and Medical Leave Act).

Make sure that a knowledgeable and experienced lawyer reviews the employee handbook and any procedures manuals before you publish them — and then ensure that your company's day-to-day practices match its written policies and procedures.

>> **Control the distribution.** Every employee who receives an employee handbook should sign a document that acknowledges their receipt of the handbook and that they have read and understand its contents. In the document, they should also attest that they're required to work under its policies and that they know the handbook is not a contract of employment in any way. Finally, the document the employee signs should include that the company, in its discretion, may change its policies in the future from time to time — and such changes will apply to them. Put the signed form in the worker's employee profile. You may need it in the event of a disciplinary proceeding or lawsuit.

You don't want the manual to circulate outside the company — and the manual needs to contain a clear statement to this effect. Some companies require departing employees to turn in their company handbooks before they leave. You may want to consider this policy as well, especially if your handbook details your operational procedures, contains trade secrets, or includes confidential or proprietary information.

Knowing what to include

Most employee handbooks follow the same general format. What differs from one company to the next are the specifics. The following list gives you a look at a typical table of contents for an employee handbook:

>> Welcome statement from the CEO or executive director

>> EEO policy statement (including prohibition of sexual and other forms of discrimination and harassment and the procedure for reporting such conduct)

>> Company history and overview

>> Employment at-will (if applicable)

>> Company mission statement and values

>> Essential company guidelines, such as work hours; attendance, timekeeping, and payroll practices; business ethics; and dress code

>> Other company policies such as a code of ethics, harassment policies, open door policies, and PTO guidelines

>> Performance evaluation process

>> Standards of conduct and disciplinary procedures (have a lawyer carefully review this section)

>> Health, safety, and security rules and procedures, including fire exit maps

>> Employee benefit information, including available health and dental insurance coverage, pension and deferred-income and retirement programs, paid time off benefits (including company holidays, vacation time, and sick days), leaves of absence, and eligibility requirements

>> Technology policies, such as email policies and social networking policies

>> Parking and transportation information, including maps

>> State-specific supplemental information, which usually is required by law

REMEMBER

This sample table of contents is just that: a sample. The employee handbook you end up with will be one of your own design. Laws are constantly evolving, especially those involving the use of social media by companies and employees. For a full understanding of what's right for your handbook, consult with a knowledgeable attorney.

WHAT ABOUT OTHER LANGUAGES?

In today's diverse, multilingual workplace, you may want to produce your employee handbook in languages other than English. Such a practice is a good idea, especially if English is a second language to many of your workers. But be warned: You need a professional translator to do the work, not a staff member who took language courses in high school. It's a legal document.

FIND ONLINE

See the Employee Handbook Table of Contents in the online tools for another sample. Also included is an Employee Handbook and At-Will Employee Status Acknowledgment.

Also, be sure to keep the big picture in mind. Don't just adopt policies because I refer to them in this book or online. Think about the guidelines you want to govern your workplace given the culture you're striving to create. This isn't a mechanical exercise — it's an exercise in creating the guidelines you want to apply to your employment relationship with your workers.

Playing it safe

Whatever else your employee handbook does, make sure that it doesn't do any of the following:

» Make promises you can't keep.

» Publish procedures you don't follow or can't enforce.

» Say anything that someone may construe as discriminatory.

» Use the phrase termination for just cause. If this phrase is used, be sure you're prepared to give up at-will employment and specify exactly what you mean by just cause.

One last piece of advice: Always include a disclaimer that emphasizes that the handbook is a general source of information and not for anyone to construe as a binding employment contract, and that employment contracts can be created only with a written document signed by authorized company representatives.

» Understanding the key components of a total rewards system

» Clarifying exempt versus nonexempt employee status

» Evaluating pay raises, bonuses, and other incentives

» Helping employees see the total rewards package

Chapter **11**

Ensuring a Competitive Total Rewards System

Early in my career, the first time I received a total rewards statement from my employer, I remember looking at it and thinking, "The benefits I get from this organization are worth *how* much?!" I knew that the organization offered competitive pay and benefits, learning and development opportunities, an ongoing performance management program, and more, but seeing all these benefits outlined so clearly as a total package had a big impact. It created an awareness of the total rewards package beyond my compensation, and up until that point, I hadn't had visibility into the comprehensive nature of the benefits provided.

Communicating total rewards is an essential part of your strategy to motivate and retain employees — and it goes well beyond compensation and benefits. It's also a vital part of your value proposition as an employer. If a new hire is surprised by their total rewards statement, it means that they didn't grasp the rewards that were communicated during the hiring process, and that means that candidates are not hearing all the reasons why they should come work for you.

This chapter outlines the key components of a total rewards system with a detailed focus on compensation. Chapter 12 rounds out the total rewards picture with a focus on team member benefits. Across both chapters, I highlight best practices and key considerations for each part of an organization's total rewards system.

Understanding What a Total Rewards System Is

A total rewards system is an integrated reward and motivation system encompassing three key elements that employees value from their employment:

- » **Compensation:** Most employees, regardless of their title or role within the organization, have a general expectation regarding their compensation. There are a range of pay strategies that provide incentives and encourage retention, including paid time off.

- » **Benefits:** Medical and dental coverage are what generally come to mind when discussing employee benefits. Many other value-added benefits can also be offered within benefit plans. Employee assistance programs, life and disability insurance, wellness and health incentive programs, and retirement benefits such as 401(k) plans are also ways to expand the offerings to employees. A 2018 survey by risk management and insurance brokerage firm Willis Towers Watson revealed that 78 percent of workers said they would stay with their current employer because of the benefits it offers.

- » **Work experience:** The overall work experience and the programs available are an important part of the total rewards equation. This includes creating a positive work experience for leaders inside and outside of work, implementing a strong performance and recognition system, and ensuring learning and development opportunities for team members.

An employee's total rewards combine both the monetary and nonmonetary benefits the employee earns at a company. The best strategy combines compensation and benefits with personal growth opportunities inside a motivated work environment.

Designing and implementing a total rewards strategy requires a large-scale approach that drives organizational change. Senior leadership buy-in is critical for the success of a total rewards strategy. Your project team should be made up of decision-makers as well as front-line employees to ensure that your approach is well-rounded and fits the needs of everyone at the table. If you operate in a union environment, it is important to understand that collective bargaining may affect the implementation of your strategy.

Many organizations calculate the value of each employee's individual total rewards and present it to them on a total rewards statement, either during annual performance reviews for employees or along with an offer letter for candidates. This helps give employees a better understanding of all the internal programs their organization has set up to help them personally and professionally, as well as better recognize the value they get by working for the company.

This chapter focuses on the specifics of your compensation and benefit programs. Chapters 12, 13, and 14 address the benefits and the work experience. It's the combination of all of these HR processes and systems that impacts your team members' relationships with the organization, so it's important to view them all as part of the system to support team member success and engagement.

Compensation: Setting the Foundation

The quality of your business's compensation and benefits packages plays a major role in your ability to recruit and retain employees. Compensation and benefits are foundational to your total rewards system. If you aren't competitive in those areas, you'll have a hard time attracting and keeping people. But it's important to note that trying to compete on compensation alone isn't a winning strategy either. If that's the only driver, you aren't going to be successful.

Your goal isn't to know everything that anyone can know about employee compensation. As you take on the task of managing your company's HR function, though, you do need to remain aware of changes taking place in this critical area and best practices to support your team members and their success.

REMEMBER

So, what is HR's responsibility in building a compensation plan? Generally, in your HR role, you don't need to decide how much a particular individual should be paid. Your responsibility, instead, is to communicate options available for building a compensation system. It's your job to make sure that your compensation and benefits are competitive enough to keep your top employees from being wooed away by companies that claim to offer more attractive packages.

You need to be both consistent and flexible in your compensation practices. The two may sound contradictory, but they actually go hand in hand. Consistency means that you have a logical plan and structure to everything you do in the areas of compensation and benefits. That way, you don't inadvertently create employee discord by giving the impression that you're showing favoritism or acting capriciously. Flexibility means that you're doing your best — within reason — to adapt to market dynamics and align with employee performance and impact.

The intended end result of balancing these two factors is a wage and salary structure that not only gives your employees equitable compensation but also focuses on the market realities of your industry and business.

Determining Your Compensation Philosophy

A compensation philosophy is your organization's approach to setting salary ranges and paying your employees. Compensation strategies are not one-size-fits-all. You need to consider what's best for your organization now and in the future by determining your compensation philosophy. These sections outline the importance of naming your compensation philosophy and provide best practices for how to formulate yours.

Keeping your eye on the prize

Creating an effective compensation philosophy requires a constant eye toward the long-term needs and goals of your business. The three major compensation philosophies are leading the market, lagging the market, and matching the market. In other words, do you want to be ahead of the competition, behind it, or aligned with it?

Your objective is a well-thought-out set of practices that helps ensure the following results:

>> Employees receive a fair and equitable wage for the work they perform.

>> Payroll costs are in line with the overall financial health of your company.

>> The basic philosophy of compensation is clearly understood by your employees and has the strong support of managers and employees alike.

>> The pay scale for various jobs in the company reflects the relative importance of the job and the skills required.

>> Pay scales are competitive enough with those of other employers in your region and industry so that you're not constantly seeing competitors hire your top employees away.

>> Compensation policies are in line with state and federal laws involving minimum wages and exempt or nonexempt classifications.

>> Compensation policies are keeping pace with the changing nature of today's labor market — particularly in recruiting and retaining your company's top performers.

Squaring away your philosophy and passing the test

Here are some questions you may want to ask yourself as you formulate your compensation philosophy:

>> Are you going to make your basic salaries simply competitive with the going rate for employers in your area and/or in your industry or higher?

>> Are you going to establish a structured pay scale for specific jobs in your company, or are you going to tie salaries to individuals, basing pay on the qualifications and potential of the person filling the job?

>> To what extent are the monetary rewards you offer your employees going to take the form of salary, performance bonuses, or benefits?

>> Are salaries based on employee performance or on other factors, such as how long staff members stay with you or what skills or credentials they bring to the job?

>> Are you going to award bonuses on the basis of individual performance, tie bonuses to company results, or use a combination of the two?

Keep in mind that no specific answers are right or wrong for every situation. What's important is that your compensation philosophy considers your company's mission and goals. If your goal is to become the dominant company in your industry within five years, you'll probably need to offer generous wage-and-benefit packages to attract the people who can fuel your growth. And you may need to pay highly talented employees a little more than market value today so you can reap the benefit of their contributions three or four years from now. If your goal is to improve productivity, you most likely want to tie compensation to performance and productivity.

Identifying the Key Components of Employee Compensation

Employee compensation includes everything employees receive in exchange for their work, including base pay, bonuses, and incentive pay, as well as benefits. The following list offers a quick overview of the key aspects of employee compensation:

>> **Base wage or salary:** The base wage or salary is simply the salary or wage — before deductions and other incentives — that employees receive for the work they do. (If you want to get really technical, you generally use *wages* as an umbrella label for all forms of pay, including hourly rates, day rates, commissions, and salaries. More specifically, salary typically describes the pay arrangements of employees who receive their compensation as a flat weekly, biweekly, or monthly amount, regardless of how many hours they work.)

>> **Benefits:** Benefits are items that you offer to employees in addition to their base wage or salary. Examples include health insurance and retirement plans (refer to Chapter 12 for more details).

>> **Bonuses and incentives:** Generally speaking, any payment made to reward performance, attendance, productivity, tenure, a specific result, or other work-related behavior is an incentive. Bonuses are just one form of incentive. Additional forms of incentives include prizes, awards, and special sales incentives.

>> **Commission:** This term refers to a percentage of the sales price of a service or product that salespeople receive in addition to (or in lieu of) base wages. Commission arrangements include the following:

- Straight commission with no salary.

- Commission combined with a base salary.

- A draw. Technically, a *draw* against future commissions is an arrangement in which the salesperson receives a set amount on a regular basis, regardless of how much commission is actually earned during that period. If your salesperson (most typically someone new in their role) never hits their stride, they'll accumulate a large negative draw, which may be difficult to pay back.

Bonuses, incentives, and commission are all components of variable pay; your use of variable pay is an important part of your compensation strategy. It allows you the ability to remain competitive and create a system in which employees have greater earning potential beyond their base salary. But because base salary is a big portion of the compensation equation, it's important to be thoughtful and strategic in your approach. In the following sections, I provide insight and support in how to best establish a pay structure that's equitable and competitive and supports your business goals.

Setting pay levels in your organization

One of the main tasks in any effort to create an equitable and effective wage and compensation system is to develop a consistent protocol for setting pay levels for every job in your organization. In setting the actual pay scale for specific jobs, you have several options.

The more essential a job is to the fundamental mission of your company, the higher its job value and, thus, the higher its pay range is likely to be. Job value can be determined by using any of these popular job valuation methods (although they aren't the only methods).

Job ranking and leveling

How this approach works: You make a list of all the jobs in your company, from the most senior to entry-level employees. Then you group the jobs by major function — management, administrative, production, and so on. Working on your own or with other managers, you rank jobs by the degree to which they provide value to the company. Eventually, you produce a ranking or hierarchy of positions. In the process, you create a measure of internal equity. As a result, employees feel that they're being treated fairly. Keep in mind that you're not rating individuals — you're rating the relative importance of each job with respect to your company's revenue goals.

The rationale: In large companies, you may want to use a reasonably structured approach to decide what pay range to apply to each job. The more systematic you are as you develop that structure, the more effective the system is likely to be.

The downside: Creating and maintaining a structure of this nature takes a lot of time and effort.

Market data and pay trends: "The going rate"

How this approach works: You look at what other companies in your industry (and region) pay people for comparable jobs and set your pay structure accordingly. There are a number of helpful sources for determining pay ranges. The U.S Bureau of Labor Statistics is a good source. Others include the staffing company Robert Half, Salary.com, Glassdoor, Payscale, Indeed, SalaryExpert, and the job postings of your competitors. In addition, many organizations utilize compensation survey databases such as Culpepper to determine pay ranges. It allows you to submit your own data and place data cuts based on industry, employee count, revenue and so on, and also allow you to search hybrid roles, which mitigates the challenge noted in the downside bullet.

Rationale: The laws of supply and demand directly affect salary levels. Benchmarking salaries (and benefits) is important to ensure that you're paying people competitively.

The downside: Comparing apples to apples can sometimes be difficult in today's job market. Many new jobs that companies are creating are actually combinations of jobs in the traditional sense of the word. As such, they can prove difficult to price, because you can only go by how other companies pay. Still, it's a good starting point.

Collective bargaining

How this approach works: In unionized companies, formal bargaining between management and labor representatives sets wage levels for specific groups of workers. These are based on market rates and the employer's resources available to pay wages.

The rationale: Workers should have a strong say (and agree as a group) on how much a company will pay them.

The downside: Acrimony arises if management and labor fail to see eye to eye. In addition, someone else — the union — plays a key role in your business decisions. Also, in this system, employees who perform exceptionally well can feel shortchanged because less proficient colleagues in similar positions receive the same pay.

Adopting a pay structure

Salary structures are an important component of an effective compensation strategy and help ensure that pay levels for groups of jobs are competitive externally and equitable internally. A well-designed salary structure allows you to reward the skills, knowledge, and talents team members bring to the company — and not the nature of the positions they fill. In this section, I fill you in on some of the ways businesses design their pay structures.

Variable pay system

Variable pay systems link a percentage of a position's pay to defined performance and accomplishment targets.

How the system usually works: You establish a base pay rate and define group and individual objectives as a variable salary component. Some systems set base pay at about 80 percent of the possible compensation under the variable system. You can base proportions of the variable component on the attainment of departmental or company objectives and on individual achievement.

Advantages:

>> It imposes a direct relationship between pay and production.

>> It guarantees employees a stable base income, while providing incentives for superior performance.

>> Some forms of variable pay, such as profit sharing, provide employees with flexibility and allows the organization to reward employees through profit gain rather than operational expenses.

Disadvantages:

>> If employees can't meet performance targets, it can lead to morale problems in an economic downturn.

>> If the criteria for variable pay isn't defined accurately, it can result in the improper implementation of the pay structure.

Offering competitive compensation is key to attracting top talent to your organization. But after employees are onboard, salary levels don't stay competitive for long. As employees develop new skills and increase their knowledge of your business, they become increasingly valuable. Their value in the marketplace increases as well, meaning that they become attractive targets for other companies. To keep your best and brightest, you need to figure out fair (and affordable) ways to augment what you pay them — a variable pay structure allows you to do that. As you're building a variable compensation structure, ensure that the program meets the following criteria:

>> **Results-oriented:** Employees must accomplish something to receive variable compensation.

>> **Fair:** The rules for variable compensation are clear and enforced equitably.

>> **Competitive:** The variable compensation program rewards extra effort and superior performance.

Broadbanding

With *broadbanding,* you reduce a lengthy series of narrowly defined base-pay categories to a few broad salary ranges or pay bands. These pay bands are how you define the target pay for employees within job grades. For each level, a company should decide the low-end and high-end of the pay that level will command.

A traditional salary range is commonly 30 to 40 percent. It's common for top salary grades (in other words, for executives and top management) to have a wider range (sometimes greater than a range of 40 percent) and for the lowest salary grades to have the narrowest range (sometimes smaller than 30 percent).

How the system usually works: You boil down a cluster of related jobs into one pay band. For example, say you currently have six different job titles and pay groups for your administrative staff (office assistant, office manager, receptionist, executive assistant, administrative assistant, and senior administrative assistant), with base salaries ranging from $37,000 to $65,000 a year, depending on job title. Under broadbanding, you eliminate all job titles and salary ranges and combine everything into one band — administrative staff — with the same overall pay range as before but with no hard-wired connection between specific salaries and job titles.

Naturally, pay bands are wider at executive level positions, whereas entry-level bands are narrower.

Keep in mind that the actual salaries you pay don't change. You may still have one person earning, say, $50,000 and another earning $37,000. On the other hand, managers now have the option of basing pay on factors that derive from job performance or some other criteria, as opposed to job title. Managers also have the option of moving employees around as the work requires — according to the employees' skills — without needing to worry about job titles.

Advantages:

>> Gives managers flexibility in setting base salaries and work assignments

>> Eliminates bureaucratic barriers to transfers and employee development (such as job titles)

>> Eliminates unnecessary distinctions between similar jobs

>> Lets managers reward superior performance more easily

Disadvantages:

>> It may prove disconcerting to long-time employees who may see broadbanding as a threat to their status.

>> It can result in inconsistent compensation decisions across departments.

>> Unless guidelines are clearly established, management can be open to charges of favoritism or discrimination.

>> In unionized industries, you can implement the system only through collective bargaining.

Taking individuals into account

You pay people, not positions. So, sooner or later, you must program into your salary decisions those factors that relate solely to the individual who is to perform the job. The following list describes the key individual factors you may want to consider in finalizing your compensation system:

>> **Experience and education:** To a certain extent (and in particular occupations more than others), you see a fairly reliable correlation between employee productivity and their education level and experience. Be careful, however, not to take this principle too far. More education and greater experience don't always translate into better work. People who are overqualified for positions, for example, can prove less productive than individuals with less experience or less education. The key here is to make sure that a logical connection exists between the employee's education and experience and the basic requirements of the job.

>> **Past job performance:** In theory, at least, you should pay more to workers who can demonstrate that they produce more. The challenge is putting this simple idea into practice. To do so effectively, you need to address the following questions:

- What barometers are you using to measure job performance, and how do they tie into your strategic objectives? If you're evaluating customer service specialists, for example, are you interested in quantity — the number of inquiries handled in a specific time frame — or are you more concerned about the satisfaction level reported in customer surveys? If you're evaluating the performance of technical service personnel, are you going to key pay levels to technical proficiency or their ability to interact with others?

- Who's responsible for measuring performance? Is it the employee's immediate supervisor, or do you use a team-based approach to performance evaluation? What recourse do employees who take issue with your evaluations have? If they don't think the performance criteria are fair, can they take their case to someone other than their supervisor?

- Are the performance criteria you're using to reward performance discriminatory in any way? In other words, does any aspect of your company's job performance criteria favor one gender over another, individuals under 40 years of age compared to those 40 and older, or one ethnic group over another?

>> **Seniority:** Length of service has long been a factor in the pay scales in most industries — unionized industries in particular. The rationale is that loyalty is valued and should be rewarded. The downside: No strong evidence suggests that seniority and productivity in any way directly correlate.

>> **Potential:** Some companies justify higher pay for certain individuals because they consistently demonstrate the potential to become exceptional producers or managers. This consideration is generally why comparatively unskilled, inexperienced college graduates may receive extra compensation if they enter management trainee programs.

The payroll/revenue ratio: What's an optimal balance?

Regardless of the compensation system you set up, you must make sure that your company can afford to carry the costs. No optimal ratio exists between payroll costs and revenues, but whatever you decide needs to be a structure you can handle comfortably. Employees should feel that their salaries are reasonably well insulated from the ups and downs of your business. Given a choice, most employees may be willing to take home a little less on a yearly basis (within reason) in exchange for the reassurance that they're going to receive their pay regularly throughout the year.

Most business consultants tell you that the key issue in determining an appropriate cost/revenue ratio is how much of a profit margin you realize on your products or services. The general rule is that between 15 percent and 30 percent of your gross sales should go to payroll. However, this can vary by industry. Companies that operate on relatively high margins (50 percent or higher) can absorb higher payroll costs than can companies operating on smaller margins.

Considering state wage and hour laws

The states have varying policies governing the determination and payment of wages. In general, state laws require employers to pay wages

>> At prescribed intervals, such as weekly, biweekly, semimonthly, or monthly (so-called *pay frequency*)

>> Within prescribed periods of time after the close of each interval, such as no later than seven days (so-called *pay timeliness*)

The wage and hour laws of many states also restrict the types of deductions that employers may take from an employee's paycheck. Although it's typically lawful to automatically deduct taxes (withholding taxes, Social Security, unemployment taxes, and state disability insurance payments) that are forwarded to a government, other deductions often may be barred outright or allowed only with a signed authorization from the employee. Deductions subject to an outright bar can include, depending upon the state, product breakage and cash shortages. In most cases, employers should get employee approval before withholding amounts from their paycheck for benefits such as medical coverage, life insurance, 401(k) contributions, or other employee-paid benefits.

WARNING

Wage and hour laws can be very tricky to comply with, and federal laws may or may not correspond with the requirements of state laws. This is an area where you're wise to consult with an experienced and knowledgeable attorney.

Differentiating between Exempt and Nonexempt

The three main purposes of the Fair Labor Standards Act (FLSA), enacted in 1938 and amended several times since then, are to

>> Establish a minimum wage

>> Provide overtime (typically at one-and-a-half times the regular rate of pay) for work in excess of a weekly standard (typically 40 hours)

>> Set minimum standards for child labor

Included in the FLSA are special rules for determining whether a position is eligible for exemption from the FLSA's overtime and minimum wage standards. Thus was born a key distinction between exempt and nonexempt workers.

WARNING

Compliance with wage and hour laws can be very complicated. Employers should consult with an attorney who is knowledgeable and who has experience with such laws. Don't try to soldier through this heavily regulated area without legal counsel.

Classifying workers: Who's exempt and nonexempt

The rules that distinguish exempt and nonexempt employees focus on their job duties and forms of pay. *Exempt employees* are those whose primary duty is to perform specified tasks and who, depending upon the particular exemption, exercise discretion and independent judgment. Typically, exempt employees receive a fixed salary, without regard to the quantity or quality of their work. In some instances, especially in the entertainment industry, exempt employees may receive a fee rather than a salary.

Nonexempt employees are those who don't meet the exemption requirements. They may receive pay in any form (for example, an hourly rate, a piece rate, a salary, or a commission), but employers must reduce that pay to an hourly rate for each workweek in which they work overtime. Employers must make this conversion, because overtime typically is a rate per hour and because that rate typically must include (or blend) all forms of pay for work performed.

The rules for distinguishing exempt from nonexempt employees are technical and fact-based. Basing exempt status on job title or job description, salary level, job complexity, access to confidential information, or safety sensitivity isn't safe.

In addition, the burden is on the employer, not the employee, to justify exempt status. Moreover, the back pay, interest, and other damages that can flow from misclassifying your employees can be large, going back two or three years. Keep in mind that individual states can, and often do, create higher standards for exempt status than those imposed by the FLSA. Some states impose higher damages or penalties for misclassification, and some states look back more than two or three years. For these reasons, you should consult an attorney when drawing lines between your exempt and nonexempt employees.

WARNING

An employee can't waive their right to overtime. So, even a signed agreement saying an employee won't receive overtime is meaningless. The employee can later claim that nonexempt status.

Keep in mind the following guidelines as you're classifying workers:

>> **Analyze jobs to determine actual duties.** Focus on day-to-day activities and correlate them with the requirements of the law. Compare what the employee actually does with the formal job description. Lawsuits can arise as a result of conflict between the two.

>> **Correct problems when you find them.** Don't wait for a lawsuit to drop in your lap or a government inspector — municipal, state, or federal — to walk in

the door. Bear in mind, though, that a voluntary reclassification of positions can, in and of itself, trigger a lawsuit by those who claim that the reclassification has exposed prior noncompliance.

» **Keep accurate records.** You need to keep accurate time records for all nonexempt employees. If a dispute arises as to whether an employee worked overtime, the employee probably will win unless the company can produce an employee-completed time sheet showing otherwise.

» **Don't allow employees to work off the clock.** There is no point to going from the frying pan to the fire — going from improperly classifying someone as exempt to underpaying them as nonexempt. Remember this basic rule: If you knew or should have known that a nonexempt employee was working, you must pay for that time, even if the employee didn't write it down. You can impose discipline for working unauthorized hours, but this is tricky because, if you resort to discipline, you must do so in a way that doesn't discourage anyone from writing down the hours for which they're entitled to pay.

THE BOTTOM LINE ON OVERTIME

Overtime often is an integral part of today's nonexempt jobs. Employees in many industries depend on the extra money they make in overtime wages to support their standard of living. No one disputes that relying on overtime work certainly makes sense in many situations. The question you need to ask yourself is whether overtime is the best option for your company in any given situation.

Responding to temporarily increased demand by putting existing workers on overtime can be less expensive than hiring new employees. Of course, cost savings from using overtime are true only for a short period of time. A steady diet of overtime to increase production can have negative long-term consequences. Excessive, long-term overtime can increase the rate of on-the-job accidents, erode employee morale, and cause family pressures. Also, a steady diet of overtime may suggest, at some point, the possibility that adding staff actually will decrease your compensation burden because a new hire may cost less than the recurring overtime.

You're best-off viewing overtime as a stopgap strategy, reserving it for short-term situations, such as when people call in sick or take vacations, or when the workload increases in the short term. If the need becomes constant, consider adding a new employee or filling the gap by using contingent workers (see Chapter 4).

Contemplating other legal issues

The following list gives you a brief look at federal laws that address discrimination, as well as how much you pay your workers. Don't forget to check your local and state regulations, too.

>> **The Equal Pay Act of 1963:** This law prohibits unequal pay to men and women doing the same job, assuming that the jobs require equal skill, effort, and responsibility and that employees perform the jobs under similar conditions. Most states have similar statutes. The law permits a few exceptions, such as seniority, merit pay, or productivity, so check with a lawyer.

>> **Civil Rights Acts of 1964:** Title VII of this law prohibits wage (and other employment) discrimination on the basis of race, sex, color, religion, or national origin. The U.S. Equal Employment Opportunity Commission (EEOC) enforces this law.

>> **Age Discrimination in Employment Act of 1967:** As amended in 1978, this law bans wage (and other employment) discrimination for employees ages 40 or older, including pay increases, bonuses, and benefits. One of the most common violations is the denial of pay increases to people nearing retirement to avoid increasing retirement benefits that are based on salary. The EEOC enforces this law, too.

>> **The Americans with Disabilities Act of 1990:** This law prohibits discrimination in compensation (and other employment terms and conditions), including access to insurance, against qualified applicants and workers on the basis of disability.

>> **The Davis-Bacon Act of 1931, the Copeland Act of 1934, the Walsh-Healey Act of 1936, and the Anti-Kickback Act of 1948:** These four laws focus, in different ways, on the compensation policies of companies with federal contracts. Each law has its own wrinkle, but the basic purpose is to ensure that employers pay prevailing wages and overtime while prohibiting excessive wage deductions and under-the-table payments by employees to obtain work.

>> **The Wage Garnishment Law:** This law prohibits employers from firing workers whose wages, for whatever reason, are subject to garnishment by creditors or a spouse. In most cases, it also limits garnishments to no more than 25 percent of an employee's take-home pay.

For more information on the first four laws in the preceding list, see Chapter 17.

Focusing on Pay Raises and Base Salary Increases

Many organizations have budget dollars set aside each year for pay increases. Some budget for various types of pay increases that may occur throughout the year; others budget a flat amount that includes all types of pay increases in one lump sum. According to a 2022 Willis Towers Watson survey, annual merit increases in the United States averaged around 3 to 4 percent. Following are the most common types of pay increases:

» **Cost of living increases:** Organizations sometimes give pay increases to help offset inflation. For instance, if annual inflation increases by 2 percent, it may be wise to also increase your employees' salaries by 2 percent so they can still support their basic living costs.

» **Merit increases:** Merit pay raises, or *performance-based pay raises,* are given as rewards for excellent work by an employee. Employers use these types of increases to keep top-performing employees engaged and motivated, and let them know, in a very tangible way, that they are appreciated. The WorldatWork Salary Budget Survey 2019–2020 showed that organizations budgeted a 3.6 percent pay increase for high performers, 2.5 percent for middle performers, and 0.6 percent for low performers.

» **Promotions:** Pay increases are typical when an employee receives a promotion (more responsibility and a new job title), and sometimes even if the employee takes on more responsibility within the current job description.

» **Market pay adjustment:** Organizations adjust pay when they determine that the rates they are paying for certain jobs are not competitive enough to attract or retain employees. In many cases, wage surveys are used to determine whether a company is paying competitively in their geographic location or industry.

» **Equity pay increase:** An equity increase is used to ensure that employees receive equal pay for equal work. This has been an emphasis particularly in combating the gender wage gap. In 2021, research form Payscale found that women earned 82 cents for every dollar earned by men, and that similarly, racial pay gaps are prevalent, as well.

Bonuses

Bonuses are one-shot payments that are typically tied to the achievement of a result or a condition being met (such as staying with the company). They come in a variety of flavors:

>> **Annual and biannual bonuses:** These bonuses are one-time payments to all eligible employees, based on the company's results, individual performance, or a combination thereof.

>> **Spot bonuses:** Spot bonuses are awarded in direct response to a single instance of superior employee performance (a particularly successful suggestion, for example). Employees receive the bonus on the spot — that is, at the time of the action that warranted the bonus or immediately thereafter.

>> **Retention bonuses:** You make such payments to persuade key people to stay with your company. These bonuses are common in industries that employ hard-to-recruit specialists. They're also effective in retaining top managers or star performers.

>> **Team bonuses:** These bonuses are awarded to group members for the collective success of their team.

WARNING

Employers must be aware that the amount of a bonus may — depending on certain circumstances — need to be included in determining an employee's regular rate of pay, which is the amount of pay upon which overtime pay is calculated. Mistakes can violate federal or state wage and hour laws. A knowledgeable attorney can help you navigate this tricky area.

Employers also need to be aware that the timing of payment of a bonus can determine whether the IRS views the bonus as providing deferred compensation, which can trigger application of special tax rules. A knowledgeable benefits attorney can help address tax issues relating to bonus plans.

Other incentives

The following sections outline some other common incentive programs, besides bonus programs.

REMEMBER

Where I cover employee benefits in Chapter 12, I discuss a number of retirement plan options you can offer your team members. I mention some of them in this section as well because these plans can be viewed as incentives or retirement plan benefits, depending on how they are structured and how the employee intends to use them.

Profit-sharing plans

Profit-sharing plans enable the company to set aside a percentage of its profits for distribution to employees. If profits go up, the employees get more money. You can vary these programs by allocating profit sharing on a department or business-unit basis. Employees who stand to share in the company's profits have an extra incentive to work hard and be more aware of avoiding waste and inefficiency. After all, it's their business, too.

Profit-sharing plans fall into one of two categories:

>> **Cash plans:** Payments are distributed quarterly or annually.

>> **Deferred plans:** The company invests the profit-sharing payment in a fund and then pays out an employee's share when they retire or leave the company.

Deferred plans offer significant tax advantages to both the company and employees. On the downside, deferred plans can have less effect on productivity. In some cases, the worker doesn't actually see the profit-sharing money, except as a figure on paper, until retirement. A profit-sharing plan that is set up to defer compensation until termination of employment or retirement can be either a tax-qualified retirement plan or a nonqualified deferred compensation plan. Both types of programs are common, and neither requires the employer to have actual profits. Detailed rules under the Internal Revenue Code and ERISA may apply depending upon how the program is structured.

WARNING

Whenever the profit-sharing plan provides for the receipt of income in a year after it's earned, there's a deferral of compensation, and the plan will be subject to complex tax laws. You should exercise caution before locking in any contractual obligations and consult an employee benefits or tax attorney for counsel.

Stock

Stock in the company is an incentive that publicly traded firms (in addition to firms planning to go public or private companies who don't have imminent plans to go public but may likely be acquired) may choose to offer their employees. *Stock option plans* give employees at publicly held companies the right to purchase shares in the company at a time of their own choosing, but at a price that is set at the time the option is awarded. Employees are under no obligation to exercise that option. However, if the stock price goes up, employees can buy the stock at the cheaper price and either hold on to it or sell it for the current value, thereby earning a profit.

Stock options also have given small, growing companies a way to attract top talent without having to pay high salaries. These plans have become commonplace in fast-growth industries such as technology.

If your company is thinking about offering equity as an overall benefits package, there are certain aspects of the process everyone must be aware of. For privately held companies offering stock ownership as an incentive, it's a good idea to consult with experts who can assist you with the available equity options and methods for valuing the company and the shares offered. If you're publicly held, you need to make sure that you have an organized plan and mechanisms in place that won't dilute the value of the stock to nonemployee stockholders. Bear in mind, too, that these programs must comply with tax laws and with Securities and Exchange Commission (SEC) regulations.

What's fair versus what works?

Instituting policies for raises, bonuses, or other incentives that people don't understand and that neither managers nor employees buy into can backfire and do more harm than good. The following list offers guidelines to help you avoid these pitfalls:

- » **Set clear rules.** Whether you're dealing with an incentive system or a merit-raise program, everyone must understand the rules that govern the rewards program. Key information includes who's eligible for the program, what they must do to receive the reward, who decides on those who benefit, and the size of the reward.

- » **Set specific targets or goals you can quantify.** If you're going to establish incentives, make sure that you set a specific target: "125 percent of our annual sales quota," for example, or "more than 500 pieces per day." Specific numbers eliminate arguments and misunderstandings.

- » **Make the goal worthwhile.** If the incentives aren't attractive, they're not really incentives. So gear the reward to the group whose performance you're seeking to enhance. Think about setting up different rewards for varying levels of achievement — for example, a 4 percent increase for an average performer and an 8 percent increase for a top-notch employee.

- » **Don't ask for the impossible.** Such terms as killer goals may sound highly motivational, but you may only discourage employees if they think they're simply unattainable. Not only can that dampen their motivation and effort, but it also costs you credibility. That's not to say there's anything wrong with "stretch" goals, but they should be attainable.

- » **Don't make promises you can't keep.** Never promise a bonus or incentive you're not sure you can afford.

Communicating Your Compensation Philosophy and Total Rewards

Studies show that the average employee doesn't fully understand their compensation package. They either don't know how to access the materials that explain their compensation or don't understand them because the information is confusing or not presented in a helpful way. In particular, it's important to brief managers and supervisors on your company's pay systems so that they can effectively explain, administer, and support your policies. Managers and supervisors need the following information:

>> Your company's compensation philosophy

>> The way to handle and refer employee questions and complaints about their compensation

>> The legal implications of all compensation policies

You also need to advise employees of the company's pay policies and how those policies affect them individually. You need to communicate and fully explain any changes in these policies promptly. Employees need to know

>> How compensation decisions are made

>> How they can raise their own income through performance and promotion

>> How to voice questions or concerns about their pay

Building a compensation system isn't a one-time event — like all aspects of HR, it's a process that is continuously evaluated and updated. The key steps in keeping it updated are as follows:

>> Obtain and review competitive data at regular intervals.

>> Review — and adjust if necessary — salary ranges at least annually.

>> Look over position success profiles regularly and adjust based on disparities between actual work performance and the formal description.

>> Evaluate the performance appraisal system. One common problem is that too many employees get superior ratings.

>> Review salary systems in terms of your company's financial condition to determine whether the system is in line with the company's financial health and is tax effective and efficient.

>> Periodically measure and rate productivity and determine whether any links exist between productivity increases (or declines) and pay policies.

FIND ONLINE

TOTAL REWARDS: LET EMPLOYEES KNOW WHO'S PAYING

With the smorgasbord of benefits offered by companies today, wouldn't it be great for your employee recruitment and retention efforts if everything could be grouped together in one easy-to-understand "basket"? That way, workers could readily see how much time, money, and other resources you're investing on their behalf.

Materials distributed to employees during the annual enrollment process likely already show part of the picture. A more comprehensive look can take into consideration compensation, benefits, work/life accommodations, and even taxes paid on behalf of employees.

This idea of holistically reporting to employees what their employer is doing on their behalf is sometimes referred to as total rewards. The goal is to ensure that employees understand what they're getting from the company and the associated value.

If you decide to create a statement of the broader benefits you provide, make sure that you've gone through the thought processes I describe in this chapter to align your benefits with what employees actually value. If you haven't taken this step, the effect of a report you issue could be the opposite of what you intend: It could make your team aware that little you do for them has real meaning to them as individuals. In short, a total rewards statement may be a good idea for your business; just be sure to approach it carefully and be realistic about what it actually portrays about your company.

A case can be made for including Social Security and unemployment insurance in your total rewards statement. These are so common that your employees probably don't consider these programs as "benefits." That means they may not realize how much your company is paying on their behalf. If you don't want to include this in your total rewards concept, you may want to list your company's contributions right on the employee's pay stub, next to deductions from the employee's gross pay. In some states, this and other categories of information may be required under applicable wage and hour laws. If you contract out your payroll, your contractor may already have the software to do this.

See the online tools for a draft Total Rewards Statement. Keep in mind that the statement you prepare can be more comprehensive than the example online. You also may use the total rewards statement to provide an explanation and amplification of how each benefit works and its value to the employee. Just be sure that the statement you prepare is an accurate reflection of your offerings and policies.

» Reviewing the basics of employee
   benefits

» Grasping the intricacies of insurance
   offerings

» Making benefits administration
   easier

Chapter **12**

Putting Together the Right Benefits Package

As employers strive to retain and recruit the best talent in a tight job market, there's an increasing focus on health benefits and patient-centered care. Employers have found that quality employee benefits can help them differentiate themselves and remain competitive as they seek ways to address recruitment and retention challenges. Nearly half (48 percent) of the more than 9,600 U.S. employees surveyed by Willis Towers Watson in 2022 said healthcare benefits were an important reason they chose their current employer.

You have a lot to think about when managing benefits for your team members — administrative details and government regulation, not to mention pressure to reconcile employee desires with the financial realities of your business. However, a comprehensive package of employee benefits is a critical component in recruiting and retaining talented teams. It's by no means an inexpensive undertaking, but the payoff is more than worth the cost.

Much of the complexity in benefits planning and administration today is due to the changing face of the workplace and changing expectations. Today's diverse workforce has many needs, and this diversity extends to the benefits workers want. Add to this a wide range of laws and healthcare and retirement plan options, and you quickly see how complicated it can be to create and implement effective benefits programs.

As challenging as all of these factors seem at first glance, you have opportunity here as well. After you get your arms around this area of HR, you can do a great deal of good for your employees and your company. And, best of all, if you know what you're doing in building and promoting a competitive benefits package, you can greatly strengthen your company's ability to attract and retain top talent. That's what this chapter is all about.

Addressing Key Trends in Benefits Management

You can define a benefit as any form of compensation that isn't part of an employee's basic pay — and that isn't tied directly to either job requirements or performance.

Specific employee benefits today take a multitude of forms ranging from multiple-option healthcare coverage and tuition reimbursement to childcare and mental health and fertility benefits. Other benefits include pet insurance, caregiving benefits, and identity theft protection. Exactly which benefits you offer and how much of your payroll expense goes to pay for them are decisions your company's financial health and business philosophy must determine. Your job in taking on the HR function is to make sure that both your company and its employees are getting the best bang for their benefits bucks.

The world of benefits administration is changing rapidly. Between shutdowns, home offices, and the great resignation, the Covid-19 pandemic has shifted employee priorities regarding their relationship to their work and employer. Employees are increasingly more concerned and proactive about safeguarding their physical and mental well-being, work-life balance, and financial health. This shift is challenging employers to reevaluate their current benefit packages and consider new ways of meeting employee needs.

The following sections provide a quick glimpse of three key trends.

Considering the continued increase in healthcare costs

The average American spends a considerable amount of money on healthcare each year, and healthcare costs — premium increases, higher deductibles and copays, and soaring prescription drug prices — continue to rise.

To offset the rising cost of employee benefits, organizations are asking employees to assume a larger portion of the overall benefits tab. For example, in the all-important realm of healthcare costs, the typical employee's contribution has risen considerably. Companies are now finding innovative ways for employees to "earn" a percentage of their benefits premium with programs such as committing to remain tobacco free or performing a health risk assessment.

Focusing more on mental health

Mental health has become a rapidly growing area of attention when it comes to employee benefits. With the hardships faced throughout the Covid-19 pandemic, employers and employees are recognizing and placing more concern on mental health than in the past. According to a 2022 study by The Conference Board, 88 percent of companies offer some sort of program that supports emotional well-being (including mental health resources and Employee Assistance Programs), up 23 percent from 2021.

Lifestyle Spending Accounts

A Lifestyle Spending Account (LSA) is an employer-funded benefit that provides employees funds for specific categories of goods that are generally outside the scope of what's covered under a group health plan. LSAs may cover expenditures like fitness memberships, athletic equipment, home office expenses, and much more. Employers control the amount of funds they contribute and what types of expenses the funds can be used toward. In return, employees receive taxable financial support for areas they traditionally had to pay for themselves.

Examining the Basics of Benefits Coverage

Offering most employee benefits is voluntary. You're under no legal obligation to provide them with five notable exceptions: Social Security and Medicare, unemployment insurance, workers' compensation insurance, Family Medical Leave Act (FLMA) protection, and health insurance (for organizations that employ 50 or more full-time employees). Note that some states require additional benefits; for instance, disability pay is required in states such as New Jersey and California and some states have other types of paid or unpaid leave requirements, so check your state requirements to comply.

The following sections take a brief look at the five benefits that are required across all states:

Social Security and Medicare

The Social Security tax is a percentage of gross wages that most employees, employers, and self-employed workers must pay to fund the federal program.

Payroll taxes finance Social Security and Medicare. Your employees typically contribute 7.65 percent of their gross take-home pay to fund both programs. Federal law obligates your company to match that amount. (The Social Security tax rate for those who are self-employed is 12.4 percent.) The first 6.2 percent of the tax that goes to the Social Security fund is assessed only up to a specific income ceiling — $160,200 in 2023. Any income over that limit isn't subject to Social Security tax. No ceiling exists, at present, on the 1.45 percent Medicare tax. These rules are subject to change.

TIP

Check out *Social Security For Dummies,* by Jonathan Peterson (John Wiley & Sons, Inc.), for much more information on the complex rules surrounding Social Security.

Unemployment insurance

Unemployment insurance provides basic income for eligible workers who become unemployed through no fault of their own.

Individual states run the unemployment insurance program, which was established as part of the 1935 Social Security Act. The federal guidelines are rather loose. Except in a handful of states (Alaska, Pennsylvania, and New Jersey) that expect employees to pay a small percentage of the cost, employers pay for their workers' unemployment insurance. The cost to employers is generally based on the company's *experience rating* (how frequently its former employees receive payments through the program). The more people you lay off, the greater your potential assessment becomes.

TIP

The experience-rating method of calculating employer unemployment costs is yet another reason for your company to avoid cycles of new hires in flush times and layoffs whenever demand sags. It's also a good reason to use contingent workers during times of reduced business or to handle normal workload peaks and valleys. In addition, it's important for a company to regularly pay unemployment insurance taxes. This fact may seem obvious, but in recent years, a number of companies have behaved illegally.

Workers' compensation

Workers' compensation provides protection for workers who suffer injuries or become ill on the job, regardless of whether the employee or the employer was negligent. It pays medical bills, provides disability payments (income replacement) for permanent injuries, and distributes lump-sum death benefits.

Workers' compensation is an insurance program. Some states permit private insurance — if your company can demonstrate financial capability to state authorities, you may choose to be self-insured. Other states require you to contribute to one state-managed fund; still others permit a mixture of state and private insurance. Generally, however, contributory systems are experience rated: The number of claims that employees file against your company determines your rates. Good workplace health and safety practices, therefore, pay off.

Some employers, especially those with large numbers of remote team members, have integrated workers' compensation programs into health-insurance programs. Keep in mind, though, that certain laws — federal and state — can make such a combination difficult to manage. As with other areas related to employees who work away from a specific office, thoroughly explore this option with an attorney.

WARNING

If you include the 50 states, the District of Columbia, Puerto Rico, and the Virgin Islands, at least 53 separate workers' compensation programs currently exist. You need to consult with your lawyer, insurance carrier, and state officials to determine your own liability. Workers' compensation, with very limited exceptions, is a no-fault system: No matter who's to blame for the illness or injury, it still covers the employee. If your company operates in more than one state, you must adjust your workers' compensation policies according to local rules. If you run into legal problems, you most likely must retain lawyers licensed to practice in the state in which the problem arises.

Family and Medical Leave Act (FMLA) Protection

The Family and Medical Leave Act (FMLA) entitles eligible employees of covered employers to take unpaid, job-protected leave for specified family and medical reasons. Covered employers are private-sector employers with 50 or more employees, and all public employers. The FMLA provides eligible employees with up to 12 weeks of job-protected, unpaid leave during a 12-month period for qualifying family and medical reasons, and to handle qualifying exigencies; as well as up to 26 workweeks of unpaid, job-protected leave in a single 12-month period under the Military Caregiver Leave. Qualifying reasons would include the birth of a child, dealing with a serious or chronic personal illness, or caring for an immediate family member with a serious or chronic illness.

Note: In addition to benefits under the FMLA, some states and local jurisdictions require paid/unpaid family leave and/or paid/unpaid sick and safe leave. Employers must review their obligations under applicable state and local laws.

Taking a Healthy Approach to Insurance

Health insurance is today's most expensive employee benefit. Without a doubt, it's also the most difficult benefit to administer, not just because of its cost but also because of the many options available and the challenges companies face balancing two seemingly contradictory objectives: keeping costs down while at the same time meeting employee needs.

The Affordable Care Act (ACA) provides that any organization that employs 50 or more full-time employees will be subject to a tax assessment unless they provide full-time employees with sufficient healthcare coverage to meet ACA requirements. These organizations are also required to report the value of health insurance on employee W2-forms, and they also have to file the appropriate forms with the IRS, providing details regarding the cost and types of health coverage offered to their employees. Not offering sufficient or affordable health insurance to full-time employees can result in an assessment and possible penalties from the federal government.

Health insurance is a very important aspect of employee benefits, so the following sections delve deeper into this topic.

Looking at the flavors of health insurance

The number of healthcare plans available today is enough to fill a book — a book that, given the changing world of healthcare, would no doubt be out of date quite quickly. Following is a bit of information on the three most prevalent healthcare plan options. Bear in mind that these options (in fact, the entire structure of employer-provided healthcare) may change rapidly, given the pressure on companies to control healthcare costs.

Fee-for-service plans

Fee-for-service plans are insurance programs that reimburse members a stated amount for designated healthcare services, regardless of which practitioner or hospital delivers the service. Under some fee-for-service arrangements, members pay the bills themselves and then submit their claims to the carrier for reimbursement. Under most plans, the physicians or hospitals assume the responsibility for filing and collecting on claims.

Fee-for-service plans have two fundamental parts:

>> **The base plan:** The base plan covers certain defined services, usually in connection with hospitalization — an appendectomy, for example, but not routine mole removal.

>> **The major medical:** Major medical covers such services as routine doctors' visits and certain tests.

Health maintenance organizations

Health maintenance organizations (HMOs) offer a wide range of medical services but limit your choices (both in medical practitioners and facilities) to those specialists or organizations that are part of the HMO network. Each person whom the plan covers must choose a primary physician (sometimes known as the *gatekeeper*), who decides whether a member needs to seek specialty services within the network or services outside the network.

As long as employees stay within the network (that is, they use only those facilities and medical practitioners who are part of the HMO network), the only additional cost to them if they undergo any procedure that the plan covers is a modest co-payment. HMOs differ in their out-of-network policies. Some are highly restrictive. Others allow members to seek care outside the network but only with the approval of the gatekeeper; members who use approved services outside the network may assume additional costs (up to a predefined deductible) for each out-of-network visit.

Preferred provider organizations

Preferred provider organizations (PPOs) are similar to HMOs but with several key differences:

>> The plan has a designated provider network, and employees who obtain treatment from providers in the designated network have a lower cost-sharing requirement than for services received outside of the designated network.

>> Employees have a wider range of choices as to whom they can see if they experience a medical problem than they have in an HMO plan.

>> PPOs typically require no gatekeeper — members can choose to go outside the network as long as they're willing to assume the additional costs, up to the agreed-upon deductible.

>> The premium and other out-of-pocket costs to employees for participating in a PPO are usually more than the costs to participate in a comparable HMO plan.

Weighing the options

In recent years, many companies have altered the options they offer. The traditional fee-for-service plans are still available, but most companies today make it most advantageous for employees to choose HMOs and PPOs, which are also known as *managed-care programs.* HMOs and PPOs provide the same benefits as the traditional fee-for-service plans but set limits on which practitioners and which facilities employees on the plan can use to receive maximum benefits. Some managed-care programs provide no benefits at all if employees go outside the approved networks.

REMEMBER

When deciding which type of plan to carry for your employees, you need to consider the following factors:

>> **Extent of coverage:** The procedures that health insurance plans cover can vary widely, but most plans are required to provide coverage for essential health benefits. Plans offered by employers with 50 or more full-time employees need to provide affordable minimum essential coverage at minimum value in order to avoid the employer shared responsibility penalty under the ACA.

>> **Quality of care:** The quality of medical services that members of managed-care programs receive has become an issue today for an obvious reason. Employees covered by these plans are obliged to use only those physicians or facilities designated by the plan's administrators. Therefore, you must make sure that any managed-care program you choose has high standards and a quality reputation. In addition, check to see whether the National Committee for Quality Assurance (www.ncqa.org) certifies that program.

>> **Cost:** In shopping for your company's health insurance, keep in mind that you always get exactly what you pay for, regardless of the particular option you choose. Insurers generally base their pricing on three factors:

- The number of people the plan covers

- The demographics of your workforce (average age, number of children, and so on)

- The amount of deductibles and co-payments

>> **Ease of administration:** A key factor in your choice of insurance carriers is the ease with which you can administer the program. The best plans, for example, offer an easy-to-use website.

WARNING

Although you can save some money by using in-house resources to handle administration, servicing your benefits can require a major commitment of staff time and financial resources. If you decide to assume this responsibility, make sure that you have the administrative ability.

Rising costs: Staying ahead of the game

The good news about contemporary healthcare is that society takes its well-being very seriously. People of all ages are leading healthier and longer lives. But a major part of taking better care of themselves means more trips to doctors for examinations, more preventative procedures, and when necessary, surgery. All these factors point to a pragmatic financial reality: Healthcare costs will continue to rise. The numbers bear this out. The average costs that U.S. employers pay for their employees' healthcare will increase 6.5 percent to more than $13,800 per employee in 2023, up from $13,020 per employee in 2022, according to professional services firm Aon.

The message here appears to be this: Don't expect the cost of keeping employees healthy to level off any time soon.

In many ways, issues related to healthcare strike right to the core of a company's responsibility to its employees. And there's no question that, depending on culture, history, and financial resources, different companies approach the matter of healthcare in different ways. Some see increased government involvement as an answer to rising costs. Others point to a benefit realignment in which employees bear more of the responsibility for healthcare costs and provider choices. You need to keep up with all these developments but also understand what companies are currently doing to contain healthcare costs.

REMEMBER

One key step is to encourage employees to stay healthy. Conducting regularly scheduled wellness seminars; distributing literature; and offering a wealth of information on topics such as stress management, nutrition, sleep, and other health-related subjects can go a long way toward decreasing healthcare costs. Some large companies go further, building on-site facilities that offer exercise equipment and even spa services. Some even provide financial incentives for employees who quit smoking, lose weight, or maintain a regular exercise schedule. Smaller firms can take many of these actions, perhaps including discounts on memberships at local health clubs. Be aware, though, that wellness programs are heavily regulated, and there are separate rules under ERISA, HIPAA, the ACA, the ADA, GINA, the Internal Revenue Code, and state law that may come into play in designing a workplace wellness program. Work with a knowledgeable benefits lawyer to confirm that your program complies and that proper notices are issued to your employees.

This commitment to ensuring a healthy employee base fits in with much of what I cover in this chapter. HR can play an important role in creating and nurturing a culture where employees are urged to take good care of themselves. Be on the lookout, for example, for managers and employees who work themselves to the brink of exhaustion and end up getting sick. Although dedication is valued, rarely is a short-term productivity gain worth the long-term expense.

SIX WAYS TO MINIMIZE HEALTHCARE COSTS

Even though it's true that you pretty much get what you pay for in a healthcare plan, you can adopt a few strategies to help you save money without compromising the quality of your employees' medical care. Here are some guidelines to keep in mind:

- **Offer a high deductible health plan (HDHP) in tandem with health savings accounts (HSAs) funded by employees and/or employers.**

- **Encourage active benefits participation:** Employers can help limit overall health costs by making employees active participants in their healthcare. This means encouraging employees to improve their health literacy, research treatments, and do price comparisons.

- **Manage drug benefits.** Many companies have eliminated co-pay arrangements for prescription drugs, opting instead for plans that require coinsurance and/or deductibles on a cost-sharing basis. One cost-cutting aspect is to provide preferred coverage for generic drugs. Some plans offer reduced costs to participants who elect home delivery by mail for long-term prescription needs instead of purchasing these items at a local pharmacy.

- **Change plans or how they are funded.** By shopping smart and comparing plans, you can investigate ways to make your benefits package stronger and more attractive to current and prospective employees — ideally, while also cutting costs.

  A more drastic option for reducing health costs is restructuring how plans are funded. For instance, a self-funded plan may be more cost-effective than paying a monthly premium for a fully insured plan. Other options include level-funding or reference-based pricing models, each of which carries its own set of administrative rules and legal constraints. Funding decisions should not be taken lightly and should be based on several factors, such as the size of an organization, risk tolerance, and financial stability.

- **Consider working with a benefits consultant.** Bringing in an outside benefits expert to analyze your company's healthcare needs and recommend the best approach to health insurance may cost you money in the short run, but the recommendations can more than offset the initial expense. Another option is to find a local insurance agent who specializes in medical insurance and ask that person to recommend the best program. Just make sure that the programs recommended to you have an established track record. Bear in mind, too, that while some benefits consultants charge on an hourly basis, others act as insurance brokers and get a commission (anywhere from 3 percent to 10 percent). If you're a good negotiator, you may persuade the broker to make price concessions.

- **Establish wellness programs.** Wellness programs that encourage employees not to get sick in the first place are a growing benefits trend. These initiatives can not only keep healthcare costs down for companies but also promote healthier behaviors that result in reduced absenteeism. Be aware, though, that having these programs in place can raise privacy and perceived discrimination issues, especially among people with hard-to-manage health issues such as obesity or smoking. If care is not taken in establishing them, workplace wellness programs can shift costs to those with the greatest healthcare needs and potentially violate federal antidiscrimination and privacy laws and other regulations.

Retirement plans

The business environment has changed radically in a single generation. Rarely do you see cases of one employee working at a single company for an entire career. In response, retirement plans have become much more flexible and portable. And because many companies no longer offer defined benefit (for example, corporate pension) plans, employees are seeking ways to personally remain in control of this important aspect of their careers and financial security.

Retirement plans that companies offer their employees generally fall into two categories:

>> **Defined benefit plans:** In a *defined benefit plan,* employees know the amount they'll get out of it (the benefit). The company chooses how to invest its employees' money and guarantees the amount the employee will receive at retirement. The most common type of defined benefit plan is a traditional pension plan.

>> **Defined contribution plans:** In a *defined contribution plan,* employees know how much they put in (the contribution) but don't know how much they'll eventually be able to take out. Typically, employees choose from a list of available investment vehicles and direct the investment of their retirement account. The payout depends on how those vehicles have performed when the time comes to make withdrawals. The most common type of defined contribution plan is a 401(k) plan.

TECHNICAL STUFF

Companies can offer a hybrid of defined benefit and defined contribution plans. An example is a cash balance plan, which combines some of the elements of a 401(k) plan and a defined benefit plan, such as a pension. According to the U.S. Bureau of Labor Statistics, the individual account feature of a cash balance plan makes it resemble a defined contribution plan. From an employer perspective, however, these plans are defined benefit plans because the employer doesn't actually fund the individual accounts but rather keeps a common fund sufficient to pay all future benefits.

Defined benefit plans

Generally limited to large, established companies, *defined benefit plans* provide a fixed benefit after retirement, usually calculated by a formula that considers salary level and length of service. The employer can fully fund these plans (noncontributory) or require employee contributions (contributory).

Advantages: Employees can count on a fixed, set amount of retirement income. The plan encourages employee loyalty and retention.

Disadvantages: These plans aren't generally portable — employees can lose some or all benefits by changing jobs. The funding obligations for these plans vary depending on numerous factors and can fluctuate significantly over time. Administrative costs can be high, too, and pension liabilities can significantly affect a company's balance sheet.

Overall, defined benefit plans are becoming much less common than they used to be. According to consultant Towers Watson, defined contribution plans (see the next section) are becoming nearly universal among employers. In a 2012 report, Towers Watson cited reasons why companies have shifted away from defined benefit plans, including competition, cost reduction, and an intent to improve employee satisfaction. (See "Employer contributions to retirement plans," later in this chapter.)

Defined contribution plans

Defined contribution plans are the primary alternative to defined benefit plans and basically involve individual accounts for each participant. The 401(k) plan is the classic defined contribution plan, but others are profit-sharing plans and employee stock ownership plans (ESOPs).

Employees can contribute their income to a 401(k) fund, deferring taxes until they withdraw the income (when, presumably, they'll be in a lower tax bracket). There is an annual limit on the amount employees may contribute, with a higher limit for older employees to "catch up" on their retirement savings. For example, for 2023, employees may contribute up to $22,500 into a 401(k) plan, and employees who are age 50 and older can contribute another $7,500. The plan may be designed with additional limits as well. If the plan document permits plan loans, employees may borrow within certain limits against their investment accounts. The plan may permit certain other withdrawals while the employee is still employed, for example, starting at age 59½. Some companies augment or match what their employees set aside in defined contribution plans. (See "Employer contributions to retirement plans," later in this chapter.)

Advantages: These plans are highly popular with employees. They also offer favorable tax treatment, lower administrative costs than traditional pension plans (usually), and portability — employees can take most or all funds with them when they change jobs.

Disadvantages: These plans offer no guaranteed payouts. Investment risks fall on employees. Employees face heavy tax penalties (10 percent) for early withdrawals unless for limited reasons, such as disability.

Many employees are now offering a Roth 401(k) in additional to the traditional 401(k) plans. Traditional 401(k) contributions grow on a tax-deferred basis, while Roth 401(k) dollars grow completely tax-free. That's good news for your team members who are contributing to a Roth 401(k) — once they put money into their account, they're done paying taxes on it.

Employer contributions to retirement plans

As employers replace their defined benefit plans with defined contribution plans at only a portion of the cost — and potentially only part of the benefit — many employers make contributions to a profit-sharing or 401(k) plan. According to the Society for Human Resource Management, a company has a number of options in the way it goes about this: no contribution, nonelective contributions, or matching contributions. A nonelective contribution is one an employer makes regardless of whether the employee contributes to the plan.

401(K) PLANS: SMART SHOPPING TIPS FOR EMPLOYERS

These days, many financial institutions are aggressively marketing 401(k) plans to employers of all sizes. These organizations usually also handle virtually all administrative details for employers. Finding a 401(k) vendor isn't hard, but choosing the best one for your company can be a challenge. In fact, the governing laws impose fiduciary duties on the employer or others who handle plan administration and investments. That means that you must act solely in the interests of plan participants and beneficiaries when administering the plans, selecting and monitoring investments, and using any plan assets to pay fees to third parties. The law imposes a very high standard on employers in this regard.

(continued)

(continued)

Here are some questions to ask any potential 401(k) provider:

- Are the management fees reasonable? Compare them with other plans and find out exactly what you're paying for.

- Are the investment options all from the same family of funds, or can the employee choose individual funds from different companies?

- How easily and frequently can employees switch their investments — between an equity and a bond fund, for example?

- How often do participants receive account statements?

- Does the plan offer a full range of investments, from conservative to moderately risky? The more choices employees get and the broader the range of those choices, the better the plan can meet employees' varied investment needs and goals.

- What's the reputation of the 401(k)-plan vendor? How long has the vendor been offering and managing 401(k) plans? How have the investment options in the plan fared against similar options? Stack the plan's equity funds alongside similar equity funds to see how they compare.

- How good is the vendor's documentation for your employees — its brochures, investment-option explanations, and so on? Keep in mind that many employees require solid, easy-to-understand advice and guidance.

- Can the vendor support IRS and Employee Retirement Income Security Act (ERISA) reporting? See the upcoming section, "ERISA and other legal issues."

- Does the provider offer self-service capabilities so that employees can access their accounts online to make changes?

Because an employer's directors and officers face potential personal liability for mishandled 401(k) plans, smart employers establish investment committees and generally structure their mandate through a carefully drawn charter.

FIND ONLINE

See the online tools for a 401(k)-plan summary called "A Look at 401(k) Plan Fees," one of many publications addressing retirement planning that is available from the U.S. Department of Labor's Employee Benefits Security Administration

ERISA and other legal issues

Your company is under no legal obligation to provide a retirement plan for your employees. If you do offer a plan, however, you're subject to the regulations of ERISA — the Employee Retirement Income Security Act of 1974.

Since its passage, ERISA has created significant administrative requirements that small businesses often feel the most. Subsequent laws have modified some of ERISA's provisions. In addition, the Internal Revenue Code imposes detailed requirements on all retirement plans, both plans that qualify for favorable tax treatment and retirement plans that provide deferred compensation for executives and other highly-paid employees. For example, qualified pension or profit-sharing plans you offer need to meet the following requirements, among many others:

>> The plan can't exclude most employees who are older than 21 or require an employee to complete more than one year of service in order to participate in the plan.

>> Employee contributions must be 100 percent vested at all times.

>> Vesting for employer contributions must fall into one of the following two categories:

- **Cliff vesting:** Under this vesting approach, the employer's contributions aren't vested at all until a stated number of years. At that time, the employer's matching and other contributions become the complete (100 percent) property of the employee.

- **Graded vesting:** Under this vesting approach, the employer's matching and other contributions become the property of the employee *in increments* until the employee is fully vested. After a stated number of years, employees are permitted to own a certain percentage until full vesting occurs.

>> You must fund qualified retirement plans at least annually, with defined benefit pension plans' funding requirements calculated on the basis of future obligations.

>> Also, in the case of a defined benefit pension plan, your company must be part of and pay for ERISA's government insurance fund to help protect employees from the possibility of the pension plan dissolving.

>> Special rules apply when your retirement plan is invested in your company stock.

>> You must meet ERISA standards for the people who administer the program. As noted earlier, ERISA's fiduciary duties apply to anyone who exercises discretionary control over the plan or its assets. That means that all decision-makers are subject to ERISA's exacting requirements. Individuals who breach their duties or engage in certain prohibited transactions with benefit plans can be held personally liable.

>> Employers must report pension operations to the government and inform employees of their pension rights and the status of their pension plan. All plans are required to file an annual report on the Form 5500, filed through the Department of Labor's eFast system.

Sampling the Rest of the Benefits Smorgasbord

Businesses frequently offer a number of other benefits. Here's a rundown of the most common benefits and what you should know about them.

Dental insurance

Dental insurance has become an increasingly popular employee benefit and is expected by most employees. In 2018, 79 percent of the U.S. population had dental benefits, the majority of which were sponsored by employers, according to the National Association of Dental Plans' (NADP's) 2019 "Dental Benefits Report: Enrollment." The 2018 NADP "Survey of Employers" indicates employers also recognize the desirability of dental benefits, as 87 percent of those surveyed felt dental benefits are essential or a differentiator.

Companies sometimes offer dental care as part of a health-insurance package and occasionally as a separate policy or an add-on. Costs and deductibles vary widely by region and by extent of coverage.

Generally, these plans cover all or part of the cost of routine checkups, fillings, and other regular dental procedures. They also may cover orthodontics or extensive restorative dentistry (usually with stated limits). Most dental plans have deductibles and typically require the employee to pay at least part of the cost of each visit or procedure.

Vision care

Most benefit plans restrict vision coverage to routine eye exams, with some discounts provided for glasses and contact lenses. Most also impose a ceiling on how much is covered toward the purchase of lenses, frames, and contact lenses. These plans, moreover, don't cover serious eye diseases and other conditions that, in most cases, the employee's regular health-insurance policy covers.

Family assistance

The much-documented increase in the number of two-income families, single working mothers, domestic partners, and employees who care for both children and aging parents has led to an accelerating demand for childcare and eldercare assistance from employers. You can expect the need to intensify in the years ahead. The following list describes some ways in which companies provide this benefit:

>> **Childcare:** Beyond offering flexible schedules for employees with young children, some companies provide on-site childcare (daycare). This is a great idea in theory — the convenience to the working parent is obvious — but only a handful of companies provide a daycare facility at the work location itself. The big problem is cost — liability insurance, in particular. Another obstacle is that state and county authorities extensively regulate on-site childcare centers, including the amount of play area required and the ratio of childcare workers to children.

>> **Eldercare:** As people live longer, many employees must care for their aging parents or other relatives. As a result, some businesses are providing elder-care benefits to help employees meet these obligations. Support ranges from partial reimbursement for eldercare specialists and emergency in-home care to allowing employees to enroll adult family members in their healthcare plans.

>> **Contracted daycare for children and seniors:** The company contracts with one or more outside providers to provide services for the children and parents of employees. This approach is becoming more prevalent, but it also mandates a good deal of responsibility. When your company selects a particular provider, you vouch for that provider's quality of care and services.

>> **Vouchers:** Vouchers are simply subsidies that you pay to employees to cover all or part of the cost of outside childcare. Voucher systems are the simplest form of childcare assistance to administer.

>> **Dependent care reimbursement accounts:** These accounts enable an employee to use pretax dollars to pay for dependent care.

>> **Accessible fertility benefits:** These are typically part of the group health plan. Sixty percent of employees said that family-forming and fertility issues have impacted their work performance, according to the National Infertility Association, and 77 percent said they'd stay with their employer at their company longer if fertility benefits were offered.

>> **Adoption assistance:** Many companies offer adoption assistance (which can be nontaxable to some degree) and surrogacy benefits (which are taxable). Both are non-ERISA benefits and outside of the group health plan.

Time off

Although many employees take the practice for granted, paying employees for days they don't work — whether for holidays, vacation, sick days, or personal days (now often lumped together as *paid time off (PTO)* — is an important benefit that your employee handbook needs to spell out. Each company has its own philosophy, but the following list offers general observations about paid days off:

>> Most companies provide employees with a fixed number of paid holidays per year, such as New Year's Day, Independence Day, Thanksgiving, Christmas, and so on.

>> The number of vacation days granted each year may vary by length of service. According to the Bureau of Labor Statistics in 2021, more than one-third of private industry workers received 10 to 14 days of paid vacation after one year of service. After ten years of service, 33 percent of private industry workers received between 15 and 19 days of paid vacation. In both cases, the remaining workers received fewer vacation days.

>> Vacation accrual policies differ widely from one company to the next. Some companies enable their employees to bank vacation time. Others require employees to take all vacation time during the year in which they earn it. The more popular option is to enable employees to accrue vacation time, but be careful — this policy can leave you with huge liabilities for unused vacation time that you may need to pay in cash if the employee retires or leaves your company. Where lawful, hedge your bets by capping the maximum amount that can accrue.

>> Some companies combine sick time, personal time, and vacation time into a single paid-time-off program.

The most important point here is that state authorities heavily regulate employee time off. In some states, for example, the law requires companies to allow employees who don't use accrued vacation time in a single calendar year to carry it over to the next year. In such states, vested vacation benefits are treated as a form of wages, so that a policy of "use it or (eventually) lose it" amounts to the failure to pay wages in violation of wage and hour mandates. In other states, this type of policy is permissible. Make sure to consult legal counsel regarding the lawfulness of your policy in the state(s) in which you operate, as well as potential tax issues that may arise when employees are provided a choice as to whether to roll over unused PTO.

Leaves of absence

A *leave of absence* is an arrangement whereby employees take an extended period of time off (usually without pay) but still maintain their employment status. They resume their normal duties when the leave is over. Employees either request or are granted leaves of absence for a variety of reasons: maternity, illness, education, travel, military obligations, and so on.

When a particular law doesn't apply to a leave of absence, the specific policies you adopt regarding such leaves of absence are within your discretion. In such cases, it's up to you to determine how long employees can stay away from the job without jeopardizing their employment status. You decide what benefits will be maintained and what job, if any, will be guaranteed them when the leave is over. For benefits subject to ERISA, such as all retirement plans and welfare (medical, dental, vision, life, disability, and so on) benefits plans, the continuation of benefits during a leave of absence is governed by the terms of the written benefit plan documents. In addition, specific laws, such as the Affordable Care Act (ACA), the Consolidated Omnibus Reconciliation Act (COBRA), and the Family and Medical Leave Act (FMLA) can apply and impose requirements on continued eligibility for certain benefit plan coverage during a leave of absence.

However, very often, the law governs a leave of absence. For example, many leaves of absence related to certain military circumstances and family and health situations are covered by the federal Family and Medical Leave Act (FMLA) and, often, analogous state leave laws. The FMLA, passed in 1993 and amended in 2008, applies to companies with 50 or more employees. Eligible employees are entitled to take up to 12 weeks unpaid leave per year for any of the following reasons:

>> To care for newly born or newly adopted children (note that this right extends to both parents)

>> To care for a child, parent, or spouse with a serious health condition

>> To attend to a serious health condition that makes the worker unable to perform their job

>> Because of any qualifying exigency arising out of the fact that the spouse, son, daughter, or parent of the employee is on covered active duty (or has been notified of an impending call or order to covered active duty) in the armed forces

Also, the FMLA requires covered employers to grant an eligible employee who is a spouse, son, daughter, parent, or next of kin of a current member of the armed forces (including National Guard or Reserve) with a serious injury or illness up to 26 workweeks of unpaid leave during a single 12-month period to care for the service member.

Under FMLA regulations, you must maintain the employee's health coverage, at the same level, under any group health plan for the duration of the unpaid leave, and you must restore the employee to the same or equivalent job when they return. The law also requires you to post and deliver notices advising workers of their rights under the law. Note that various states may have similar family and medical leave and/or pregnancy and/or baby-bonding leave requirements, while other states (California and Connecticut, for example) provide greater leave rights or benefits to eligible employees. The FMLA imposes requirements on the administration of other benefits as well that may require continuing to give the employee credit for service while on an FMLA leave of absence, and continuing benefit eligibility to the same extent as the employer does for other types of leaves.

WARNING

A leave of absence, with job restoration at the end of the leave, may be required as a form of reasonable accommodation to disabled employees under the Americans with Disabilities Act (ADA) and/or under equivalent state laws. Also, if an employee requests leave time in connection with a disability, and your company is covered by the ADA, you have a legal duty to engage, in good faith, in an interactive process (discussions and so on) with the employee. This process is aimed at identifying whether your company can provide a reasonable accommodation to enable the employee to perform their essential job functions — and that one accommodation may end up being a leave of absence. A lawyer can help you in this area, including the related question of what, if any, benefits must be continued during the period of a leave that is provided as a reasonable accommodation. Also consult an experienced lawyer if you are unclear, in any given situation, whether a particular leave of absence may implicate legal leave of absence protections.

FIND ONLINE

See the online tools for the following federal FMLA forms:

>> Employee Rights and Responsibilities Under the Federal Family and Medical Leave Act

>> Certification of Health Care Provider for Employee's Serious Health Condition (Federal Family and Medical Leave Act)

>> Certification of Health Care Provider for Family Member's Serious Health Condition (Federal Family and Medical Leave Act)

>> Certification of Qualifying Exigency for Military Family Leave (Federal Family and Medical Leave Act)

>> Certification for Serious Injury or Illness of Covered Servicemember — for Military Family Leave (Federal Family and Medical Leave Act)

>> Notice of Eligibility and Rights & Responsibilities (Federal Family and Medical Leave Act)

>> Designation Notice (Federal Family and Medical Leave Act)

Sick days

Formal sick leave policies generally limit how many sick days the company is willing to pay for (anywhere from 6 to 12 days per year). In addition, companies usually impose a limit on the number of sick days that employees can take in succession (after which employees may be entitled to nonpaid leave of absences). Most companies have short-term disability plans that kick in either immediately following an accident or on the eighth calendar day after the onset of an illness. Short-term disability ends after a predefined interval (typically either three or six months after it has started), at which point long-term disability may begin.

Sometimes companies offer a reward for employees who don't use their allotment of sick days — for example, a cash payment for a percentage (usually half) of an employee's unused sick leave at the end of the year or if they leave the company. Many companies have choice-time-off (CTO) or personal-time-off (PTO) plans that combine vacation and sick days.

Failure to formulate and communicate to all employees a formal sick-day policy can be dangerous to the health of your company. If you have a loosely defined policy that sets no limits on paid sick days, for example, you may run into legal problems if you ever decide to discipline or fire an employee who's clearly abusing your guidelines. The employee may argue that you treated them more harshly because of a protected status (like their religion or nationality) than you treated other employees who did not have that same protected status. Without a record of consistently administering a sick-day policy, you may have a more difficult time defending against such a discrimination claim.

Both the federal FMLA and the federal ADA (and/or similar state laws) may be implicated if employees who used paid sick days in connection with FMLA absences or for reasons related to disabilities are disqualified from a cash reward due to such absences. Also, some states require employers to allow employees to take a portion of their sick days to care for ill family members. An attorney can help you analyze these issues.

BENEFITS FOR COMMON-LAW SPOUSES, SAME-SEX SPOUSES, AND DOMESTIC PARTNERS

Extending benefits to common-law couples, same-sex married persons, and domestic partners (either opposite-sex or same-sex nonmarried partners) is a common practice across the United States. This benefit speaks powerfully to the ways corporations have become aware of the changing lifestyle arrangements of many of their employees.

(continued)

(continued)

Though no official, nationally recognized set of requirements determines eligibility for domestic-partner benefits, here are a few possible eligibility requirements to consider using if you decide to offer them:

- Both partners occupy a common residence, as proven by a lease or title deed, for at least six consecutive months.

- Both partners are at least 18 years of age and not related by blood.

- They have a joint bank account or joint credit cards or can provide other evidence of shared financial responsibility.

- They're registered as partners in a state or locality that permits registration of domestic-partner relationships.

For qualified retirement plans, the term *spouse* is required to include same-sex spouses and common-law spouses. For other benefit plan purposes, most employers define spouse based upon the law of a designated state. Based upon the current status of federal law, most benefit plans recognize common-law and same-sex spouses within the definition of spouse.

Your business may be in a state where common-law or same-sex marriages are legal. Where these marriages are legal, both partners are afforded the same status — including employee benefits for spouses.

This is one area where it's prudent to talk with an attorney if you have any questions or concerns.

Looking Closer at Employee Assistance Programs

The Society for Human Resources Management (SHRM) defines an Employee Assistance Program [EAP]) as "a work-based intervention program designed to assist employees in resolving personal problems that may be adversely affecting the employee's performance." Between the rise of remote work, the continued challenges related to the Covid-19 pandemic, and the tumultuous political climate, it could be argued that EAPs have never been more vital. It is a well-known fact that happy and healthy employees are more productive employees, and the cost of not providing this type of assistance can be enormous. According to the Center for Prevention and Health Services, workplaces lose $79 billion to $105 billion each year due to employee mental illness and substance abuse disorders, so an EAP provides a safe place for employees to get the support they need.

Here's just a sampling of areas in which EAP providers can assist employees:

» Stress management and conflict resolution

» Social, psychological, and family counseling

» Referral to legal services

» Preretirement planning

» Termination and career transition services (sometimes called *outplacement*)

» Alcohol and substance abuse

» Mental-health screening and referral

» Gambling addiction and other compulsive behaviors

» Marriage counseling

» Financial issues and credit counseling

» Bereavement

EAPs are generally subject to regulation as ERISA plans, unless they don't provide substantial medical benefits. For example, if your EAP only provides referrals and no more than three counseling sessions, it may be exempt from ERISA.

The number of third-party EAP service providers has grown dramatically, so employers can select from a wide list of EAP providers. There are many promising options — it all depends on what you hope to achieve with your employee assistance program.

You can obtain a list of EAP providers in your region by getting in touch with the Employee Assistance Professionals Association (www.eapassn.org). Another suggestion: Check with your local business associations, chambers of commerce, and other businesses in your area for referrals.

REMEMBER

When the time comes to make a choice, here's what to do:

» **Check references.** As you would with any outside provider, carefully check references and make sure that the staff members of EAPs you're considering have the required training, certifications, and licenses. Companies normally do this during the request for proposal (RFP) process, comparing factors such as average call-center wait times and the level of medical and psychological education of staff before they sign up for a particular service. Ask providers to demonstrate the quality of their care through surveys or case studies.

» **Clarify fees.** EAP costs can vary widely, but in most situations, a basic per-employee fee can range anywhere from $12 to $20 per year, depending on the number of employees in your company. This fee is frequently adjusted on a yearly basis depending on how extensively your company actually uses the services. Ask about additional charges, such as referrals to therapists. The EAP's base fee should cover everything, including materials and administration.

» **Check with your health insurer.** Your health-insurance policy may be required to provide mental-health benefits and substance use disorder benefits that are on par with your medical and surgical benefits. If you are not currently providing those benefits, you may want to upgrade your benefits.

WARNING

If you offer an EAP, remember that confidentiality is essential for legal and practical reasons. Employees must have confidence that they can talk privately to a counselor without repercussions (information reported back to a supervisor, for example). The Americans with Disabilities Act (ADA) prohibits using information on employees' health problems in a way that would negatively impact their jobs. If your EAP is a group health plan under ERISA, the Health Insurance Portability and Accountability Act (HIPAA) also protects health-related data from inappropriate intrusion. Your EAP contracts should provide for this confidentiality.

Making Administration Easier: Five Ways to Help

Benefits administration can get very complex. The good news is that these five simple principles can make the job of administering benefits in your company less stressful.

» **Remember that one size doesn't fit all.** With businesses more diversified than ever, employees bring a wider range of values, desires, and expectations to their jobs. As a result, you need to constantly evaluate which mix of benefits works best for your company and its broad spectrum of employees.

TIP

The point is that your benefits offerings need to be broad and flexible enough to appeal to a variety of diverse groups. However, your job isn't to make assumptions about which benefits will appeal to which people. The single most important thing that you can do to win employee support for your program is to involve them as much as possible in all aspects of the plan, particularly as you're deciding which options to offer. If your company is small enough, you can keep your employees in the loop informally — simply by meeting with them regularly to discuss your benefits package and whether it's meeting their needs. If you have ten or more employees, however, a survey is a better option. Instead of asking employees to list benefit options that are important to them, provide them with a list of options to rate on a scale of one to five.

>> **Get to know your programs cold.** You and the people who work with you in benefits administration need to have a thorough knowledge of your benefits package and the topic of benefits in general. Otherwise, you can't explain your offerings to employees, help employees sort out problems, or make the best benefits choices for your company. At the very least, you need to be able to write a brief description (in simple, clear language) of all the programs that your company offers. And regardless of your level of experience in HR, you should make it a point to stay current. Be on the lookout for seminars and short courses that are offered nearby and make sure that you route important benefits articles that appear in HR journals or business publications to all those accountable for or interested in benefits administration.

>> **Make benefits education a priority in your onboarding program.** Making sure that your employees have a thorough understanding of their benefits options should be one of the main priorities of your onboarding program. Take the time to develop an information package that spells out what you offer but doesn't overload employees with overly detailed information. Make sure that your programs are properly described in summary plan descriptions and all other mandated notices. Make sure that the person who handles the benefits side of the onboarding program can answer the most frequently asked employee questions. (For more on onboarding, see Chapter 10.)

>> **Monitor your program for problems and results.** Don't make the mistake of waiting for resentment and dissatisfaction to build before you do something about aspects of your benefits package that aren't working. Whether you do so informally through conversations or through some other means, such as a survey, make sure that you're attuned to employee attitudes, particularly about health insurance.

>> **Provide feedback and problem-resolution procedures.** If you haven't already done so, establish formal mechanisms to receive employee comments and complaints and set up a system to resolve problems. Many problems aren't really problems at all but misunderstandings that stem from miscommunication. Try to develop some means of tracking problems through various stages of resolution. (One method is to use a form that lists the complaint and includes spaces for the various steps you need to take to resolve it.) The benefits complaints that employees voice most commonly today involve denial of health-insurance claims. Note that due to HIPAA

privacy concerns, complaints about health benefit claims should not come to the employer but need to be provided only to the plan administrator so they can be handled confidentially according to the rigorous privacy requirements that apply. Use employee feedback as a resource to periodically revise your communications about benefits.

employee work and the impact

» Allowing for flexibility in *how* team members get the job done

» Highlighting corporate social responsibility

» Using team-building exercises to promote meaning and purpose

» Using employee surveys to gauge the mood of the organization

» Checking out more ways to drive purpose and meaning

Chapter **13**

Creating a Meaningful Employee Experience

You may heard the saying, "happy employees make happy customers." The research is clear: The employee experience impacts the customer experience. According to 2022 research from Forbes and Salesforce, companies that deliver great employee and customer experiences are growing almost twice as fast as companies that stumble in both areas. Of the executives surveyed, 70 percent agreed that a better employee experience leads directly to a better customer experience. Because of this, companies that are appropriately attuned to creating a supportive, nurturing work environment stand the best chance for long-term growth. What appear to be opposite ideas — unwavering attention to business results, coupled with an environment focused on the team member experience — go together like bees and honey. Your skill in linking the two can go a long way toward building a first-rate organization.

Across organizations in all industries and of all sizes, leaders are recognizing the importance of the employee experience. In this chapter, I explore how to do that most effectively.

Understanding Your Team's Emotional Needs: Providing Purpose and Meaning

In general, people's relationship with work is changing. While my grandfather's generation worked for a job, today, the goal is to engage in a career that is fulfilling. Work and life are much more integrated today, which naturally changes the way employees think about their work.

Employee purpose refers to a couple of things: the way employees feel about their work and the way their personal values correspond with the organization's. In other words, employee purpose creates a connection beyond the work the employee is doing.

A sense of purpose is integral to any successful work environment. After all, if employees embrace a purpose-driven mindset as they go about their work, they're more likely to be engaged, resulting in not only higher performance and productivity, but overall levels of job satisfaction, as well.

So what can you and your organization do to develop and foster a sense of purpose in the workplace? *Connect what employees do with the impact of their work.* In other words, you can help foster a sense of purpose in your employees by helping them understand how what they do impacts the organization. Employees want to feel like what they do matters. By creating a sense of meaning and purpose in what your employees do, companies can help their employees find the motivation to engage with their jobs most fully.

Goodbye, 9 to 5: Creating a Flexible Environment

As people's relationship with work evolves, so do employee expectations. Smart leaders know that work-life flexibility is essential for a healthy, thriving, productive culture. This flexibility is also referred to as *work-life integration, work-life balance,* or *flexible work arrangements.*

Quite simply, work–life flexibility allows team members to do what they need to do in all aspects of their personal lives (be at home when their kids get off of the bus, take an elderly parent to a doctor's appointment) during traditional work hours. During the Covid-19 pandemic (and still today) a large number of employees shifted how they accomplish their work (virtually at home versus in an office) and many came to appreciate this arrangement. Because of this, many organizations have adopted a work-from-anywhere (WFA) philosophy particularly in those situations in which productivity hasn't suffered. And because of this shift, employee expectations have changed — more people are looking for organizations that offer flexibility.

The following sections take a closer look at work–life flexibility, including what forms it can take and how your organization can incorporate one that works for the business and for team members.

Considering the different ways that work-life flexibility can be implemented

A company's ability to attract and retain employees with the expertise it requires relates increasingly to the human side of the day-to-day working experience — the general atmosphere that prevails in the workplace. This includes, in particular, the extent to which company practices help people balance the pressures they face at work with the pressures they are encountering in their personal lives.

Work–life integration focuses on results rather than the location and time at which the employee does the work. In other words, productivity is key. Here are ways you as the employer can help employees achieve workplace flexibility while striving to achieve company goals:

>> **Flextime:** Flextime is any arrangement that gives employees options with regard to structuring their workday or workweek. In the most extreme (and rarest) form, employees decide for themselves not only when they work but also for how long. More typically, though, employees working under flextime arrangements are expected to be on the job during certain core hours of the workday. They're given the opportunity to choose (within certain parameters) their own starting and ending times — as long as they work the required number of hours each day.

For example, say that you have a six-person customer service department, and the phones are answered from 9 a.m. to 7 p.m. The peak period — when the most calls come in — is between noon and 3 p.m. You can institute a flextime arrangement that obliges all six customer service representatives to be in the office from noon to 3 p.m. but also gives employees the latitude to work together to set up their own eight-hour days so that the department is never left unstaffed.

- **Compressed workweek/condensed schedule:** Under this arrangement, employees work the normal number of hours but complete those hours in fewer than five days. The most common variation of the compressed work week is the so-called 4/10, in which employees work four ten-hour days rather than five eight-hour days.

- **Job sharing:** As the term implies, job sharing means that two part-time employees share the same full-time job. Salary and benefits may be prorated on the basis of what portion of the job each worker shares. Apart from the obvious consideration (both people need to be qualified for the job), a successful job-sharing arrangement assumes that the employees can work together harmoniously to make the arrangement work.

- **Remote work:** Remote work, which may also be called *working from home* or *working from anywhere,* includes any work arrangement in which employees — on a regular, predetermined basis — spend all or a portion of their workweek working from home or from another noncompany site.

- **Permanent part-time arrangements:** The hours in these arrangements usually vary from 20 to 29 hours per week, with employees sometimes allowed to decide which days they work and how long they work on those days. The key attraction of this arrangement is that the employees may be entitled to company benefits, albeit on a prorated basis.

- **Freelancing:** Employees work on a contract/project basis of their choosing.

- **Unlimited PTO (paid time off):** Employees are encouraged to take the personal time they need without counting days.

- **Alternative scheduling:** This entails setting nontraditional work hours (for example, not 8 to 5) such as starting earlier or later in the day to avoid the commute or meet school schedule demands.

THE INS AND OUTS OF REMOTE WORK

Remote work (working from home and working from anywhere arrangements) has become the norm for many employees, intensified as a result of the Covid-19 pandemic. According to a 2022 survey by McKinsey & Company, nearly 6 in 10 (58 percent) of employees say they're able to work from home at least one day a week. Another 35 percent work from home for the entire week. Only 13 percent say they could work remotely but choose not to do so. The data is clear: Remote work is here to stay, and it's important for organizations to create an environment and a culture in which remote team members feel they're part of something and understand the importance of their role in moving the business forward.

Paying attention to legal implications

As with all business decisions, you need to contemplate the legal impact of any alternative work arrangement. With certain groups of employees (hourly employees or unionized workers, in particular), flexible arrangements can easily run counter to existing agreements. You should check, for example, the laws on overtime pay before adopting a compressed schedule for any employee. In California, for example, overtime is calculated on a daily basis rather than on a weekly basis. Some states permit compressed workweeks as long as they're created and administered according to strict regulations.

Also, the U.S. Department of Labor, Internal Revenue Service, and other federal or state authorities may challenge your classification of a former-employee-turned-contractor, which could result from some phased retirement arrangements. If the employee returns to function in the same essential role, performing the same job duties, they may be deemed an employee by a government agency — potentially triggering numerous employment and tax consequences, including possible penalties — regardless of your characterization of them as a contractor.

Separately, one condition for employees to qualify as exempt from overtime and other wage and hour mandates is the receipt of a predetermined amount of pay (either per week or on a less frequent basis) that does not change because of variations in the quantity of hours worked. Employees otherwise classified as exempt can lose that status under a job sharing or phased retirement program if their pay drops below the statutory minimum.

Making alternate arrangements work

In theory, alternate work arrangements offer a win-win situation. Flexible scheduling policies improve the overall employee experience, increase morale and job satisfaction, reduce absenteeism, reduce turnover, and minimize burnout — and with no measurable decline in productivity.

That's the good news. The downside is that these arrangements don't work for every company or for every position. An effective alternate work arrangement is dependent on the company's commitment to support such an arrangement, in addition to the nature of the work and the employee. So, the practices may have to be carefully implemented with some legally sound ground rules. In addition, instituting a policy of alternate work arrangements involves a good deal more than simply giving your employees a broader selection of scheduling options. The process needs to be carefully thought out. It must be implemented with consistency, patience, and discipline because you can easily ruin a good thing. The following sections offer some guidelines if you're thinking of setting up a flexible scheduling policy in your company.

Be willing to rethink processes

Implementing a successful flexible work arrangement policy requires far more work than merely changing when jobs get done. More often than not, alternate work arrangement policies need to be accompanied by changes in how the work actually gets done and, in particular, how people are supervised.

So, when considering new work arrangements, think about this question first: How will the work itself be affected by the new scheduling? All subsequent decisions should be based on the answer to that question.

Establish clear guidelines

Flexible work arrangement policies don't have to be set in stone. At the very least, though, you need a set of guidelines that serve as the basis of the program. Here are some specifics:

>> **Make sure that the flexible work arrangement policies your company develops are logically keyed to the nature and demands of your business.** Based on the products and services you're offering to your customers, how can you create a sense of flexibility within your scheduling expectations?

>> **Be consistent.** Decisions regarding flexible scheduling should be based on the nature of the job as opposed to the needs of the individual. You can certainly be lenient and account for the special needs of employees, but you can sabotage a formalized flexible work arrangement policy by making too many exceptions.

>> **Make sure that managers and supervisors have some say in policy development.** Bear in mind that supervisors are always affected by the scheduling patterns of the people they manage.

>> **Have clear employee eligibility guidelines in place.** Some examples include demonstrated work experience with little or no supervision, a positive performance record, and tenure or experience in a job. It's difficult to manage an employee remotely or working a flexible schedule who is not meeting performance expectations or needs constant supervision. Most new employees or those newer in their role need on-the-job training or mentoring to be able to fully perform. If they're working from home, learning from others may be too difficult.

>> **Create a culture that supports remote team members.** In other words, ensure your organization's environment supports team members who work remotely. The following are specific ways to ensure that happens:

- **Set a foundation of trust and psychological safety.** Ensure that leaders have focused time to address the needs of remote team members and that it's comfortable for team members to vocalize challenges and tensions.

- **Prioritize meaningful work.** Help remote employees to see the impact their work has and ensure they are doing work that is adding value.

- **Establish regular meeting rhythms.** Ensure that managers are meeting regularly with remote team members to stay connected to them.

- **Schedule some face time.** Ensure there are opportunities throughout the year to engage face-to-face with remote team members.

Considering phased retirement options

One option that has become quite popular in recent years is the notion of a *phased retirement,* or allowing tenured employees to gradually ease their way out of the organization by reducing the number of hours they spend on the job. This plan has many positives. Phased retirement gives your company the ability to retain the valuable institutional knowledge of long-standing employees that would otherwise walk out the door with them. It also provides a better means of transitioning job responsibilities.

In many cases, phased retirement simply means lowering an employee's workload and training their replacement. But another approach is for the employee to technically retire and then continue to work for your firm on a contract or consulting basis. Given the number of Baby Boomers expected to leave the workforce in coming years, a phased retirement option can be extremely productive for both employer and employee.

WARNING

As I note earlier in this section, alternative arrangements can present new legal issues. Check with your legal counsel or state labor department to see whether flexible scheduling violates state or local laws and, in particular, how certain arrangements may affect overtime obligations. Also, employees who work at home for the majority of each workweek may need to receive notices and posters otherwise available only at the employer's offices.

Ensuring leaders are leading flexible scheduling policies well

Leaders set the tone in all organizations, so to ensure a culture that allows for flexibility, you must encourage leaders to be in tune with the work styles and personal needs of their team members. Individual needs vary, so I suggest you view each employee as an individual, which may require you to set up a system for managers to inventory (perhaps on a spreadsheet) the needs of individual team members. This will allow visibility to team member needs and a way for you to choose most effectively solutions to adopt.

In addition to focusing on individual needs, consider these additional workplace flexibility best practices:

>> Focusing on results — accomplishing goals — rather than how the goals are achieved; providing more autonomy on how and when the employee completes their work.

>> Being clear and transparent about the expected results. It's impossible to hold a team member accountable for an expectation that hasn't been set.

>> Encouraging creativity and the sharing of ideas; this creates an environment of collaboration and a sense of "we are in this together" versus a siloed mindset.

>> Creating an environment where employees feel comfortable taking time off for things that matter to them; in this kind of environment, employees are much more open about their needs.

Regardless of how thrilled your employees may be with a flexible work arrangement, the policy itself will face rough sledding if it doesn't have the enthusiastic support and involvement of both senior management and line supervisors.

Addressing Corporate Social Responsibility

Another way to create a meaningful work experience for employees (and all stakeholders) is by letting them know that the company they work for is a force for good — that it has a purpose beyond making money. Today, the way a company gives back to its community, positively impacts the environment, and acts for the greater good — not just a greater profit — is critical. That's why the corporate social responsibility of a business is important.

Corporate social responsibility (CSR) refers to a company ensuring its actions are accountable to everyone it deals with — customers, stakeholders, and the broader world. The data is clear — employees want to work for organizations that are socially responsible. A 2022 Mercer study reports that 96 percent of employees expected their employer to balance financial results with social issues, diversity and equity, and environmental impact.

An organization can be cognizant of its impact on society and practice corporate social responsibility. Here are some examples:

>> Putting ethics first in all interactions with customers and employees

>> Providing safe, reliable products

>> Demonstrating a commitment to diversity, equity, and inclusion

>> Making charitable contributions

>> Volunteering in their community and virtually

>> Demonstrating environmental stewardship and reducing carbon footprints

>> Being what employees consider an overall great place to work

Looking at a few of these a bit more closely, organizations with a commitment to CSR maintain an equitable, inclusive workplace that leverages the diversity of its team members. They provide employees with salary and benefits that are administered fairly. A solid corporate citizen is also ethical in all its interactions with clients, customers, suppliers, and others.

A good corporate citizen also is keenly aware of the environment. That can translate to using energy-efficient equipment whenever possible, designing or refurbishing facilities along "green" environmental guidelines, and taking other steps to limit a company's carbon footprint.

Additionally, a good corporate citizen urges its employees to do their part by giving back and volunteering in their communities. Many companies go beyond mere encouragement by providing paid time off to allow employees to help causes or charities they deem worthwhile. Some companies even institute a "volunteer day," when staff from throughout the organization attend a philanthropic event as a group.

A report from SHRM's Research Institute says that 47 percent of U.S. organizations offered community volunteer programs in 2022. Offering volunteer opportunities not only impacts team members in a positive way, but they also have a positive impact on organizations. Here are some of the multiple benefits (to organizations) to offering volunteer opportunities:

>> **Strengthening company culture:** Volunteering is an opportunity to build a service-mindset, empathy skills, and collaboration within the team.

>> **Attracting and retaining talent:** Employees want to work for organizations that are giving back, so offering volunteer opportunities is a recruitment and retention strategy. A 2019 Havas Group report notes that employees who volunteer are 32 percent less likely to leave the organization.

>> **Strengthening your employer brand:** The same Havas Group study also reports that 77 percent of consumers support brands who share their values. Offering volunteer opportunities is an example of an organization's values in action and provides credibility.

The research is clear: Companies that are committed to corporate social responsibility enjoy greater employee productivity, higher morale, and longer employee retention. Being a positive force in their local communities helps them attract the best employees, build closer relationships with customers, and build and reinforce a good reputation. Overall, CSR is a thoughtful and practical way to give back.

Building Teams to Connect People and Drive Collaboration

Not only is teambuilding a key approach to satisfying company goals, but it's also an element of a positive work environment for many employees. None of us are as smart as all of us, and good leaders know that it is through the leveraging of team strengths that we best accomplish our goals.

Collaboration is the watchword of today's workforce, and yet collaborating as a team isn't something that comes naturally to everyone. As a leader, it's helpful to highlight the importance of teamwork and demonstrate every day how and why teamwork is critical within your particular organization. Leaders need to model cooperative behavior, recognize people who are collaborating well, and advocate for tools and performance measures that support collaboration.

Even assembly lines are affected by collaboration, as more employees are trained to address line breakdowns and more jobs become interdependent. Many people enjoy the intellectual stimulation and the chance to build their problem-solving skills that working on a team offers. Working in teams makes a job more interesting.

Companies have long embraced team-building exercises as a way to promote collaboration — and at the same time bring fun and connection into the workplace. Even activities that aren't purely for team building, such as group learning and development, can have the added benefit of helping a team build camaraderie. Here are the key elements to bring teamwork most effectively to life within your organization.

Ensuring a shared vision

So how can you most effectively instill a team approach in your organization? It starts with a shared vision — this gives teams something to rally around. In other words, what are team members working together toward?

In their book *The Leadership Challenge* (published by Jossey-Bass), James Kouzes and Barry Posner define a shared vision as an "ideal and unique image of the future for the common good." Team leaders have a responsibility to bring clarity to where it is the team is going — the ideal and unique image of the future that serves the whole. Naming the future vision is inspiring because it gives team members something to strive for together.

Prioritizing the key drivers of effective teamwork

The key drivers of successful teamwork are trust, communication, and effective leadership. While the shared vision is the tie that binds team members and provides a collective responsibility for success (or failure), without trust and communication, the team will have difficulty functioning effectively.

Trust provides the foundation from which to lead through the inevitable challenges and conflict that arise, while strong communication within the team ensures that members lean into and address challenging situations and keep each other informed along the way.

When there is trust within the team, team members naturally express their unique ideas without fear of judgment or criticism. Differing opinions can take brainstorming to the next level. Members respect each other fully and are open to hearing what others have to say, even when they disagree. A culture that values trust and communication makes it easier for teammates to collaborate and build upon their individual skills, ideas, and experience.

Effective leadership instills a focus on team-building and facilitates ongoing team development and connection. A successful team is usually led by an individual who is trusted and respected by its members. Such leaders unify members toward the shared vision by providing focus and guidance. They also offer encouragement and motivation to keep the team engaged, even amidst challenges.

Effective teamwork is a key to business success. No matter how large or how small your organization is, if you are working together as a team, you have a stronger position. By fostering an environment that enables successful teamwork, you increase productivity and produce better solutions to problems.

Employee Surveys: Keeping Tabs on Company Morale

In many cases, particularly if your company has fewer than 50 employees, you don't have a hard time getting a good read on the general atmosphere in the workplace. You're able to personally connect with team members and leaders enough to observe how employees interact with one another, how they feel about the way they're treated by senior management, and whether morale is rising or falling.

But if your company is larger, periodically conducting a more rigorous employee survey can be exceedingly valuable. Not only can you gain a comprehensive sense of how employees feel about your company, but you also convey the message that you genuinely want their opinions and feedback. That can make employees feel valued and allow you to adjust policies and procedures based on your findings. In the long run, it can lead to greater employee engagement and retention.

TIP

Here are some tips on conducting employee surveys:

» **Be considerate about the timing of the survey.** Don't conduct surveys during holidays when many employees may be taking days off. Avoid exceptionally heavy workload periods.

» **Think carefully about your goal and objectives before crafting your survey questions.** Why are you conducting the survey? What do you want to uncover? How will you use the information?

» **Share survey goals and objectives with employees but do so in language that's relevant to them.** In other words, instead of using HR terms such as "We want to assess employee engagement levels," say, "We want to hear your thoughts since we merged with Company X."

» **Give the survey a trial run.** Before you unveil your survey to the entire company, test it out on a small group of employees to see whether your questions are appropriate and what you can refine.

» **Assure employees that their comments are anonymous.** They'll be more likely to be honest and forthcoming.

» **Communicate to employees the results of the survey in a timely manner and act, as appropriate, when employees make recommendations.** Let employees know how their input has affected company policy. Surveying your employees, setting expectations that change will occur from their responses, and then taking no action can have a negative impact.

FIND
ONLINE

WARNING

To get an idea of some of the questions you may want to ask on such a survey, see the Employee Opinion Survey in the online tools.

Employee survey information may need to be disclosed during litigation. It's a good idea to consult with an attorney before initiating your own survey or the sample survey online. Also, employers need to be prepared to address serious concerns raised in survey responses such as comments about perceived discrimination or harassment. The anonymous nature of surveys makes it difficult to respond, but inaction may be worse.

Taking the pulse of your workforce more regularly

Don't limit your use of employee surveys to those conducted over longer periods of time. More regular pulse surveys can also provide valuable insight into employee attitudes and opinions and send an important message to your team that you care about their ongoing feedback.

True to its name, a pulse survey is designed to measure the "heartbeat" of a company by examining such issues as engagement, learning and development needs, support from leadership, and opinions regarding pay and benefits. Because pulse surveys can be given semi-annually, quarterly, or monthly, they allow you to keep an eye on any significant trends or developments.

Pulse surveys differ from conventional surveys in a number of ways. In addition to being conducted more frequently, they're often shorter and more focused on one or more particular issues. For instance, a pulse survey may include just five or ten numerically rated questions and one or two open-ended questions. Also, pulse surveys can be administered to one group of employees one time and another group another time. This offers a broad array of perspectives without the risk of burning out employees on too many surveys that are conducted too often.

Pulse surveys are valuable on several levels:

>> They can offer an early warning system, bringing up issues that may develop into significant problems if left uncovered until a more comprehensive employee survey is conducted.

>> Because they're more focused, pulse surveys also can encourage employees to think carefully about particular issues they may have never given much thought to.

>> Conducting pulse surveys lets employees know that you consider these issues important and worthy of their feedback.

>> They foster an ongoing sense of communication between you and your employees. You're conveying the message that you value what they think and are eager to regularly solicit their ideas.

Like a conventional survey, it's important that employees understand that pulse surveys are completely anonymous. That makes employees comfortable in being as candid and forthright as possible.

FIND ONLINE

The online tools include a Sample Pulse Survey.

Exit interviews

When you're trying to take the temperature of the organization and determine how best to create a meaningful work experience, some of the most candid employees are often those who are leaving your company. To gain valuable ideas about improving your working conditions and making the workplace more inviting, a best practice is to conduct exit interviews with employees who have resigned or are otherwise voluntarily leaving your company. (People you've had to fire — though potentially the most candid of all — are not good subjects for two reasons: They're unlikely to cooperate, and if they do, their input will probably be overly negative rather than constructive.)

FIND ONLINE

For an Exit Interview Questionnaire, see the online tools.

Stay interviews

Many organizations have adopted the practice of conducting stay interviews from current team members to find out what keeps them at the organization. And the best person to facilitate the stay interview is the employee's manager — it's a great opportunity for the manager to connect with the team member and understand their experience within the organization.

REMEMBER

Instead of asking why an employee is quitting, a *stay interview* focuses on what motivates the employee to stick around, what could be better about their work experience, and how they envision their future with the organization.

Stay interviews should focus on how your employee feels about the work they do every day and the value of their contributions. The stay interview is *not* a time to share status updates about to-dos and projects. Some common questions include the following:

>> What do you like *most* about your job?

>> What do you like *least* about your job?

>> What keeps you working here?

>> If you could change something about your job, what would that be?

>> What would make your job more satisfying?

Here are a few best practices when conducting stay interviews:

>> Ensure that it's conversational and informal.

>> Ask questions so that team members feel open and psychologically safe to speak freely.

>> Don't respond or react to any of the feedback with judgment or defensiveness. This is an open space for the team member to share.

>> Ensure that it is a two-way dialogue (again a conversation) versus a job interview. This is a connection opportunity between the employee and their manager.

>> Don't combine stay interviews with performance reviews to ensure that the focus is solely on the employee's work experience and needs.

>> Ask questions that address both the positives and negatives of an employee's position as well as questions about working for the company as a whole.

Creating a Meaningful Work Experience — More Ways to Do So

A workplace that's designed to keep employees happy and productive helps pay for itself in many ways, such as greater employee engagement and productivity. Some larger companies go as far as creating in-house gyms complete with rock-climbing areas! Although the snazziest perks may be beyond the reach of many small and mid-size businesses, following are examples that a number of companies offer.

WARNING

Be careful to ensure that any perks you offer are deservedly distributed and don't violate any laws. When granting time off, for example, consult with an experienced lawyer about any impact on exempt employees of a partial-day absence; deducting an amount of salary because of a partial-day absence may compromise the employee's status as exempt from overtime laws and other wage protections. In addition, some employees may not see this as a perk. Some state laws mandate that employees be afforded a certain amount of time away to attend their children's school-related activities. Finally, some bonuses — including referral bonuses — may be required (by the U.S. Department of Labor) to be included in the wages used to calculate overtime.

Providing access to exercise facilities

A healthy workforce is more energetic and productive. Healthy employees also have less downtime due to illness. Many companies promote employees' health and well-being by providing on-site exercise facilities or access to exercise facilities. These can include weights, a variety of exercise machines, and locker rooms and showers. An unused portion of the company's building can make an ideal site for an in-house workout space. If that's not an option, many companies offer complimentary or subsidized memberships at nearby gyms.

Having access to mental health services and preventive care

In a 2019 BetterUp survey, 83 percent of employers said they believed their company's wellness program had a positive impact on workers' health, and 84 percent believed their programs had a positive impact on productivity and performance. Providing mental health clinical services and preventative care, such as therapy, coaching, and mentorship, is an important strategy in supporting your employees' mental health.

Providing tuition assistance or reimbursement

Most employees want to feel they're moving forward with both their lives and careers. A tuition assistance or reimbursement program can help make that happen. Here, you pay for part or all of your employees' tuition, covering anything from college and university classes to more specialized training and seminars. The employee feels valued, while you, in return, have a professional with a growing array of knowledge and skills.

Designating relaxation spaces

Give your employees a safe space to relax and unwind during their breaks. This helps them refresh and re-energize so they can be ready to work when they return.

Offering employee sabbaticals

Sabbaticals were once limited to scholars and college professors, but some companies now offer them to their employees. Encompassing both paid and unpaid forms of leave that can last several months, sabbaticals often are offered to employees who have been with a company for a number of years. Generally, employees on sabbatical can do pretty much what they want, including traveling, learning a new language, or reconnecting with family and friends.

A study in the *Journal of Applied Psychology* found that people who take sabbaticals not only experience a decline in stress during their time away but also have less overall stress after returning to work. On the other hand, you'll likely have to rearrange staffing or work responsibilities to pick up the slack for the absent employee. Of course, this may allow you to provide development opportunities to those employees who fill in for the person on sabbatical.

Note that some states severely restrict an employer's flexibility to offer sabbaticals by controlling their frequency, duration, and permissible uses.

LOW-COST EMPLOYEE PERKS

Smaller companies can't afford all the perks larger firms can provide, as a rule. But attractive employee perks don't have to be expensive. Here are some inexpensive, but no less appealing perks to create a more meaningful work experience:

- **Movies:** These can either be a group outing or complimentary tickets.

- **Game time:** Some companies provide foosball, table tennis, or pool tables in their break rooms.

- **Employee referral bonus:** If an existing employee recommends a new hire who stays on the job for a certain amount of time — usually 60 or 90 days — give the referring employee a cash reward.

- **Healthy snacks:** Encouraging regular workouts? Your employees need energy to make the most of any exercise regimen. Fuel that fire by offering healthy treats — whole-grain muffins or energy bars, fruits, juices, and the like — daily or even once a week.

- **Free learning and development opportunities:** Professionals often speak for free (to promote themselves) on topics such as investment planning or ways to relieve stress. Make sure that attendance is voluntary.

(continued)

(continued)

- **Employee appreciation programs:** Help employees feel recognized for their efforts by creating an employee appreciation program. The type of program you use will depend on your company's and employees' unique needs. For instance, you may decide to give gift cards to employees' favorite stores when they finish a big project, or you may decide to honor a work anniversary by sponsoring a public outing.

- **Company celebrations during work hours:** Celebrate company wins by hosting company parties during work hours. If your employees usually help customers face-to-face, consider closing your business to the public for a few hours. Or, you can have a party room where employees can enjoy the party when they're not with customers.

- **Paid volunteer days:** Consider giving employees a set number of days they can get paid to volunteer outside of work. This job perk can be a great way to promote community relations (as discussed earlier) and provide a meaningful way to take a break from work. To document employee participation, have them send you a confirmation email from the organization they volunteered for.

- **Commuting assistance:** Provide a stipend to cover public transit passes to help staff defray the costs of traveling to and from the office; give car commuters free or subsidized parking.

Saying Thank-You: Focusing on Team Member Recognition

Another important way to create a meaningful work experience is to recognize team member accomplishments. Team member recognition includes a varied group of offerings and incentives that, taken as a whole, are designed to celebrate all sorts of employee achievements. In some ways, you might see them as feel-good measures, but the benefits of recognition go beyond simply inspiring goodwill. Letting employees know that you value their contributions also increases productivity and innovative thinking. But recognition can't be a rare event. It has to be a positive feedback loop woven into each and every day.

Defining employee recognition programs

An *employee recognition program* is an acknowledgment — either formal or informal — of an employee's or team's behavior, effort, or business result that supports the organization's goals in ways that have gone beyond normal expectations. Examples include

- » Exceeding expected sales levels

- » Obtaining new contracts or business

- » Going beyond productivity quotients

- » Solving a particularly problematic issue or situation

- » Reaching certain lengths of service

Just how employees are rewarded or recognized for outstanding performance varies from one company to another. Some companies continue to use something as simple (and inexpensive) as a certificate or plaque marking the achievement, but cash and gift certificates are also popular. Registration for a job-related conference or a paid membership to an association is also a good choice.

When deciding which rewards your company will use, be mindful of potential tax and overtime implications. Depending on the amount, the gift may need to be taxed as income to the employee or it may need to be included when calculating overtime rates for nonexempt employees. Generally, a payment is in the nature of a gift if its amount is not measured by or dependent on hours worked, production, or efficiency. A lawyer experienced in wage and hour law can help you determine when an extra payment to an employee should, or should not, be included in the regular rate of pay, as well as other complex compensation issues.

Your employees benefit from recognition programs — and so do you!

Your employees benefit in the following ways:

- » **Greater motivation:** Employees who know they stand to be rewarded for outstanding performance approach their jobs with greater enthusiasm and creativity. The opposite is unfortunately also true: Not being appreciated is a common reason departing employees cite when deciding to move on to a business where they feel that their efforts are more likely to be recognized.

- » **Peer acknowledgment:** Chances are, employees who get word of a coworker's achievement will take the time to offer their own congratulations. It's hard to imagine an employee who wouldn't welcome the acknowledgment.

- » **Empowerment and inclusion:** Employee recognition programs can make staff members feel that they're a greater part of a company rather than just the recipient of a regular paycheck. That moves loyalty beyond just a financial appeal.

Employee recognition programs also benefit the business by

>> **Reinforcing positive behavior:** If employees excel, others will notice. That can help others raise their performance in the hopes of being recognized as well.

>> **Lowering stress levels:** If the emphasis is on the positive rather than an overriding concern about snafus, employees are likely to feel less overwhelmed by their job responsibilities.

>> **Increasing customer retention:** Higher employee motivation levels typically carry over to satisfied customers and clients. Those you do business with inevitably notice employees who bring a commitment and enthusiasm to what they do. Unfortunately, a disgruntled or frustrated employee can stand out to customers just as much.

Getting the fundamentals in place

Now's the time to put an employee recognition program in place. How do you want to run it? Even the best program doesn't run itself. You need to make sure that you have a workable foundation. Here's a checklist to get you started:

>> **Make sure that people know about it.** One of the key duties of the person managing a recognition program is to publicize it. Mention it in your employee communications, such as an employee magazine or company intranet.

>> **Set up a budget.** How much do you want to spend? You'll need to ensure that your programs are affordable for the business. In considering this question, don't forget that money and tangible rewards aren't everything to employees. It's a good idea to set up a formal program, while also encouraging managers to informally recognize employees when and how they see fit. Some managers may overlook doing this if they know the company has an official program in place.

>> **Make your recognition efforts an investment, not an expense.** Any program you set up shouldn't be a line item like a company retreat, but rather part of your operating costs that can't be cut. It's that important.

>> **Make sure that it's aligned with your overall business strategy.** For instance, if your goal is to cut expenses, reward people who suggest and implement money-saving ideas.

>> **Encourage line managers to weave it into their regular schedules.** They should be encouraged to make recognition a habit. Encouraging the heart is a cornerstone of good leadership. Even a simple thank-you can have a big impact.

>> **Make it fair.** If only a few select employees are regularly singled out, that can breed resentment and jealousy among others. Spread the recognition as equitably as possible.

>> **Make it mean something.** Bonuses, raises, and other financial rewards are always welcome, but the research shows that meaningful recognition is personal. Extra time off, a complimentary meal, and other means of saying "thanks" or "job well done" can mean just as much. The bottom line: Whatever you do to recognize performance, be sure that the recipient will genuinely appreciate it. It's all too easy to see through recognition that's cosmetic and little more.

>> **Make recognition go beyond a slap on the back.** However rewarding your words may be, sometimes it's nice to spice them up a bit. Picture the employee going home and telling their spouse: "Virginia stopped by to say thanks for the great job on the contract. And check it out — dinner for two at that new Thai restaurant!" Powerful stuff.

>> **Create a culture of recognition.** Encourage team members to recognize each other and tell stories of good works during team meetings. By engaging the team in recognition, it becomes part of your ways of working — part of the culture.

>> **Solicit employee feedback.** Ask staff whether they value your recognition approach. If they want changes, what would they be? For instance, what sorts of rewards do they feel really mean something? The greater the connection people feel with the recognition, the more involved they'll become.

LOW-COST EMPLOYEE RECOGNITION PERKS

Not every employee recognition award has to be pricey. Here are several budget-conscious alternatives:

- Time off or extra vacation days
- Dinner at a local restaurant (or a "lunch on me" coupon)
- A designated employee-of-the-month parking spot or transportation/commute reimbursement
- Tickets to the movies or a sporting or cultural event
- A bouquet of flowers
- A department picnic or dinner to celebrate the achievement
- Golf or tennis lessons (or instruction in the sport or pastime of the employee's choice)
- A book by the staff member's favorite author

An additional note: If you do hand out employee recognition awards, they may be subject to taxation by the Internal Revenue Service. Seek legal advice if you need help determining which awards are taxable. Some employers tack on a little extra to offset an employee's tax liability.

Administration and communication

Even an established recognition program doesn't run itself. You need a capable administrator. If you're handling your company's HR function, that point person may well be you. If not, it's helpful to have one person charged with the administrative and technical duties of running the program. That makes overall administration and troubleshooting that much easier.

One of the key components of sound program administration is communication. Don't let yours exist in a vacuum. Even the most appealing employee recognition program will prove ineffective if employees don't know that it's available. Make sure that your staff members know which programs are in place and what the criteria are for who receives awards. Many firms use company communication forums for updates. A recognition program will be more successful if it has support from all levels of management — and employees are made aware of this. Senior management buy-in and joint ownership ensures that the effort doesn't sit solely — and potentially languish — on one person's (or department's) shoulders.

Handing out awards: The importance of publicity

Although recognition can be handled in a personal one-on-one setting, it's often more effective to make the event public — in a variety of ways. That can help maintain enthusiasm and high levels of participation.

Publicly offering kudos gives employees the recognition they deserve. Consider the following advertising venues for publicizing award recipients:

>> The company website

>> The company social media pages

>> The company intranet

>> The company newsletter

>> The annual report

>> Staff meetings

>> Company-wide emails/communications

>> Town Hall meetings

Evaluating results

As I mention earlier in this section, employee recognition isn't just a feel-good activity. It's wonderful if your employees feel great about your program, but you also need to make sure that you're getting the results you want from it. Measure productivity, retention, and other barometers alongside the implementation of employee recognition programs. If those numbers are up and can be correlated, the plan is having an impact.

4

Developing Talent

Focus on the right growth experiences for your team members based on the personal and professional goals of your team and business.

Develop leaders through career pathing, mentoring, coaching, and succession planning efforts.

Manage employee performance ongoing with regular check-in and focused feedback.

Chapter **14**

Providing the Right Growth Experiences for Team Members

I n Chapter 1, I establish that your employees *are* your business, and much of this book focuses on how to maximize the talent in your business to support your business success and growth. After all, businesses don't go; people do, so this chapter outlines how *best* to support the growth and development of your team members.

Understanding What Talent Development Is

Talent development is the part of the talent management process that ensures team members grow in skills and experience and contribute to the organization by accomplishing their goals over the long term. Talent development is the organizational process of positioning team members for career advancement in a way that aligns with the company's mission and the team member's career aspirations. It's about aligning them with the *right growth experiences* to develop their skills and better position them to accomplish organizational goals.

Meanwhile, *talent management* is the broader strategy of maximizing the talent within your business. Talent management encompasses all the human resources and talent processes related to attracting quality candidates, effectively onboarding new team members, and retaining employees. Talent management is strategic. Talent development is specific.

Here, I delve deeper into talent development — recognizing the goals of talent development and making sure all your employees are being given opportunities for growth.

Recognizing the goals of talent development

The primary goals of talent development include the following:

>> **Creating a high-performance workforce that allows the company to achieve its objectives:** It's simple: Empower team members by providing what they need to succeed, and you'll reap the rewards. Team members can't perform well if they don't have the skills and knowledge required to succeed in their role. When learning and development resources and opportunities for further growth are available, team members are more likely to accomplish and exceed objectives.

>> **Reskilling/upskilling employees so the company can continue to be competitive:** According to a 2021 Gartner study, 58 percent of employees will need new skills to successfully do their jobs in the coming years. This makes development essential for organizations and employees. *Reskilling/upskilling* is helping employees develop a new skill or skills to be successful in a different position or support a new focus within the organization. For example, an organization may reskill a workforce when a system changes from a manual one to an automated one.

- » **Increasing employee engagement and retention:** With the Great Resignation making competition for talent fiercer than ever before, improving employee retention is top of mind for organizations across industries, and prioritizing talent development can help. Prospective employees often report opportunities for growth and promotion as top drivers for exploring new jobs. Talent development initiatives are an important part of your retention strategy as they drive engagement and connection to the business. In addition, developing talent internally and equipping employees to take on expanded responsibility and/or new roles can save dollars that it would take to bring in external talent. The cost of replacing an employee who leaves a company averages anywhere from one-half to twice their annual salary, so efforts that promote employee retention and internal growth offer a significant return on investment.

- » **Attracting quality candidates to the organization:** For job candidates, career prospects and future opportunities are an important part of evaluating a potential employer. An organization's reputation for developing its employees is a powerful recruiting tool. In 2021, *Inc.* found that growth and training opportunities are a major draw for 90 percent of job applicants. Implementing talent development initiatives can entice the best candidates to apply for positions within your business.

- » **Improving your succession planning:** Retention is an important business strategy as you want to keep the talent that runs your business. That is the goal of succession planning, and talent development initiatives help by collecting and analyzing data about employee performance and potential that can used when promoting team members and getting them ready for advanced roles.

- » **Improving legal compliance:** Talent development initiatives are an important part of creating a safe, inclusive, and nondiscriminatory work environment, so in addition to the growth of team members and the business, they contribute to better legal compliance.

Talent development (for all of the reasons noted above) is an increasingly important part of every company's business strategy, regardless of size. Talent development activities include growth experiences such as mentoring and coaching, skills-based training, leadership development, succession planning, on-the-job learning, and more. Throughout the rest of this chapter, I share the must-haves for all talent development activities, discuss the differences in different types of growth experiences, and reinforce the importance of measuring success across all talent development initiatives. Chapter 15 continues the conversation on talent development with a focus on career growth and leadership development.

Note: Most HR professionals use the terms *training, learning,* and *talent development* interchangeably, and even though there is much overlap, I address them differently. Talent development is the umbrella for all employee growth experiences. Training and learning are specific activities to support the growth and development of team members. Training and/or learning refers to activities a company offers employees to help them become more proficient at the tasks and the skills necessary for success in their role.

Ensuring talent development initiatives are connected to other HR activities

The key is connection — ensuring that the skills/competencies you are developing through talent development programs are the same skills/competencies you are hiring for and that these skills/competencies are the ones being measured through performance management.

In order to be relevant and effective, all talent development activities must be intertwined with other HR and talent processes and the company's long-term business goals. Business leaders responsible for talent development work closely with senior managers, supervisors, and employees themselves to stay connected to what's happening in the business. It's critical to ensure alignment between the talent development programs being offered and the skill sets necessary to keep organizations competitive.

In Chapter 5, I highlight the importance of defining the skills necessary for success in the position success profile and through the definition of organizational core competencies. Documenting your core competencies into a framework provides clarity and visibility to leaders at all levels around what success looks like. These core competencies can then be used to ensure that your talent development activities are developing the right skills.

Creating a Learning Culture

It takes more than a curriculum of well-designed, well-delivered learning and development workshops to make a talent development program successful. What's needed most of all is an organizational culture that values and supports continuous learning and development. There's no single formula for creating such an environment. Clearly, though, it's hardly a coincidence that companies frequently singled out for their commitment to employee development are headed by chief executives who are themselves strong advocates of employee learning and growth.

I once worked for an organization whose owner encouraged all team members to "work harder on themselves than their job." He knew that team members who were focused on growth and development and committed to improving their skills would move the business forward. If the organization's leadership and culture encourage a growth mindset, talent development efforts to support the growth of team members will become a regular part of working within the organization.

Here's a brief look at some of the best practices found in companies known for their outstanding talent development initiatives. You may want to use them as a checklist against what is currently going on in your company.

>> **A mission statement** that incorporates continuous learning as a core value. Beyond this, there also should be a steady flow of communication from senior management that reinforces this commitment.

>> **A systematic approach** to identifying the skills and knowledge needs of managers and employees that are explicitly connected to business objectives and goals.

>> **An administrative support system** that makes it easy for employees to gather information about education and learning and development programs, to relate them to their needs, and to arrange the time in their work schedules to take advantage of those offerings.

Assessing Your Needs

The place to start with determining your broad talent development needs is with the skills/competencies outlined in your position success profiles and/or your competency model. Before implementing any talent development initiatives, you must answer these questions to ensure that you are focused on the *right* growth experiences for your team:

>> What are the strategic goals of this business — both long term and short term?

>> What competencies do employees need to achieve these goals?

>> What are the current strengths and weaknesses of the workforce relative to those competencies?

>> What improvements can training be expected to offer that differ from day-to-day supervision?

>> What kind of a commitment — in money, time, and effort — is your company willing and able to make to provide necessary training?

After you have clear answers to these questions, you're more prepared to act, which the following sections help you do.

Determining the right growth activities

Follow these steps to gauge the right talent development activities:

1. **Identify the business need.**

   What is the expected performance to support organizational goals?

2. **Determine the gap.**

   What is the gap between the expected and actual performance (how the team member is performing today)? In this step, it's important to identify what it is that is getting in the way of employee success. There are a variety of ways to collect this information:

   - Direct observation

   - Questionnaires/surveys

   - Consultation with people in key positions, and/or those who have specific knowledge

   - Interviews with team members

   - Focus groups (targeted conversation with six to eight employees)

   - Assessments

   - Team member work samples

3. **Identify the right talent development activities to fill the gap:** What talent development activities can be provided to help team members meet expected performance standards?

Working through this process helps to ensure the following:

>> How talent development will improve productivity and the bottom line

>> What, specifically, team members need to focus on for growth, as well as what will improve success and performance

>> An understanding of the link between organizational issues and learning

Incorporating the four ingredients for growth

Before outlining the specific ways to develop the talent in your organization, it's important to clarify *how* growth happens. After all, growth is what you're after. You aren't interested in learning for the sake of learning; you're interested in growing team members to support them as individuals and to support business growth. So how does growth happen?

Regardless of the talent development activities used within your organization, you need to ensure the following factors are woven into *any* growth experience — the must-haves:

>> **Time:** Development is a process, not an event. It happens over time, as team members struggle through the learning curve and take on new skills. You must allow time for growth to happen, or it will be stunted.

>> **Focus:** There must be clarity on *who* and *what* is being developed through the process. Focus = growth, and if you try to focus on too many skills or irrelevant skills, you'll miss the mark.

>> **Accountability:** Research from the Association of Talent Development (ATD) proves the impact of accountability. Committing to someone that you will follow through on the goal you've set increases your likelihood of accomplishing the goal to 65 percent. Having a specific accountability appointment with someone you've committed to increases the likelihood of accomplishing the goal to 95 percent.

>> **Psychological safety:** The environment in which team members are developing must be one in which they feel safe letting their guard down, failing, and struggling through the learning curve.

Comparing Online and In-Person Learning

Online learning is exactly what it sounds like: Classrooms and subject materials are all covered virtually. Options in online learning are continually increasing. It can be accomplished via an online learning platform, an online conferencing tool, online videos, and so forth.

In-person learning is the traditional way of learning, where students attend face-to-face workshops or learning sessions at a specified time and location.

There are obvious benefits and drawbacks to both in-person and online learning. It's important to carefully evaluate the pros and cons before making a decision that will affect your team members' growth and, ultimately, career. The key is to determine what works best for your employees' schedules, learning needs, and your overall financial situation.

Tables 14-1 and 14-2 point out some of the advantages and disadvantages of in-person and online learning.

TABLE 14-1 **In-Person Learning**

Advantages	Disadvantages
Being face-to-face creates a greater sense of connection among participants.	Participants have to congregate in a physical location.
Hands-on learning provides better opportunities to practice new skills.	Participants must adhere to a specific class schedule, which may interfere with their job or other meetings.

TABLE 14-2 **Online Learning**

Advantages	Disadvantages
Participants can join from any location via the internet.	Skill development may be impeded by the lack of hands-on practice.
Participants can work at their own pace and repeat content if needed.	Participants lack the opportunity to get help from one another.
Scheduling is flexible.	The lack of structure may cause procrastinators or very busy employees to put off attending.
More accessibility options, such as captioning, text-to-speech, and so on are available.	Technology isn't infallible. The Internet goes down, the screen freezes — you get the idea.
Virtual learning is less expensive, especially if it allows you to avoid travel expenses.	Participants, especially those who work remotely, may look forward to attending an event with coworkers.

REMEMBER

In order for online learning to be successful, it needs to be managed and monitored, just like in-person learning. If you simply upload a slew of learning and development courses and encourage team members to have at it, you shouldn't expect it to do much good. The good news is that online learning is easy to monitor through the many online learning platforms that exist. Quizzes and exams can be incorporated to assess comprehension. Encourage — and maybe even offer incentives — to employees who complete online learning. When providing online learning, set aside specific times so that team members feel encouraged to temporarily stop their day-to-day tasks to complete an online course.

Identifying the Right Talent Development Activity Given Your Needs

After recognizing the skill or competency you want to develop to support your organizational goals, you can identify the learning approach that works best for your team members.

Learning is a highly individual process. As a result, you must remain skeptical of taking a one-size-fits-all approach. Formal learning and development programs still abound, but numerous other delivery methods are available as well. What follows is a brief look at the range of approaches that are possible today. It's also important to note that many of these options happen in combination to create a variety of learning methodologies for employees.

Implementing formal learning and development programs

Formal learning and development (L&D) programs are the most traditional and familiar form of talent development. Employees are part of a cohort who are led through a targeted development program by a facilitator. These programs can be delivered in a variety of ways — in-person, virtually through online learning or videoconferencing, or via a combination of both (referred to as a hybrid development offering). Facilitators can include internal leaders and/or external partners.

The primary advantages to formal learning and development programs (apart from their familiarity) are that they provide ample opportunities for group interaction and social learning, and they give facilitators a chance to motivate the group and address the individual needs of each team member.

Formal L&D programs need considerable administrative support to be effective (coordinating schedules, reserving space for in-person sessions, ensuring appropriate technology for virtual sessions, and so on). Also, organizations that are bringing remote team members into the office for the learning can incur major expenses (travel and lodging, for example), which aren't directly connected to the learning experience.

Encouraging participation in conferences and public seminars/learning events

Professional association conferences and seminars can provide a wealth of information on a broad array of topics and professional issues and provide an opportunity for team members to network and learn from other professionals within your industry. Often, associations rotate the location of such events from one city to another, and many are held online (or have a virtual attendee option). That can make it more convenient for certain members to attend, depending on the proximity of the conference or seminar.

Associations are well aware of the issues that are most important to their members, and they tailor programs accordingly. Conferences and seminars also offer opportunities to meet other members to exchange insight and ideas.

Like other learning options, however, the cost of travel and lodging can be a significant issue. Additionally, because some conferences can be quite large, one-on-one interaction with speakers and other people leading the program can be difficult if not impossible. Plus, topics may be more generic and not relevant to your organization or business goals.

To circumvent the travel expense issue, you may be able to identify local professional associations or user groups offering training that could benefit your employees. These may not be as comprehensive as an annual conference, but an after-work lecture or presentation can still be valuable.

You also can encourage employees to attend topic-specific workshops that are organized and run by learning and development companies. These public seminars usually are held at a public site, such as a hotel or conference center. Companies that stage these seminars typically market them through direct mail or advertising. Recognize, however, that most public seminar offerings are, by necessity, generic. Similar to large industry conferences, the topics covered don't necessarily have direct relevance to your particular company. Another problem: inconsistent quality from one seminar to the next.

Offering executive education seminars

Seminars and workshops offered by universities and business schools are targeted, in most cases, to middle- and upper-level leaders. Typically, they cover a wide range of both theoretical ideas and practical pointers for putting these principles into practice.

Instructors are usually faculty members with a high level of expertise. These kinds of seminars are a good opportunity for attendees to network and share ideas.

However, courses at the more prestigious schools can take the executive away from the office for more days than desired. They're also expensive — in some cases as much as several thousands of dollars (including room and board) for a course lasting several days.

TIP

Choose these courses wisely. Make sure that events cover management concepts and techniques that are relevant or applicable to your firm's business focus and culture.

Mentoring

Some skills, such as the development of interpersonal skills, aren't easily taught in the classroom or through online courses. In fact, some skills aren't taught well in groups at all. Enter employee mentors. Just as appointing a more experienced employee to serve as a mentor for a new employee can help the new hire acclimate to your work environment, well-chosen mentors can assist staff at any stage of their careers with longer-term developmental learning.

In a mentoring role, an employee who excels in a given area — customer service, for example — can help less-experienced employees discover how to smoothly interact with customers and colleagues or develop additional skills that require more long-term and individualized attention than a classroom or online course can offer. Mentoring also helps people build interpersonal, or people, skills.

Mentors also can serve as valuable training facilitators for high-potential employees you may want to groom to eventually take over key roles in your company. (I touch on this in Chapter 15.) This is no small advantage. As firms brace for significant turnover among their most experienced employees due to the eventual retirement of many Baby Boomers, such arrangements may become increasingly important as a means of passing on valuable expertise to less-experienced workers and preparing them to take on positions of greater responsibility.

In short, the opportunity to have a close confidant is a valuable — and appealing — form of talent development.

Professional coaching

While the focus of mentoring is learning from a more experienced leader, the focus of professional coaching is asking the right questions to help the team member work toward their goal. A professional coach is someone who supports professionals and guides them in pursuing personal or professional goals. The International Coaching Federation describes professional coaching as the process of "partnering with clients in a thought-provoking and creative process that inspires them to maximize their personal and professional potential." In the business world, this is a collaboration through which employees and managers can develop new skills, create a clear career path, and improve their performance with the help of a professional coach.

There are a number of different coaching formats to choose from, including group coaching, one-on-one coaching, and even online coaching.

One distinction in coaching formats is between individual coaching and collective, or group, coaching. The difference between these two is really dependent on the goal you want to achieve. For example, if the goal is to help a high-performing individual, a new manager, or an executive either improve soft skills or overcome certain challenges they're facing in the workplace, individual coaching is best. Especially in the latter situation, it's critical that the individual feel comfortable and open to change. This can only be achieved in a one-on-one setting.

If you want to successfully introduce a wider change within your organization, whether you're going through an organizational transition or want to improve diversity and inclusion throughout your organization, collective or group coaching can help you shape attitudes and mentalities in the same direction.

While mentoring and coaching are important and valuable talent development activities, in Chapter 15, I provide additional insight into both mentoring and professional coaching in supporting team members on their career paths.

Additional talent development tools

The following sections present some other tools you may consider using.

Microlearning

"I don't have time" is a common response when team members are asked why they don't participate in learning and development activities. Calendars are full and attention spans are limited, and this makes it challenging for team members to find and make the time for learning amidst their day-to-day activities. For these reasons, microlearning — short (3 to 5 minutes), focused learning — is a popular tool to support ongoing development within organizations.

Microlearning, also referred to as *nano learning, bite-size learning,* or *micro-training,* is online content that is delivered in a short, succinct manner, focusing just on what the employee needs to know. It is ideal for focused 3-5 minutes of informal learning in bite-sized chunks, rather than developing skills that require in-depth learning.

For example, many organizations use microlearning in their onboarding process, including short bursts of learning on compliance, data security, and other industry-specific regulations. Another example includes the use of microlearning in a distribution facility to reinforce the importance of safety and moving products without accident or injury — shift workers may be required to spend

3 to 5 minutes playing a game answering questions about important safety features within the workplace.

Holding lunch-and-learn sessions

Some employees learn best in a more relaxed environment. Many businesses have adopted the concept of a lunch-and-learn session, in which a team member or someone from another company gives a brief seminar-style presentation while refreshments are served. It doesn't even have to be a full lunch. It's a simple, cost-effective way to bring team members together and provide a quick burst of learning on an important topic to your business.

Implementing individual development plans (IDPs)

An individual development plan (IDP) is a great way to personalize the development of each team member. It's a document that outlines the projected growth for an employee. It's an agreement between an employee and employer that certain skills should be improved or learned, or that overall performance should meet a certain standard by a specified time.

A best practice in the use of IDPs is for the team member to own the development of their IDP in collaboration with their manager; this helps to ensure that the plans are customized to each employee's needs. Encouraging the development and ongoing review and update of the IDP demonstrates that you care about their growth and provides a defined development track for team members to follow.

The specifics of an IDP can vary greatly depending on the job and the goals of the team member. Some IDPs are standard documents for all employees. Sometimes, they are created when employees are specifically tasked with showing improvement. Either way, they are a helpful talent development tool as they document specific areas for growth and add accountability for the employee.

Pair these plans with regular one-on-ones with supervisors or managers to ensure development stays on track. The IDP is only as valuable as it's followed, so it's important for managers to discuss the contents of the IDP ongoing. During one-on-ones, managers should discuss any challenges the employee is facing and provide guidance so there is continual conversation about their growth — this helps to instill a culture of learning.

FIND ONLINE

You can find a sample IDP template in the online tools.

Knowing What Makes for an Effective Talent Development Program

In this section, I cover some of the factors that most often influence the effectiveness of a program, regardless of which form it takes.

Team member readiness and preparation

You should consider the extent to which participants are open and receptive to the concepts that are covered in the training. Do they know *why* they have been selected? Do they agree that the objectives will be helpful to them?

TIP

Do your best to communicate to all potential participants the specific learning objectives of the course and how they'll benefit *prior* to the learning event. Make sure that supervisors who've recommended that certain employees attend the program communicate to those employees why that decision was made.

The applicability and relevance of the subject matter

The success of any program hinges largely on whether participants believe that what they're being taught has direct relevance to the day-to-day challenges they face in their job.

TIP

Take all reasonable steps to ensure that the workshop focuses on issues that are the most important to employees who are in the program. If you're using an external partner, make sure that the facilitator and/or program manager (often with external partnerships, you'll have both a facilitator delivering the content and a program manager who is administering the program) are aware of those issues. Arrange to have examples and exercises customized, making ideas easy to relate to.

The overall learning experience

Consider how interesting or entertaining the learning event is, content notwithstanding. The typical adult attention span is 10 to 15 seconds, so the content needs to be engaging and capture the attention of the learners.

TIP

Learning events should be as interactive and participant oriented as possible. The best courses use a variety of learning tools: discussion, simulation, and exercises.

Reinforcement of concepts

Follow-up is critical. Devise techniques to reinforce the skills learned in the seminar and apply them to the job or task at hand. Instead of stand-alone sessions, a best practice is to provide a learning series where shorter sessions are conducted over a few months' time, during which participants handle projects in between sessions and assignments. This approach is particularly effective for emerging leaders or high-potential talent. Individuals are more likely to retain, apply, and improve if they learn through a series of activities and experiences.

TIP

Provide relevant homework and exercises between sessions. Ask participants to create follow-up plans during or at the end of a session. Class participants also can form a community post-session, sharing ways they've successfully applied what they've learned in their day-to-day jobs.

But Is It Working? Measuring Results

As the person in your company responsible for the learning and development efforts, you can safely assume that you're going to be called upon at some point to answer a simple question: Are we seeing results from our efforts?

HR professionals have long wrestled with the problem of quantifying the results of a process that doesn't readily lend itself to quantifiable measures. It's generally acknowledged, for example, that one of the primary benefits of employee development is that it enhances morale. But how do you measure the bottom-line benefits of morale? Not easily, to be sure, but you can look to team members for feedback and track and measure important aspects of the employee experience to gauge the impact of talent development programs.

It's virtually impossible to isolate the impact of a talent development program, but by tracking multiple data points, you can gauge progress over time and tell a compelling story about your team members' growth.

First, ask your employees how they're doing and solicit their feedback on your talent development program. You can send out employee surveys asking them to give your learning modules, manager meetings, and other programs a grade. Ask them what works and where there's room for improvement. Then, see what changes you can make.

TIP

Employees' answers to the following survey questions immediately following the learning event can help you gauge its effectiveness:

>> Were the topics covered in this learning event directly relevant to your job?

>> Was the facilitator sensitive and responsive to the needs of the group?

>> Were the instructional materials easy to follow and logical?

>> Would you recommend this program to other employees?

REMEMBER

The feedback you receive is useful but limited. Post-learning surveys measure initial reactions and offer little insight into the long-term value of the development efforts. Because of this, it's important to observe the accomplishments or behavior of employees in the weeks and months after the learning event or to follow up with the individuals' supervisors for their assessment. Do those who had leadership development, for example, report lower turnover rates? Have employees who enrolled in a technical skills course shown noticeable improvement in their mastery of a certain software program? Do more trainees win promotions than the average employee base? Drawing a direct correlation between training and job performance isn't always possible, but this type of hard data can be invaluable when making the argument for additional talent development resources and can reinforce the value of the development that is being offered.

Another way to gauge the impact of talent development programs is to dig into the data. If assessment data is used within the development program, analyzing pre- and post-assessment data is a helpful way to measure progress and provide valuable insight to employees about their growth.

In addition, you can look to other HR and Talent metrics to help tell the story of progress on learning goals. Whenever possible, use metrics that are compelling to the business. Your chosen metrics will greatly depend on the purpose of the program, but they may include such factors as tenure, succession or next-level readiness, promotions, employee engagement levels, and production rates. The following HR metrics are commonly used to help tell the story of growth over time:

>> Employee engagement

>> Employee retention

>> External versus internal hiring rates

>> High-performer turnover rates

>> Promotion rates

If your talent development program is robust and impactful and meets the needs of employees and the organization, you'll see that reflected in the data. Team members want organizations to invest in their development, and they'll be more likely to engage, stay, and reach for promotions if yours does.

Chapter **15**

Pathing Careers and Developing Leaders

One of the chief responsibilities of your role as a people-focused leader is finding and recruiting the best people. But after they're onboard, it's every bit as important to help your staff keep growing professionally.

Companies that view ongoing leadership and career development as something employees should do on their own are missing valuable retention opportunities. Your team members — particularly your top performers — should be able to visualize their potential to advance and take on increasing responsibility within your organization. Employees clearly value this guidance from their organizations. Even before the Great Resignation and its challenges in keeping good talent, employees were waking up to the importance of career pathing.

LinkedIn's 2018 Workplace Learning Report found that 94 percent of employees would stay longer at a company that invested in their career. The message is hard to miss: Employees want to know how to grow and advance with an organization. You can help them by creating career development programs that show them how they can translate their professional interests, preferences, and strengths into long-term careers with your organization.

Even though the umbrella for this chapter is on career development (supporting the advancement of team members and career growth), I focus this chapter on the specifics of career pathing and leadership development for good reason. Leadership development is about enhancing influencing skills and building leadership capability at all levels in the organization. Career pathing is the process of aligning organizational talent priorities with team member career growth. It's driven by the team member's interests, career aspirations, and skills.

Don't get distracted by different terminology because it trips up many business leaders (talent management, talent development, career development, leadership development). The key is this: In order to get and keep great talent, you must have processes and programs in place to grow and develop them. This chapter focuses broadly on building leadership capability throughout the business over the long term and specifically highlights career pathing as a way to do that.

Understanding Why Career Development Matters

Today careers are often viewed as jungle gyms with multiple entry points, lateral moves, and a lot of options, versus the historical view of careers as ladders. Career development today encompasses moves in all directions with a focus on growth and impact. It's an attitude that reflects the variety of opportunities all around. Instead of advancing upward, the encouragement for team members today is to embrace a more networked career in which they're likely to move across, then up, then across again. The focus is not on the position title, but instead, the focus is on growth: developing skills and engaging in the right experiences aligned with individual career aspirations. Organizations should approach career development with this in mind.

This approach to career development is a win-win for the employee *and* the employer. Employees acquire know-how that benefits their careers both immediately and in the future. In the eyes of employees, this is no small advantage. A 2017 study by Glassdoor found that employees cared less about compensation and benefits packages and more about the company's career development opportunities, culture and values, and the quality of senior leadership.

Your support of employees' ongoing development shows them they're working for an organization that cares about their growth every bit as much as they do. That can do wonders for retention rates. A business case can also be made for investing in these processes. From the company's standpoint, career development enhances your staff's ability to contribute more fully, which in turn boosts your *bench strength* (the number and readiness of employees to fill vacant leadership and professional positions) and, ultimately, your competitiveness in the marketplace.

Although you may not be able to make promises to individuals about what the future holds for them at your business, you and the company's line managers can work with employees to develop career maps that detail the steps required to achieve specific goals. An individual development plan (as I discuss in the previous chapter) can be a useful tool in this process. An IDP is a document that outlines the employee's professional goals, as well as the steps the person must take to reach them. It allows you to consistently review, update, and discuss an employee's developmental goals. When someone is ready for the next level but no position is available, an IDP can be used to identify growth opportunities within the existing position so the worker remains challenged and motivated.

If an employee is planning to make a career change and wants to develop a skill set for this new role, make sure that their plans are in alignment with the goals of the business before the time and effort is invested.

Recognizing the Value in Career Pathing

As the workforce becomes more diverse, with employees coming from a variety of backgrounds, and fast-changing job roles and ways of working becoming more mainstream, it grows ever more challenging to ensure that employees have an understanding of career paths and how they can move forward.

A career path outlines how internal movement can happen within your organization through expanded responsibility, promotion, or lateral growth (changing departments or functions). There are three simple steps to bring a career path to life:

1. **Create a career roadmap.**

   A *career roadmap* is a visual depiction of the vertical or horizontal position changes within any business function and is based on both the business goals and opportunities and team member aspirations. It shows the progression of growth over time. For example, a high potential team member in the HR/Talent function who is currently serving as a recruiter (but aspires to lead in the Learning and Development function), may have a career path that looks like Figure 15-1.

2. **Create/leverage the position success profiles for each of the positions within the career roadmap.**

   Position success profiles outline the experience, skills, and competencies necessary for success at each position, so they provide critical guidance around necessary development within the career progression. Refer to Chapter 5 for more information.

3. **Create a learning and development plan.**

   Based on the experience, skills, and competencies necessary for success in the next desired position within the career map, create an individual development plan (see Chapter 14) that outlines the specific development for the team member depending on their unique needs.

FIGURE 15-1:
An example of a potential career path for a recruiter within an HR/Talent function.

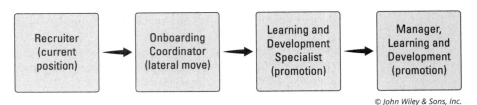

© John Wiley & Sons, Inc.

Although the team member may have obvious benefits from career pathing, your organization also reaps benefits. It can help your organization sense where the skills and aspirations are in your workforce, which can benefit recruitment and succession planning.

Leveraging Mentoring as a Tool for Growth

Mentoring is often a development initiative used within career path (and other talent development initiatives) as a way to connect team members with necessary expertise to support their growth. The most valuable (and certainly the broadest) application of mentoring is its use in fostering overall leadership and career development for your staff. That differs from its other benefits in that it takes something of a longer view — an eye toward career development that can last a professional lifetime. That means using mentoring to build attributes that are effective today as well as farther down the road.

(Elsewhere in this book, I discuss the value of mentoring in specific situations. For instance, in Chapter 10, I examine how it can help new employees acclimate and become comfortable with your work environment. Additionally, in Chapter 14, I look at mentoring in the context of a talent development tool to help employees develop skills and know-how that benefit your business.) The following sections outline how to maximize mentoring relationships within your organization.

Why and how mentoring works

As I point out in Chapter 14, some skills and competencies, particularly soft skills such as communication skills, aren't easily taught. Still, these abilities are pivotal to your staff's ability to interact with customers and with each other in the office. Mentoring opportunities are ideally suited to this kind of skill and knowledge transfer.

One reason mentoring arrangements work is that topics discussed between mentor and mentee are typically kept confidential. If an employee is having difficulty working with some of their team members, for example, they can comfortably discuss these dynamics with a mentor in a way that's not possible in a structured setting or with an immediate supervisor. This level of trust creates a psychologically safe environment that fosters growth.

TIP

Set clear expectations with mentors. Make sure that mentors bring to HR's attention any mentee concerns that could amount to unlawful harassment or discrimination, or any other possible violation of company policy.

Mentors can prove to be especially valuable resources as their mentees continue along their career development paths. For instance, a mentor can recommend ongoing learning opportunities that can best serve a mentee's career goals. If a company position opens up that represents a form of career advancement, mentors can suggest effective strategies to pursue that opportunity — or why it may not be a suitable fit.

Here are some more ways mentors can assist in your company's career development efforts:

>> **Helping to identify an employee's long-term career goals:** Many people — those in the early stages of their work life in particular — often fail to take the time to consider how they want their careers to progress over time and, for that matter, what that progress actually entails. A mentor can kick-start for an employee the process of beginning to think long term, not merely where they want to be next year.

>> **Acting as a dedicated role model:** Instead of an employee having to reinvent the career wheel, a mentor can serve as a living, breathing example. The mentee can emulate the behaviors and attributes of someone who's already taken a similar (and successful) career development path.

>> **Unlocking the power of networking:** Career development doesn't exist in a vacuum. Mentors can introduce their protégés to others who can prove to be invaluable points of contact and perhaps become additional role models.

Much like career development, which it supports, mentoring is a win-win activity. The relationship benefits not just the mentee and the company but also the mentor. In addition to bolstering their supervisory competency and leadership abilities, mentors gain the inner satisfaction of knowing that they're facilitating someone's career growth and assisting the company in cultivating a future leader. Helping employees work and interact more effectively also brings some concrete, practical career benefits to mentors. Serving in this role adds value to the organization and increases the mentor's visibility and potential for advancement.

Setting clear expectations

Developing and implementing a mentoring program (whether informal or formal) takes more than the best of intentions. First, pinpoint your specific goals and make sure that they align with the organization's goals and will benefit the employee in their current role. For example, you may want to increase retention rates, nurture employees who can help you introduce new product lines, or just make the onboarding process for new hires as stress-free as possible.

With those objectives in mind, consider what sort of mentoring arrangement may be most helpful. Do you want formal relationships — with partners in regularly scheduled contact — or do you want to operate more on an as-needed basis? Do you want to pair mentors with protégés in the same department or mix things up a bit? Also consider how the mentee's manager will remain involved. There should be some type of communication process that helps all three parties (mentor, mentee, and mentee's manager) stay engaged. Managers need to understand how they can help mentees in their day-to-day work.

Looking at the mentoring program as a whole, you need to decide who's going to lead and champion it on an ongoing basis. Also, consider your budget and how you'll measure the success of the overall effort.

Choosing the right partners — how to match mentors and mentees

The key to an effective mentoring program is to choose mentors who are temperamentally suited to the task. They don't necessarily need to be your most senior leaders. Mentors should, however, be naturally empathetic and enjoy the role of helping, connecting with, listening, and sharing information with others.

Among other attributes, ideal mentors should have

>> Excellent communication and leadership skills

>> Enthusiasm for working together as a team

>> Patience and understanding, particularly with less-experienced protégés

>> Solid connections within the organization

>> A sense of how much involvement with a protégé is appropriate and what crosses the line to micromanaging

>> Credibility as a role model for your culture and values

TIP

Here are some other suggestions on how to identify people in the company — or, in certain instances, even outside the organization — best suited to fill a mentoring role:

>> **Get recommendations.** Ask managers to recommend leaders within their teams who have the personality to act as effective mentors. Make sure that whoever they recommend has the time and capacity to devote to the task.

>> **Choose good role models.** Select as mentors those whose attitudes you'd ideally want the new employee to emulate — for example, flexible, agile, open minded, enthusiastic.

>> **Talk to managers who have expressed that they're nearing retirement or the next phase in their career.** Sometimes people nearing retirement look for someone to mentor. This isn't always the case, of course, but it may be worth checking out.

>> **Find common ground.** As you narrow down relationships to specific individuals, look for things (same schools, similar hobbies, past experience in certain industries) that can create a rapport between mentor and employee.

Although there isn't an exact science to matching mentors and mentees, consider these factors and two specific ways to identify pairs:

>> **Self-matching (mentees choose):** With self-matching, individual mentees choose the mentor they would like to work with typically from a pool of mentors. This approach creates a lot of ownership and empowerment but can be challenging if multiple mentees choose the same mentor.

>> **Program administrator matching:** With this common form of mentor matching, program managers choose the mentor-mentee match based on a set of determined criteria (skills, background, goals, and such). This allows the organization to be strategic in determining which mentors and mentees work together.

REMEMBER

It's best if a mentor is not the mentee's direct supervisor. The mentee should feel comfortable asking questions of, discussing challenges with, and soliciting advice from a neutral party who has no control over their career advancement.

Not all matches work out, and if one doesn't, it's important to address it quickly. Ask for feedback from both the mentor and mentee so you can understand each of their perspectives. This insight can be helpful for improving how you manage the matching process in the future. It's also important to quickly find a new match for both the mentor and mentee based on what they share with you. Work to help them have a positive mentorship experience.

Implementing mentoring (formal or informal)

A best practice is to provide an introductory training session for the mentors and mentees — it's ideal to bring them together for this conversation. Even the most experienced employees will get a better handle on their mentoring responsibilities with some focused direction, and mentees will be set up for success. For example, both mentors and mentees can benefit from understanding the distinction between mentoring and managing and mentoring and coaching. They also need to understand what is expected of them and what they can expect from the experience. During this meeting, everyone can get on the same page regarding goals, expectations, and other elements of the program. Cover what's required of everyone involved and how they can benefit most from the arrangement. Address meeting frequency, goals, and how long the program will last. Solicit questions from participants to be sure that no one is left in the dark on any critical issues.

TIP

If you check in at the outset to make sure that the mentoring relationship is on track, you'll be able to intervene early if there are any problems. Sometimes there's just a poor match, and people need to be reassigned. In other cases, there may be issues with time commitments or the level of mentoring being provided. If the mentor and newcomer clearly aren't hitting it off, end the relationship diplomatically but quickly. Without prejudging, try to get to the root of the problem.

Creating a Coaching Culture to Support Ongoing Career Development

Professional coaching has been widely used as a developmental tool for executives for decades, but more recently, there has been an explosion in expanding coaching access to individuals in all stages of their careers. The impact of coaching is clear, and organizations are realizing the value of coaching at all levels to support team member growth.

Before I share the specifics of how to use coaching to develop team members, I want to distinguish between the terms "mentoring" and "coaching." The terms are often used interchangeably, but they don't describe the same type of working relationship. Both share specific goals, including employee learning and career development that leads to peak performance, and the realization of full potential. However, the focus, role, and approach of mentoring and coaching are different. Table 15–1 compares the two.

TABLE 15-1   **Comparing Coaching and Mentoring**

	Coaching	Mentoring
Focus	Coaching focuses on improving a specific skill or competency in a focused time period.	Mentoring focuses on building a two-way, mutually beneficial relationship for long-term career growth.
Role	Identifying the gap between the current and desired state and helping the team member develop an action plan. The emphasis is on the team member finding the solution, not instructing or advising them.	The emphasis is on active listening, sharing specific examples in the mentor's area of expertise, making suggestions, providing guidance, and making suggestions.
Process	A structured process to help a team member accomplish a specific goal; the agenda is more specific, for a short period of time, and oriented toward certain results.	A mentee-driven process with less structure that allows for multiple areas of focus and growth over a longer period of time.

Although many organizations leverage external coaches to support the development of team members, the best way to create a culture of coaching and use coaching as a career development tool is to equip leaders with coaching skills. Using leaders as coaches is an effective way to use talent to build talent.

Employee coaching is simply supporting team members to reach a goal. Your organization can utilize it to help an employee improve an existing skill set or expand into a new one, depending on the organization's requirements. Just as coaching differs from mentoring, coaching also differs from a performance review or manager check-ins because it's ongoing, in-depth support. A coach does the following:

>> Provides positive feedback to encourage employee growth

>> Discusses the goal or challenge openly

>> Discusses solutions, approaches, or milestones

>> Establishes a plan for achieving the desired outcome

>> Sets a time and date to follow up

>> Adjusts as necessary until the employee reaches the goal

It's essential for the coach to refrain from giving the employee all the answers; the coach's role is to provide space and guidance for the employee to find those answers themselves.

Using the GROW Model to Support Employee Coaching

A model that is commonly used by leaders to coach team members is the GROW model. GROW is an acronym that stands for Goal-Reality-Options-Way Forward. It's an easy-to-use tool to support leaders at all levels in coaching team members to accomplish goals.

Think of the GROW model as a tool to help leaders lead a line of coaching questions. It helps to ensure that the coaching conversation is focused, natural, and future focused. Table 15-2 is a description and questions to ask for each part of the model.

TABLE 15-2   **The GROW Model and Coaching**

GROW	Description	Questions
Goal	Clarifies what the team member wants or where they want to go.	What do you want to have change in this situation? What's one thing you want to change? What's your vision for what it looks like? What do you want from this situation?
Reality	Establishes the current state.	Where are you now? How are you feeling? What's getting in the way? What are the issues or challenges?
Options	Explores options and discovers possibilities.	What might work best? What *can* you do now? What would it look like? How has this worked in the past?
Way Forward	Sets the path forward.	What is the next best step? What is the most important thing to do now? What are the consequences of not addressing this issue? What will you do, by when?

Building Leadership Capability Across the Business

Leadership development is a natural subset of career development. Leadership is influence, so by definition, all of your team members are leaders. The challenges, priorities, and values are different at different levels of leadership, but there is influence across the board.

Like career development itself, identifying and nurturing leaders at all levels can prove central to your business's success — and its future (as I discuss in "The Future Is Now: Succession Planning," later in this chapter).

Following is a common framework for distinguishing different levels of leadership within an organization (levels will vary based on the size and type of organization):

>> **Individual contributors** are focused on a specific role or task. They lead from the seat by influencing key stakeholders and colleagues. They are also responsible for leading up, the process of providing feedback and insight to their manager.

>> **Managers** have a major role to play in employee career growth, not just in terms of team member career pathing and development but also in understanding individual employees' personal strengths and development areas and providing a supportive sounding board for career growth ideas.

The transition from individual contributor to manager is an important one that's often overlooked. Research from The Ken Blanchard Companies shows that 60 percent of all new managers fail or underperform in their first two years in the new role because they aren't appropriately equipped to manage people. Getting results through others is very different from getting results on your own, and it requires a different set of competencies in order to be successful. This is precisely why it is mission critical to equip new managers with basic people leadership skills.

>> **Directors** are leading managers, so at this level of leadership, the focus is setting leaders up for success. Key competencies include coaching and problem-solving to eliminate obstacles and empower managers to get results through their teams.

>> **Executive leaders** are responsible for leading the business. At this level of leadership, the perspective is much broader on all aspects of the business. It's a strategic focus that includes much time spent on external factors and growing the business as a whole.

Note that the focus and priorities vary by leadership level — it's not a one-size-fits-all, so development efforts shouldn't be one-size-fits-all either. How leaders spend their time varies at each level, as well as the values they implore. While there are certainly "people leader" competencies that apply across managers, directors, and executives, there are also specific competencies that support growth at each level — these specific competencies are the focus of any targeted leadership program by level.

Defining leadership qualities that will move your business forward

Being (or developing) a great leader at any level is not a simple proposition. Every business is unique, so a leader who's effective in one setting may prove utterly ineffective in another.

For instance, if your business is more inclusive by nature, a leader who invites input and consensus would be a very suitable fit. Similarly, the top qualities of a leader in your sales group may be charisma and an eagerness to engage with others.

TIP

Focus on developing the leadership qualities that your business needs most and define them as your organizational core competencies. When you have a sense of the tailored-to-your-business leadership qualities you'd want to develop, you're well on your way to identifying people with the greatest promise. But there are additional personal characteristics and attributes that any business should look for that are good predictors of real leadership potential. These include

REMEMBER

>> **Integrity:** The last thing you want are people who may lead others into actions that don't reflect a commitment to being honest and forthright.

Your leaders set the tone for others within the organization.

>> **A knack for motivating others:** The ability to spur others into action is a key sign of someone who can lead effectively.

>> **Ability to collaborate across groups and build consensus:** A person who can't convince people to work together isn't much of a leader.

>> **Excellent communication skills:** For leaders, communication is a must. Great communicators can adapt to their audience, are clear and concise, are diplomatic with requests, use straightforward language when talking and writing, are good listeners who seek to understand, and are always trying to improve their communication style. A 2018 report by Inc. found that companies with leaders who utilized effective communication skills produced a 47 percent higher return to shareholders in a five-year period.

>> **Adaptability:** Leaders are willing to change as circumstances dictate and are comfortable with feedback — both positive and negative. This includes dealing with ambiguity, a critical skill for good leaders.

>> **Willingness to acknowledge shortcomings:** The best leaders are willing to be vulnerable. They understand where their strengths lie and where they don't (and are comfortable relying on others to fill those gaps in skill and experience).

A next step is to identify specific competencies necessary for success at each level of leadership within your business. Here are key questions to ask:

>> What is the focus for leadership at this level?

>> What are the key priorities?

>> What are the values?

>> What competencies are necessary for success at this level?

For example, a competency necessary for success at the executive level is strategic thinking, but this may not be necessary to lead at the manager level.

Determining your leadership development strategy: Factors to consider

To begin building a leadership development strategy, consider the following questions:

>> **Do you have or anticipate any leadership gaps?** Consider what may be (or will be) missing within your organization in terms of leadership attributes and characteristics. In other words, what kind of traits does it take to keep your organization humming? One factor may be the retirement of long-term team members, which can cause a gap between middle-level and senior-level leaders. This may result in a shortage of leadership talent at the senior level in your business. Some companies create *leadership tracks* that address different leadership gaps, assigning executive-level sponsors with expertise in each area to help design, socialize, and champion each track. Tracks may include such areas as leading and motivating teams, clarity in communication, or business development.

>> **How does the program align to organizational goals and strategic objectives?** How will leadership development assist your organization in meeting your goals? For instance, are you looking to grow financially, structurally, or in some other fashion? Sync your leadership development program to those priorities.

>> **Are you thinking long term?** Be sure to address both short- and long-term goals. Too often, companies think about filling a particular role and overlook longer-term needs. Focus instead on developing a "bench" of talent versus grooming people for specific roles only.

REMEMBER

NOT EVERYONE IS SUITED TO BE A PEOPLE LEADER — OR HAS THE INTEREST

It's natural to think current superstars, such as a top salesperson or marketing whiz, would make terrific managers or people-leaders, but that is not always the case. The skills required for success as an individual contributor are different than those required of managers (people-leaders).

In a similar vein, it's important to align team member ambitions to ensure they are realistic. If the top job at a law firm requires a law degree and the team member in question works in the accounting department, they may have to go to law school to gain the right qualifications. This kind of development takes time and considerable dedication on the part of the aspiring accountant/law firm CEO.

At the same time, many people don't have a desire to advance and are satisfied in their current job. A key to retaining these people is to make sure that they know that moving into a people-leader role is not the only way to advance and grow their skills in your organization.

Leadership development program options

Leadership development, mentoring, coaching, and succession planning are all linked. Most leadership development programs include some kind of mentoring, coaching, and organizational future planning. Individual activities can include one-on-one or group coaching, working with an assigned mentor, rotational assignments, job shadowing, project leadership, classroom learning (such as MBA programs, executive education, and online courses), and other options. External coaches and business school programs can be helpful (especially for larger organizations with commensurate budgets). There's an extensive external market for leadership development firms to partner with — the best firms serve as partners to come alongside you and customize a leadership development program to improve the competencies most important for your business success.

Measuring progress and success

Because the focus of leadership development is on growth, it's mission critical to build in measures throughout the program to gauge progress and measure growth. Here are some questions to help:

>> **Do participants feel they're progressing?** Ask people in the leadership program what they are gaining from the process. Do they feel they're learning and growing? How are they putting what they've learned into practice?

>> **Are their leadership activities and responsibilities increasing?** If so, how are they handling them? Do the people or departments they're managing have higher levels of productivity, customer satisfaction, and so on?

>> **What do others say?** Solicit feedback from employees who have worked with those in leadership programs. Do they feel the candidates are developing into effective leaders? If so, in what fashion? Taking employee comments in aggregate, try to measure leaders' success in terms of retention and employee engagement within their respective teams. A 360-degree leadership assessment tool is a helpful way to gain valuable data (particularly at the beginning and end of the process).

>> **Are your development efforts positively affecting overall business goals?** For instance, if one objective is to open additional branches, have beneficiaries of your leadership development efforts contributed to designing, implementing, or staffing new locations that are up and running?

>> **Is there a ripple effect?** A strong leader will also develop other leaders. Are individuals in your program reaching out to develop further talent?

>> **Are you doing enough to keep the leaders you're grooming?** Don't forget to develop and update incentives to keep candidates with the greatest leadership promise onboard. The last thing you want to happen is to invest time and resources in a promising individual, only to have that person jump ship because a more attractive opportunity surfaces elsewhere. Make sure that compensation and opportunity are sufficient to ward off advances from rival businesses. Consider creating a mentoring group to bring developing peers together from time to time so they can share experiences and progress toward their goals.

The Future Is Now: Succession Planning

In a way, succession planning is the culmination of career and leadership development. It's where you identify — from among your developing leaders — individuals who have the most potential and whose movement toward key positions, either laterally or upwardly, you want to accelerate.

Regardless of your organization's size, succession planning is an important activity. A mistake some smaller organizations make is feeling that they aren't big enough to need to boost their bench strength. Many vacancies can be anticipated and planned for, but not all talent gaps can be foreseen. No matter what your size, you can't run a business without good people ready to fill potential gaps if they occur.

If you're not currently thinking about who will fill your shoes (or the shoes of any of your senior leaders), then you're leaving a critical HR responsibility unattended. No one has an infallible crystal ball, but your organization should ponder contingencies if a key role in the organization were to be vacated.

Don't put it off!

Unfortunately, many companies don't see the urgency of succession planning. They still view succession planning as a task they'll undertake when a clear need presents itself. In an August 2021 survey from the Society for Human Resource Management, 56 percent of HR leaders said their organization didn't have a succession plan in place. Only 21 percent reported having a formal plan, while 24 percent said their organization had an informal plan.

What they're missing is that having a succession plan in place can head off confusion and uncertainty, particularly if the timing of succession is abrupt, such as a sudden resignation or death. Just as important, succession planning imbues confidence throughout a business. It provides a sense that, no matter what may occur, plans are in place to keep the company moving forward and operations going. Speak to senior managers about the importance of having a plan in place for key positions in all areas of your company — whether people are planning to leave or not.

Putting together the succession plan

Businesses manage succession in different ways based on their individual cultures. Plans cover a wide range in terms of complexity and degree of formality. But most agree that the primary goal is to create a pipeline of talent by offering top performers extra support along their developmental paths.

Smaller businesses can learn a lot from the formal policies put in place at large companies, where establishing a management succession plan is a recommended practice. Some corporations have a centralized succession planning function, whereas others empower people or teams throughout the organization to manage the function on their own.

Begin your succession plan by identifying jobs whose role in the overall function of the business is too important to remain in limbo while a search is on for a replacement of some sort. Choices should be driven with an eye on your near-, mid-, and long-term business strategies. President, chief executive officer, chief financial officer, chief operating officer, and other similar positions are the likeliest candidates. In the largest companies, the board of directors plays a key role in selecting C-level succession candidates, especially for a CEO transition. (The C in

C-level refers to "chief," as in *chief executive officer, chief financial officer,* and *chief information officer* — in other words, top-ranking executives within an organization.)

But it's not all about these C-level executives. Succession in all business-critical roles should be included in your planning. For instance, if your company leans heavily on technology (and, these days, most businesses do), you may want to add the chief information officer or other IT executive to the list. If you market your products around the world, the chief marketing officer may be another. And don't limit the field to managers only; apply your business-critical eye to all levels in the organization. For instance, an accounting firm may need to plan just as diligently for replacing a tax specialist with in-demand expertise as it does someone in a management position. When compiling your list, talk to others throughout the company to solicit their feedback and ideas.

Pinpointing succession candidates

After you've selected key positions in which you want to ensure continuity, it's time to select the individuals from your leadership development efforts who can best fill these roles. This step involves holding discussions with protégées to explain that they're being identified for positions of increasing importance (see "Creating a flexible understanding with succession candidates," later in this chapter), gauging their interest, and getting their buy-in.

When selecting succession candidates, consider not only skills but also how well individuals work with others throughout the company, particularly when they've transitioned into a position of some authority.

Here are three of the most common missteps in succession planning::

>> **Selecting a successor who is a mirror image of their predecessor:** Of course, there's a line of reasoning that suggests that, because the outgoing person was successful in the job, it only makes sense that a similar individual will carry on that history of achievement. It may seem reasonable, but the constancy of change dictates that what made one person successful in a job doesn't necessarily carry over to someone else. Instead, look at the position as it exists today. From there, match the requirements and challenges to the best-qualified candidate.

>> **Choosing a successor because their predecessor likes them:** Of course, it's never entirely misdirected to select someone with whom you and others get along, but likeability shouldn't be the sole factor in a succession decision. Qualifications and potential are the most important attributes to consider. Again, match job function to the person best suited to that role. Allow the

reality of the job requirements to direct the decision and put feelings and friendships aside.

>> **Identifying only one successor:** Avoid "anointing" someone for a role. Consider multiple candidates.

Companies sometimes discover that high-potential employees aren't eager to assume senior management roles. This is understandable, as many aspects of management involve making difficult, sometimes unpopular decisions that not everyone is comfortable with. There may also be concerns about work/life balance, travel, office politics, and general stress associated with advancement opportunity. Even top performers may not see themselves as potential leaders. By addressing possible barriers, you may be able to encourage reluctant candidates to step forward.

Selecting candidates outside the company

It may seem strange at first to consider succession candidates external to the business. Often, timing is what makes the difference. If you think you have enough time, you may be able to develop an existing employee's skills. But if your time horizon is shorter, you may need to look for an external candidate who is already somewhat prepared for the role. Still, keep in mind that there's no guarantee that person will be able to hit the ground running, and they may not be an immediate solution. They don't already know your business and may need time to mesh with the team and become acquainted with your operations.

With your existing staff, there are potential morale and retention issues to address if you bring someone onboard from the outside. What will existing employees' reactions be to being passed over for a promotion? The more open line managers are with their teams in performance and development conversations, the more easily team members can accept being passed over at that particular time. If a team member is somehow convinced they're in line for the next step, finding out that this isn't true could come as a hard blow. Make sure that existing team members have strong development plans to prepare them for the next opportunity, whether it arrives now or sometime in the future. You also want to make sure that you thoroughly vet the incoming outside leadership candidate. You can encounter morale issues if the identified person is less of a standout than you had assumed, or if they don't exhibit leadership qualities immediately upon coming onboard.

Creating a flexible understanding with succession candidates

Companies handle their interaction with succession candidates in different ways. Some hire and promote people with the message that they're being groomed either for a specific position or for a more senior but unspecified leadership role; other companies hire and promote less specifically for succession and place candidates into a *high-potential pool* (a designated group of people who are being groomed generally for higher leadership or critical executive roles).

Exactly who succession candidates are supposed to eventually replace or what positions they're preparing for may not be known to them — the choice to share this information is yours. If you do decide to reveal this, make sure that you establish an understanding that there are no guarantees, and the situation can change due to circumstances encountered by either the company or the succession candidates themselves. In addition, note that after succession takes place, either party may decide the fit is not right and reserves the right to back out. This arrangement also reduces the likelihood that the "heir apparent" will become frustrated if the person they're supposed to replace doesn't leave or retire when expected.

An approach many companies prefer today is to place emphasis not on individual positions, but on developing high potentials and letting them know that the longer they stay with the company, the more likely they are to be promoted when someone leaves. The company benefits as it maintains greater flexibility than if the preparation and investments made in individuals were designed specifically to back up a particular role or, worse, a particular person. The high-potential person benefits because they don't have to wait for just one or a finite group of people to leave. And the person who needs the backup isn't threatened that someone will be ready to succeed them before they're ready to leave.

The bottom line: Because they may eventually find that initial assumptions were too aggressive or unrealistic, many companies are reluctant to be specific with high potentials about any more than a general course of development.

Developing succession candidates

In addition to the general leadership development efforts I mention throughout this chapter, you should take the follow steps with succession candidates:

» **Expose them to other parts of the organization.** For instance, an IT person who spends a month or two learning the ropes from a finance manager will come to understand and appreciate the importance of reducing costs and improving the efficiency of processes, many of which fall under IT's purview. That broadened perspective makes for a better leader.

» **Offer other learning and development opportunities.** Although you want to offer every employee appropriate learning and development opportunities, this is even more critical for succession candidates so they can achieve their full potential. It can include varied work experience, job rotation, specific projects, and other challenging assignments. You should monitor progress carefully by evaluating how succession candidates perform in those activities. That way, you know that they'll be ready when the time comes to move up. International experience or knowledge is among the most difficult to impart. In these cases, an expatriate assignment, wherever practical, may give the best view of nondomestic operations.

>> **Consider the next person in line.** Succession planning means drawing up plans for more than just the next person up to bat. Be clear on success criteria for the future position and keep things moving by continuing to develop others farther down the pipeline. If some people seem discouraged that they weren't selected as the successor, encourage them with reminders that they're still in line for upcoming leadership opportunities. Point out that leadership openings often come out of the blue, so they need to be ready.

>> **Make it as much of a nonevent as possible.** When planned well, succession occurs smoothly and systematically. To an outside observer, in fact, it appears seamless. That is the goal of succession planning — to ensure that the business moves forward without missing a beat, despite a change in leadership.

>> **Utilize the IDP process.** Individual development plans (see more in Chapter 14) can be particularly useful in succession programs because they're customized to the individual, allowing you to work with the candidate to set specific goals and the steps needed to reach them.

>> **Consider succession planning technology.** Succession planning software applications can automate many of the tasks involved in creating a succession plan. In a nutshell, these programs allow you to readily identify upcoming succession requirements and develop necessary training and programs to address those needs. (For a full discussion of HR technology systems, refer to Chapter 3.)

Assessing succession outcomes

A succession plan is important, but it's not enough. That's because a plan doesn't develop people. They need experience, advice, mentorship, and feedback from you.

Your reviews, check-ins, and performance metrics are essential to tracking progress and keeping everyone accountable. Here are a number of barometers that can prove helpful in determining what works and what may warrant reconsideration in your succession planning efforts:

>> **Are your new leaders successful?** Are succession candidates meeting objectives and goals in their new jobs? Besides asking for a self-evaluation

from the new leader themself, also talk to the people they work with to gauge their confidence level in the new leader's direction. Again, if you identify gaps or problems in the performance in new leadership, revisit your succession process to pinpoint the source of the shortfall.

» **What do participants themselves think?** Consider making succession participants part of your evaluation process. What worked well for them? What was most impactful? What was least useful?

» **Are new leaders staying on?** As I discuss earlier in this chapter, it's just as important to retain talented new leadership as it is to develop it. Track leadership retention rates. If your best people are leaving for other companies, determine whether your compensation package is adequate by benchmarking against similar companies in similar industries and markets. Also consider whether the responsibilities of the new position are sufficient to engage highly talented leaders.

» **Is the flow of succession candidates consistent?** Succession planning should be an ongoing process. Are your efforts providing the business with a reliable supply of candidates, or are there occasional gaps that could pose a problem if an important position suddenly became available? Review your program to see if you can make it more consistent across the board.

» **Make evaluation a habit.** Just as succession planning shouldn't be an every-so-often consideration, so, too, should your evaluation be an ongoing responsibility. Not only does that allow you to maintain close touch with the results of your program, but it also lets you identify issues that may be impeding overall success. That gives you the opportunity to change and tweak elements of the program ongoing.

Even if replacing a top job seems too far down the road to be important today, don't neglect succession planning. Not only is it an important practice for identifying future leaders, but it also ensures that your top talent is highlighting and poured into.

IN THIS CHAPTER

» **Understanding what a performance management process can do for your organization**

» **Connecting the process to position success profiles and organizational goals**

» **Checking in with and assisting employees**

» **Getting a performance management program up and running**

» **Conducting employee performance reviews and following up**

Chapter **16**

Managing Ongoing Performance

F ew management practices are more basic or prevalent than performance appraisals — the mechanism managers use to evaluate team member performance. And yet, because of the way in which work is changing, the way in which HR and managers manage performance is changing, as well. Even though many organizations still do an annual or quarterly review as part of their process, new workforce expectations and innovations in technology are driving a host of changes for performance management processes.

A 2022 Gartner study reported that 81 percent of HR leaders are changing their organization's performance management process, and less than 20 percent of HR leaders believe that performance management is successful right now. These statistics support the need for changes in the way performance is managed. Yet it remains crucial that people leaders monitor the performance of direct reports, note which areas of job performance need to be improved, and then provide feedback to employees in a positive and constructive way. If these steps aren't taken, it becomes very difficult to determine how people get promoted, whether they deserve salary increases, and what specific development opportunities are most valuable to them.

So, what's the answer? Provide ongoing feedback. To do so, you need to develop a system whereby employees understand their current status and receive feedback and coaching ongoing. It's up to you to help your organization implement a structured and systematic process that considers the realities of today's workplace and the unique challenges and opportunities that exist within your business. As I point out in Chapter 11, raises, bonuses, and other types of rewards should be connected to your performance review system.

Employee success supports business success, and in earlier chapters, I highlight best practices for developing and growing talent. This chapter focuses on providing ongoing performance assessment. It emphasizes regular check-ins to ensure that team members are on track and focused on the right opportunities for growth.

Reaping the Benefits

Why should you put in the time and effort needed to create and implement an ongoing performance management process? The answer is that the long-term benefits of an effectively structured and administered performance review process far outweigh the time and effort the process requires. Here's what a well-designed, well-implemented performance management system can do for your organization:

>> Create criteria for determining how well employees are performing — and, to that end, make it clear how their responsibilities fit in with company and departmental priorities.

>> Provide an objective — and legally supported — basis for key human resources decisions, including merit pay increases, promotions, and changes in job responsibilities.

>> Verify that reward mechanisms are logically tied to performance.

>> Motivate employees to improve their job performance.

>> Enhance the impact of coaching that is already taking place between employees and their managers.

>> Establish a reasonably uniform set of performance standards that are in sync with company values.

>> Confirm that employees have the skills or attributes needed to successfully fulfill a particular job.

>> Create ongoing connection in the supervisor-employee relationship.

>> Give underperforming employees guidance that can lead to better performance.

>> Provide real-time feedback to keep employees focused on business goals and objectives.

>> Help employees clarify career goals.

>> Validate hiring strategies and practices.

>> Reinforce organizational values.

>> Assess learning and development needs.

>> Motivate employees to upgrade their skills and job knowledge so they can make a more meaningful contribution to the organization's success.

These benefits can only be realized through a performance management system that is ongoing, encourages regular check-in, and is connected to other talent activities. Figure 16-1 provides an example of an ongoing performance management process that's aligned with organizational and departmental goals. As you can see in this sample process, weekly huddles and monthly one-on-ones with team members to check in on progress drive connection and understanding so that leaders can coach team members in the moment. The key to this process is this: It's ongoing. It's not dependent upon an annual evaluation but instead, ensures that feedback and coaching on performance are a regular part of the culture.

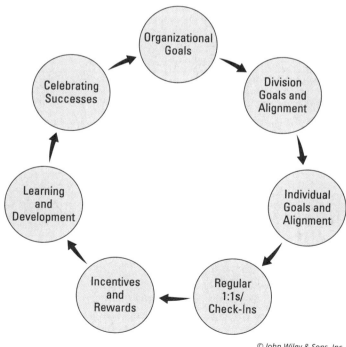

FIGURE 16-1: A typical performance review process (ongoing and linked to organizational goals).

© John Wiley & Sons, Inc.

Leveraging a Process that Works for Your Organization

The first step after you've decided either to introduce a performance management system in your organization or to change your current one is to determine what is best for your team members based on your business goals and the culture you are trying to create. All performance management systems have the same goal: to establish a systematic way of evaluating performance, provide constructive feedback, and enabling employees to grow and continually improve their performance.

The basic ingredients in all systems are pretty much the same: setting performance criteria, developing tracking and documenting procedures, determining which areas should be measured quantitatively, and deciding how the information is to be communicated to employees. Where different methods vary is in the following areas:

» The degree to which employees are clear about success criteria from the position success profile.

» How employee performance is tracked and documented.

» How performance is rated and how it aligns with corporate priorities, goals, and objectives.

» The specific types of appraisal tools used. In some cases, for example, certain approaches are more appropriate for evaluating managers and professionals than other employees.

» The amount of time and effort required to implement the process.

» How the results of performance conversations are integrated into other talent processes.

Anchoring to the Position Success Profile

When assessing an employee's performance, it's critical that the parameters you're using are fair and appropriate. The best way to ensure this is to use the position success profile as the primary guideline for assessing the employee's value to your organization. After all, the position success profile defines what success looks like in the role, so obviously, it's the place to start. Evaluating team members on criteria that fall outside of their position success profile isn't fair to them — or to you and the business.

In Chapter 5, I introduce the position success profile as the blueprint for success in a role, so the position success profile is naturally an integral part of all performance management systems because it outlines what success looks like in the position. The performance review conversation is a great opportunity to review the outcomes and competencies necessary for success in the position and identify growth points.

The two aspects of the position success profile that are most valuable in the performance management process are the outcomes (*what* was accomplished) of the position and the competencies necessary for success (*how* it was accomplished).

Determining outcomes for the position

Rather than list the tasks involved in a position, the position success profile identifies the outcomes expected, which supports a stronger performance management conversation. Outcomes are the results. When evaluating outcomes, you are evaluating *what* was accomplished. These are the most valuable and important parts of the job.

Following are some examples of the types of outcomes you may include in a position success profile (thus discuss in the performance review conversation). Outcomes should be measurable (preferably with numbers); directly lead to objectives being met; and of real value.

» Meeting or exceeding revenue, profit, and/or growth targets

» Delivering products and services that meet customers' needs

» Process changes in operations and/or product areas resulting in savings of time and/or money

» Culture improvements shown to increase employee morale, productivity, and retention

» Better collaboration or relationships among distinct teams leading to quicker and higher-quality product delivery

» Other measurable improvements that can be directly or indirectly attributed to work done

Determining competencies for success

While the outcomes help you assess *what* a team member is doing, competencies help you assess *how* they are accomplishing their goals. Competencies define the employee behaviors that lead to successful execution of job roles and responsibilities. They're used to outline an organization's performance expectations for a job or the organization's culture as a whole.

There are three types of competencies that may be captured in a position success profile, and all are helpful in assessing team member performance:

- » **Core competencies:** Core competencies are company-wide competencies that reflect the behaviors that are most important to the organization, helping to differentiate it in the marketplace. These can be company values, attitudes, or the way in which you and your employees approach your work as a holistic organization.

- » **Leadership competencies:** Leadership competencies capture the essence of effective leaders and translate into observable and measurable behaviors. Leadership competencies enable you to build and customize a leadership blueprint at all levels of the organization.

- » **Technical or role-specific competencies:** They're the skills or behaviors needed for each employee to excel at their individual job.

Aligning to Organizational and Department Goals

Team members want to add value. They want to know that what they do every day is supporting the organization's success, so it's important that managers provide help to connect the dots — how team member work supports department and organization goals.

Organizational goals communicate what's important, and when employees are clear on the goals, they can plan and execute their work based on those benchmarks. Organizational goals take the company's overall strategy and break it down into manageable chunks, providing checkpoints along the way to reach the overall strategic mark. So when working with team members to set goals, start with the organization's goals. Then, align with the department goals. That way, team members know exactly how they are contributing to the bigger picture, and as the bigger picture shifts, you can adjust team member goals accordingly.

It's critical to involve team members in the goal setting process. Unless employees are determining the goals themselves (with their leader's coaching and support), they aren't likely to buy into them or feel the same sense of ownership. A 2022 Gallup report notes that employees whose managers involve them in goal setting are 3.6 times more likely than other employees to be engaged in their work.

These sections provide additional insight into the best ways to maximize team member goals.

After your organizational and departmental goals are clear, team members are well positioned to create individual goals in support of the bigger picture. The SMART goal approach is a tool that has been used for decades to help team members and leaders create and accomplish their goals.

SMART is an acronym that stands for the following:

>> **Specific:** The goal should be specific, so that it isn't misinterpreted or confusing.

>> **Measurable:** The goal should allow you and the team member to track progress.

>> **Achievable:** The goal needs to be realistic and something that the team member can actually do.

>> **Relevant:** A relevant goal is aligned with the organizational and department goals and direction.

>> **Time-bound:** There needs to be a target date for completion.

By setting clear SMART goals, your team members have clear parameters to stive for. This allows the manager to focus their performance conversations on the right things.

Checking In and Holding Regular One-on-Ones

The best leaders know their team members — they know their strengths and weaknesses, and they connect with them regularly about their work and their needs. In a performance management model that is ongoing, leaders who are in touch with what's happening with their team members have a natural rhythm for acknowledging what's working well and what's not working as they are working toward their goals. One way to ensure an ongoing rhythm is to create a regular schedule of one-on-one meetings or check-ins with team members. These meetings can happen monthly, bi-monthly, or weekly depending on the nature of the work, the team member's needs, and the relationship between the team member and the leader. For example, new team members will naturally meet more regularly with their leader as they are building a relationship.

Regardless of the frequency, here are some keys to maximize the effectiveness of these meetings:

>> **Protect the one-on-one time — do *not* cancel meetings.** To team members, this time is important, so it must be important to the business and to the leader. Yet many leaders cancel meetings for "more important work." The leader must create space in their schedule for this time. I believe that nothing is more important for leaders to spend their time on than team members. After all, leaders get results through their team, so they must pour into them.

>> **Balance the agenda, starting with their needs.** This is time for your team member to share their experience. Give them the space to share whatever is going on with them and be a good listener. It's important that the team member owns the agenda. Together, you can set some guidelines about the goals of the meeting, but ultimately, it is time for the team member to get what they need.

>> **Use a shared document to capture notes and action items:** A shared document provides accountability for both the leader and the team member and ensures alignment on the conversation and agreement on action items.

>> **Get feedback from team members:** The one-on-one is not only an opportunity for the leader to provide coaching and feedback, but it's also an opportunity to *get* feedback from the team member on what's working well, what's not working, and what the leader can do to be more effective. This creates an environment in which it's safe to voice concerns and talk through challenges.

Just-in-Time Coaching and Correcting Course

When managers create a relationship with team members in which there's a high level of trust and a focus on achieving results, coaching, feedback, and course correction are natural. Yet many managers struggle to provide feedback and coaching. It's in your best interest to coach and develop your managers so they're equipped to provide feedback when they recognize that team members are off track or stuck. Here are the points to emphasize when encouraging managers to give feedback:

>> **Focus on why candor is important.** The team member can't improve if the manager doesn't communicate the need. Additionally, if it becomes necessary to let a team member go, a manager's failure to mention the employee's

weakness in a performance conversation can jeopardize the company's ability to defend the firing decision.

» **Stress the importance of documentation.** Managers should always be prepared to back up critical comments with specific, job-related examples. The documentation for these examples should be gathered prior to the meeting.

» **Highlight the importance of careful wording.** Managers should be made aware that the wording of criticism is every bit as important as the behavior being described. Remind managers to focus on the *behavior* itself and not on the personality quality that may have led to the behavior.

» **Encourage employee feedback.** After managers have issued any piece of constructive feedback, team members should be given the opportunity to comment. Given a chance, team members will often admit to their shortcomings and may even ask for help.

Providing feedback and coaching employees go hand-in-hand. Often when team members are struggling to accomplish a goal, they need a coach to help them identify other ways in which to handle a situation. The GROW model for coaching is a helpful tool for leaders to use in the moment (see additional detail in Chapter 15).

Celebrating Team Member Successes

Celebrating success is one of the key drivers in motivating employees in the workplace. In fact, 78 percent of employees would work harder if they were better recognized, according to a 2019 Globoforce study. Increased celebration and recognition for work well done means happier, more engaged employees who are more invested in your organization and driven to produce great work, so they're obvious additions to any performance management process. But in most fast-paced, results-driven environments, it's typical to accomplish a goal and move on to the next.

Celebrating both big and small wins highlights for team members the impact that they are having on the business. Having a sense of accomplishment brings joy to the employee and also builds a spirit of community that benefits everyone, and there are countless ways to celebrate successes. Chapter 13 discusses specific ways to recognize team members.

Launching a Performance Management Program in Your Company

When you launch a new performance management program, you need to gather input from both senior management and employees to ensure buy-in and support — after all, the program is in support of their success. You also need to make sure that the program is workable and well communicated throughout the organization. The success or failure of a performance management system hinges on factors that are based more on company issues than on the system itself. The following sections list successful guidelines.

Enlist the support of senior management

It's important to make sure early in your development process that senior management is willing to give the initiative strong support and to model the steps in the program. Explain how the particular approach you're recommending is tailored to the company's business and culture and how this process will support them in driving to a higher-performing company.

Develop a fair and practical tracking mechanism

In small companies, when supervisors and employees are working closely together, following day-to-day behavior isn't much of a problem. In larger companies, though, tracking can become a key issue. Essentially, you need a reliable and fair mechanism to ensure that the results of the appraisal are an accurate reflection of day-to-day employee performance. There are many online performance management systems that are built to address these needs. See Chapter 3 for additional information.

Here are some questions to ask yourself when determining what and how to track performance conversations:

>> What are the steps in the process, and what are managers expected to track at each step?

>> During what specific periods is behavior going to be tracked and observed?

>> What education and communication do managers need to carry out these procedures without placing undue pressure on themselves?

>> What recording mechanism will be used to document performance (a physical form, an online form, an online system, and such)?

>> Where is the documentation going to be kept and what assurances of confidentiality, if any, will be given to employees about the tracking procedure?

WARNING

There is no such thing as a perfect system. No matter how hard you try to quantify the measuring of any performance criterion, you can never remove the human element. It's not a science. Don't shoot yourself in the foot by creating a system so complicated that no one will take the time or effort to learn it.

Developing a communication game plan

Most performance management processes live or die on the basis of how clearly and openly you communicate the aims and mechanics of the system to employees. At the very least, everyone involved in the process should be aware of the following information before you actually launch the program:

>> The overall goals of your performance management process

>> How employees themselves will benefit

>> How performance criteria will be developed

>> The length of the performance periods (monthly, quarterly, annually)

>> The degree to which appraisal results will be linked to bonuses, merit pay increases, and other HR-related activities

>> What recourse employees have if they disagree with the results

>> What education, if any, will be made available to managers designated to implement the program

You can communicate this information in any number of ways. The important thing is to have a communications strategy. Make sure that everyone has a clear understanding of how the program will work and their role in ensuring the program's success.

Preparing for a negative reaction

In a well-managed company, most team members are probably meeting or exceeding expectations. However, some people simply don't respond well to critical feedback, no matter how minimal or appropriately delivered. In any performance conversation, an employee whose work is being critiqued may very well become agitated, confrontational, verbally abusive, and, in very rare instances, violent. Managers should be alerted to this possibility and be prepared with a strategy for response. Here's some advice to share with them:

>> **Within reason, let the employee blow off steam.** Don't respond, comment, or challenge the employee who's agitated or angry. In certain situations, a

calm, nonthreatening demeanor can defuse a situation. Give the employee adequate time to get past the initial reaction and cool off.

>> **Don't feign agreement.** The worst thing you can say in this sort of situation is "I can see why you're upset." It can very well set the team member off again ("You're not the one who was just told you're doing a lousy job!"). Even more important, the manager conducting the meeting *is* the company for all practical purposes; it's inappropriate, and possibly legally risky, for the manager to communicate a personal viewpoint at odds with the substantive content of the review.

>> **When the storm passes, continue the meeting.** A lack of response usually ends most outbursts, and the employee quickly realizes that they've made a serious mistake. Accept any apology and move on. If the employee simply can't or doesn't move on, take a break or end the meeting and arrange to reconvene later in the day or in the next few days.

Identifying areas for further development

What's most important following the delivery of any constructive feedback is a mutual effort between employees and managers to begin the process of making changes to help team members perform at a higher level. As part of the performance conversation, managers should identify areas for improvement and, together with their employees, build a set of workable performance development activities. These can be summarized in an Individual Development Plan (IDP) that outlines focused growth goals for the team member. See Chapter 14 for specific information on how to implement an IDP.

Performance development activities are a way to help employees better achieve the job objectives set at the start of the performance period. As a result, the employee and manager should revisit these objectives during this phase of the appraisal meeting to ensure that they're still on target.

Identifying Keys to a Successful Review

Although the key to a successful performance review process is ongoing feedback and check-in, the more formal review meeting is still an important part of the process for many organizations. Whether it's quarterly or annual, a more formal performance review meeting allows for documentation and alignment on how the team member is doing. This objectivity (versus informal performance conversations throughout the year) helps to support recommendations for salary increases and learning and development opportunities.

As with other aspects of your performance review process, equip managers to have these conversations. The truth is, most managers have not been trained to conduct an effective performance review session. So, although your managers may be responsible for what happens during the session, you and your HR colleagues are responsible for making sure that they're prepared for the challenge. These sections provide specific details about getting ready and having these reviews.

Preparing for the meeting

Managers should be briefed on what they need to do prior to holding a performance review meeting. The key point is to be ready — don't wait until the last minute to think about how the meeting will be handled. When your process is ongoing and feedback and coaching are natural parts of the culture, these conversations are easier. Other points to stress include the following:

>> Give employees enough time to prepare for the performance review meeting.

>> Allot enough time to conduct a productive conversation.

>> Have all documentation ready prior to the meeting and thoroughly review it.

>> The meeting place (online or virtual) should be free from distractions, and private.

>> Recognize that the goal of the meeting is not to just review the written performance review with the team member but also to engage in a two-way dialogue with them on their performance so it can be either sustained or improved.

Also, you may want to role-play how to respond to difficult questions with the manager or supervisor who will be conducting performance evaluations. Ensure that they have a phrase or message to fall back on if an employee question is difficult to answer (for example, "I want to respond to your question, but I don't want to give you inaccurate information, so I'll look into that and get back to you promptly after our meeting ends").

Conducting the conversation

If more than a handful of managers will be involved in your performance appraisal process, think about setting up learning and development sessions for them on how to conduct an effective performance review meeting. Whether you conduct this development yourself or bring in an outside company, here are the points that should be stressed:

>> Performance management is an ongoing process, and the formal performance review meeting is an extension of the environment you create and the relationships you have with team members.

- ❯❯ Providing ongoing feedback and coaching will set you up for a successful performance review meeting.

- ❯❯ The performance review meeting should always be a two-way conversation, not a one-way lecture. Feedback should be honest and genuine.

- ❯❯ Emphasis should be on what needs to be done to improve and not what was done wrong.

- ❯❯ Employees should be encouraged to comment on any observation managers share with them.

- ❯❯ Managers should know how to explain to employees the difference between *effort* (how hard employees are working) and *quality results* (whether the results of those efforts are contributing significantly to business objectives).

THE LEGAL ASPECTS OF PERFORMANCE MANAGEMENT

Depending upon how you develop and conduct it, an appraisal system can do one of two things with respect to your company's legal exposure:

- Unnecessarily expose your company to the danger of discrimination or other employment-related lawsuits

- Provide your company with a strong defense if an employee or former employee threatens a legal claim based on an unfavorable personnel action

The best defense when an adverse employment action is taken for performance reasons and the employee claims wrongful dismissal, demotion, failure to promote, or similar action is a carefully documented record of unfavorable performance evaluations, coupled with an employee's inability or refusal to carry out suggestions to correct poor work or on-the-job behavior.

At the same time, you need to be sure that your performance review system is defensible if challenged as violative of local, state, or federal antidiscrimination laws.

Following Up on Performance Review Meetings

Because the goal of your performance management process is ongoing, managers will naturally have rhythms built into their day-to-day follow-up with team members. Between performance conversations, managers should be encouraged to remain easily accessible so employees can share thoughts, concerns, or suggestions on any of the topics covered during the appraisal. Managers should understand the benefits of providing input to team members ongoing throughout the year. If feedback is ongoing, nothing in the performance conversation will come as a surprise to team members.

5

Minimizing Organizational Risk

Navigate the risks involved in hiring and leading team members by recognizing the major laws and regulations governing the employer-employee relationship.

Handle challenging situations swiftly and ethically.

Create policies and procedures to keep your workplace free of harassment and discrimination.

IN THIS CHAPTER

» Getting an overview of legal issues

» Determining your role in labor relations

» Guarding against discrimination

» Delving into disparate impact

» Understanding EEOC requirements

» Putting employment laws under the microscope

Chapter **17**

Navigating Risks When Hiring and Leading Team Members

The legal aspects of HR and business leadership are complicated, and, yes, they can be more than a bit daunting — especially when you first encounter them. The laws in place affect virtually everything you do in the field of HR: hiring, determining compensation, choosing how to evaluate employee performance, and many more tasks. All these activities carry legal implications, so the key is to mitigate risk. Failing to fully understand the law can prove costly.

You're not alone if you find this topic intimidating. However, with ample preparation (and frequent contact with legal counsel when it's called for), you should do just fine.

In this chapter, I cite what I believe to be the most up-to-date and legally sound information available, largely based on the assistance and recommendations of the prestigious law firm Ogletree Deakins. But, just like heart surgery, the practice of law isn't something you should do yourself. Consult an attorney. The information contained in this chapter gives you an overview, but it's no substitute for the specific and tailored advice that your own legal counsel can provide about your company and workforce.

Legal Matters: Understanding The Big Picture

The legal issues covered in this chapter require careful deliberation for the following reasons:

» **Daily changes:** The legal landscape is a dynamic one. Every day, federal and state governments pass new statutes; new regulations are adopted by federal and state agencies; new ordinances are adopted by local governments; and courts are ruling on existing statutes, regulations, and ordinances and developing case law. The discussions in this book help make you aware of these topics, but you still need to be familiar with the laws that apply in the states and cities where you have operations and have your own lawyer review your forms, policies, and procedures.

» **Vague definitions:** It would be nice if all laws were as clear as the posted speed limit. If the sign says the speed limit is 65, you're safe if you're driving at 64 miles per hour and know that you can get a ticket if your speed is 66. Many employment laws aren't so clear. For example, many laws specifically require you to do what is "reasonable." But what is reasonable in a specific situation? The law doesn't tell you. Just because you think you're acting reasonably doesn't mean that the courts, the administrative agencies, or your employees will agree.

If a dispute arises between you and one of your employees over whether you've acted reasonably, don't expect it to be resolved quickly by some easy-to-reach arbiter. You may instead face a long and expensive process of finding out whether your actions were reasonable. And if the court or agency eventually decides that you *didn't* act reasonably, your organization, and sometimes its individual supervisors, may be liable for large sums of money or subject to injunctive remedies, like implementing a proper policy or rehiring a terminated worker.

» **Inconsistencies:** If only one level of government were involved, and all the laws involving HR practices were adopted at the same time, you might have an easier time. But the federal government, states, counties, cities, and so on adopt laws and regulations, and they may not consult with one another.

The laws of one government or agency may contradict the laws of another. In addition, each law is adopted at a different time, and efforts aren't always made to be consistent. In fact, new laws can conflict with old laws that are not repealed.

TIP

Don't be your own lawyer. Most laws are defined, refined, and clarified by agency regulations and court rulings that cover areas that the average person wouldn't anticipate. For example, if a law applies only to businesses with 25 or more employees, does it apply to your business? That depends on how the law defines *employee*. Do owners count? Do part-time employees count? Do temporary or supplemental employees count? Do independent contractors count? What if you never had more than 23 people at a time, but because of turnover, 40 different people worked for you at various times during the last year? The answer to questions like this may depend on which law you're analyzing, and courts in different parts of the country may answer similar questions in different ways.

It sounds confusing, but keep in mind that lots of companies are surviving and thriving in this environment. You can, too. This chapter gives you common-sense guidance. However, this information is no substitute for legal advice. Get a lawyer and talk to that lawyer often.

Keeping the Peace

The extent to which you need to concern yourself with labor relations in your company, both formally and informally, depends on many factors, but two are key: the number of people in your company (because often, employment laws are triggered based on an employer's size) and whether the company is unionized.

If your company is unionized, chances are you may spend a considerable amount of your time negotiating and administering labor agreements. What's more, you're likely to be the person union representatives approach whenever they have grievances.

If you're in a nonunion company, you can't take anything for granted. People are people, and this being the case, occasional disputes will arise between employees and their managers, as well as among employees. You may have never thought of yourself as a peacemaker. Get used to the idea.

Being Aware of Discrimination

Many federal, state, and local laws make it illegal to discriminate on the basis of a number of factors, including, but not limited to, race, color, religion, sex, sexual orientation, gender identity, national origin, ancestry, citizenship, age, physical or mental disability, genetic information, military service or obligation, veteran status, pregnancy, marital status, and domestic partner status. But the laws don't stop there.

Take employee appearance, for example. Section 12947.5 of the California Government Code makes it unlawful for an employer to refuse to permit an employee to wear pants on the basis of sex. Hairstyles and textures, weight, tattoos, and body piercings also have been issues in lawsuits. Of course, discrimination laws cover many areas besides employee appearance. My point here is that no matter how trivial an issue may seem to you, *numerous forms of discrimination are unacceptable,* and it's your responsibility to be familiar with federal, state, and local laws that address discrimination.

So, how should you deal with these laws? The answer is simple: Make all your hiring, promotion, and other decisions solely on the basis of ability to perform the job, and you should generally be okay. I say "generally" because of a type of discrimination known as disparate impact (see the next section).

Knowing What Disparate Impact Means

The laws against discrimination not only extend to intentional acts by you (called *disparate treatment*), but also may cover actions that aren't intended to discriminate but have the effect of doing so, which is called disparate impact.

For example, assume that you own a trucking company. If you decide that you won't employ people of a certain race, sex, or religion, you're practicing disparate treatment, which is illegal from the standpoint of federal, state, and many local laws. Even the 2001 Patriot Act, which is primarily focused on matters of national security, takes this form of discrimination very seriously. It condemns discrimination against Arab and Muslim Americans and Americans from South Asia on the basis of religious, ethnic, or racial background.

On the other hand, suppose that you don't intentionally discriminate, but you require all your truck drivers to speak French. If it turns out that this requirement results in limited hiring of members of a certain race, sex, or religion because, for whatever reason, few members of that particular race, sex, or religion speak

French, you may be found to have violated discrimination laws because your policy created an unlawful disparate impact on the basis of a protected group. You haven't intentionally adopted a policy against a protected group, but an apparently neutral policy has had that adverse impact.

What happens if you're challenged on this policy and a disparate impact is shown? If you can then demonstrate that speaking French is a *bona fide occupational qualification (BFOQ)* for the job, then you may not be found liable for discrimination. For example, if your trucking company is based in Vermont, and all your drivers, as part of their routes, have to drive across the border into Quebec (the part of Canada where French, and not English, is the official language and appears on all signs), you may be able to establish that the ability to speak French is a BFOQ. However, if your trucking company is located in Arizona and the drivers drive only between Arizona and Mexico, speaking French may not be considered a BFOQ, and you could be found liable for disparate-impact discrimination because native Spanish-speaking applicants may lack French fluency.

REMEMBER

BFOQ has a special meaning under the law, and it may or may not match with your determination of what constitutes a BFOQ. Your good-faith belief isn't enough to guarantee that your BFOQ will stand up if challenged. A court or administrative agency reviewing the situation doesn't have to agree with you. Seek legal advice to help you analyze whether a neutral policy or practice may adversely impact a protected category and whether your reason for that policy or practice will likely qualify as a BFOQ.

Examining the Equal Employment Opportunity Commission

The Equal Employment Opportunity Commission (EEOC) is the federal agency responsible for enforcing federal antidiscrimination laws in employment. The following sections delve deeper into what you need to know about the EEOC.

Making sure you do certain things

Regardless of how disciplined you are in your company about following equal employment opportunity (EEO) principles, there are some important steps you must or should take in this area:

>> Post all mandatory federal, state, and/or local EEO-related posters.

**FIND
ONLINE**

The online tools include a poster from the EEOC entitled Equal Employment Opportunity Is the Law. It describes the federal laws prohibiting job discrimination based on race, color, sex, national origin, religion, age, equal pay, disability, and genetic information. Every employer covered by the nondiscrimination and EEO laws is required to post this notice on its premises. The notice must be posted prominently, where employees and applicants for employment can readily see it. When businesses are exclusively remote, employers may use electronic means to post the notice as a substitute to the hard copy. If an employer has some employees working on-site and other employees working remotely, the employer must post the hard copy notice in the workplace and is encouraged to post it electronically for remote employees. In this case, employers must inform employees how to access the notice electronically.

>> Depending on the size of your company (and its affiliation with or ownership by another company with enough employees to meet the 100-employee threshold) and type of organization, or whether you qualify as a federal contractor not exempt from the requirement, you may be required to prepare and file with the EEOC an annual report (known as the Employer Information Report, or EEO-1). This report sets forth certain demographic data related to your workforce, broken out into specific job categories.

>> Retain copies of personnel and employment documents (job applications, payroll records, records related to discharges, and so on), including those that may conceivably become relevant if your company is involved in a discrimination suit. The recommended minimum period for maintaining these records is three years, though particular laws may impose their own retention periods for such documents. Certain records, such as payroll records, should be kept for longer (even for seven to ten years or longer) to enable your organization to defend against claims of discriminatory pay practices originating years earlier. Modern-day technology may make electronic storage of such records much less burdensome than in years past. Also, keep on file records of hiring practices, identifying total hires within a particular job classification and the percentage of minority and female applicants hired.

Hopefully, it'll never happen, but in the event that an employee or a group of employees, an applicant or a group of applicants, or an administrative agency like the EEOC decides to file a discrimination complaint against your company, you should at least have a basic idea of what to expect.

As a preliminary matter, an individual may not file a lawsuit in court claiming discrimination under certain federal laws unless they've first filed an administrative charge with the EEOC and, in most situations, received from the EEOC a notice expressly affording them the right to proceed in court. This is true for most claims of discrimination under federal law (for example, race, sex, national

316   PART 5 Minimizing Organizational Risk

origin), though not for claims under the Equal Pay Act (see "The Equal Pay Act of 1963," later in this chapter), which may be asserted in court in the first instance. Such charges must typically be filed within 300 days of the alleged discriminatory conduct; charges alleging violations of the Age Discrimination in Employment Act must be filed within 180 days of the alleged conduct unless a state law provides a longer time frame.

Understanding what happens after the EEOC receives a claim

According to the EEOC, employees filed more than 60,000 charges of discrimination with the EEOC in fiscal year 2021. Though EEOC research indicates that the vast majority of these cases result in no benefit to the individual filing the charge, you need to understand the steps involved in case you need to interact with the EEOC. What follows is a rough description of the sequence of events that typically takes place after a claim is registered with the EEOC.

1. **The EEOC receives the charges.**

   The EEOC will, in nearly every case, accept a charge for filing. It will not do so when, for example, the EEOC simply doesn't have jurisdiction.

2. **The EEOC notifies the respondent (the employer) of the charges.**

   The EEOC promptly notifies you that a charge has been filed and provides a copy of the charge. The EEOC generally requests information about your organization and about the allegations in the charge, including a statement of the company's position in response. That notice may include an invitation to participate in an early mediation/conciliation to try to resolve the charge immediately, before a full investigation is undertaken.

   If you choose not to participate in an early mediation/conciliation, skip to Step 4.

3. **The parties may try to resolve the charge early in a conciliation/ mediation facilitated by the EEOC.**

   If you choose to participate in early mediation/conciliation, then generally someone from your company (probably you) will meet with the person who filed the charge and an EEOC staff member. The charging party gets a chance to tell their side of the story — that is, why the person feels that they are the victim of discrimination. Your company's representative then gives the company's side of the story — why, in your view, your company acted based solely on legitimate business reasons and did not unlawfully discriminate. The EEOC staff member will likely try their best to resolve the issue and accomplish a satisfactory settlement of the charge. (Note that the resolution may involve, for example, giving a dismissed employee another chance or additional severance pay.)

4. **If the parties do not resolve the charge early, the investigation begins.**

   If Step 3 is unsuccessful (or you choose not to participate), the EEOC requests that you provide the information and the position statement requested in Step 2. The EEOC may follow up this step with requests for more information, which can include telephone or in-person interviews of witnesses, a review of documents, and/or a visit to your facility.

5. **The EEOC makes a determination.**

   Generally, on the basis of the allegations in the charge, the parties' other written submissions, and its investigation, the EEOC will issue a finding on the merits of the charge and notify both parties of its finding — either of "reasonable cause" to believe that your company unlawfully discriminated against the individual or "no reasonable cause" to believe that your company unlawfully discriminated.

   In the event of a "reasonable cause" finding, the EEOC will once again solicit you to participate in a conciliation process aimed at resolving the charge (as in Steps 2 and 3). If the conciliation process fails (or you choose not to participate), the EEOC is authorized to enforce violations of federal anti-discrimination statutes by filing a lawsuit in federal court itself. If the agency elects not to litigate, it will issue to the charging party a Notice of Right to Sue, triggering the charging party's right to bring a lawsuit on the discrimination claims within 90 days.

   If the EEOC issues a "no reasonable cause" finding, the agency will issue to the charging party a letter dismissing the charge and describing information regarding the charging party's right to pursue the claim in federal court within 90 days.

In the event that the complaint leads to EEOC action, you may find yourself with a difficult choice: You have to either go along with EEOC proposals or gird yourself for a legal fight that may take years and cost your company thousands (or more) in court costs, damages, and, possibly, negative publicity.

If the EEOC doesn't take the case, the individual claimant can proceed on their own, and you may find yourself in litigation.

REMEMBER

When a right-to-sue notice is required, the individual can — and often does, when already represented by an attorney — short-circuit the administrative process by requesting an immediate right-to-sue notice, even before the EEOC has concluded its investigation. The EEOC is obligated to furnish the notice only if more than 180 days have passed since the charge was filed, but it may furnish the notice earlier. Similarly, charging parties alleging violations of the Age Discrimination in Employment Act may file a lawsuit without waiting for a right-to-sue notice, as long as at least 60 days have elapsed since the charge was filed.

Importantly, separate and apart from the federal EEOC are state equal employment opportunity agencies that are charged with very similar authority and responsibility for enforcing state antidiscrimination laws. Employees or former employees may file charges of discrimination with these agencies, just as they may with the EEOC offices, and such state agencies may investigate and act on such charges in accordance with their statutory powers — again, in a manner often quite similar to the EEOC. In fact, many states have "work-share" arrangements with the EEOC, where a charge may be deemed dually filed at both the EEOC and state agency level, but one agency agrees to lead the investigation, the results of which are accepted by the other agency. Employers must be careful to respond to state agency charges just as they would to an EEOC charge. You should consult with a knowledgeable and experienced attorney if your business becomes the subject of these investigations.

FIND ONLINE

The Discrimination Fact Sheets included at www.dummies.com/go/hrkitfordummies detail discrimination guidelines.

STAYING COMPLIANT WITH THE OFFICE OF FEDERAL CONTRACT COMPLIANCE PROGRAMS

Companies that contract or subcontract with the federal government must comply with additional regulations protecting employees and applicants. The Office of Federal Contract Compliance Programs (OFCCP) enforces Executive Order 11246 and subsequent related executive orders which require federal contractors to take affirmative action, and not discriminate on the basis of race, color, sex, sexual orientation, gender identity, religion, national origin, disability, or status as a protected veteran.

The OFCCP also enforces the Executive Order's nonretaliation provisions. The OFCCP's enforcement procedures include compliance assistance, compliance evaluations, and complaint investigations. When it finds a contractor has violated applicable regulations, the OFCCP imposes a conciliation process to seek an agreement, and monitors contractors' compliance with any such agreements. For extreme violations, a contractor may be debarred, in other words, lose its federal contracts.

Looking Closer at the Family of EEO and Other Employment Laws

More than a dozen pieces of major, HR-related federal legislation have been enacted since 1963, all relating in some way to the area of equal employment opportunity. Local, county, and state government bodies have enacted hundreds of statutes and regulations as well.

The focus of this legislation and the type of employer covered by each piece of legislation vary, and a good deal of overlap occurs. The following sections offer a quick glimpse of the key federal laws in this area.

REMEMBER

Some statutes impose posting requirements on employers, some impose requirements about specific notices that must be given to employees, and some impose both types of duties. Be sure to consult an attorney so you're aware of the notice and posting requirements applicable to your locations.

ADEA: The Age Discrimination in Employment Act of 1967

What the legislation does: Prohibits discrimination against applicants for employment and employees who are age 40 or older. Also prohibits retaliation against individuals who oppose unlawful employment practices based on age or who participate in proceedings or hearings under the ADEA. This law was amended in 1990 by the Older Workers Benefit Protection Act of 1990 (see the next section).

Who the legislation applies to: Almost any private-sector employer with 20 or more employees who worked 20 or more weeks in the current or preceding calendar year. Includes labor unions (25 or more members), employment agencies, and state and local governments.

OWBA: Older Workers Benefit Protection Act (1990)

What the legislation does: Prohibits age-based discrimination in early retirement and other benefit plans of employees who are age 40 or older and establishes a statutory regime for assessing the effect of waivers of claims under the Age Discrimination in Employment Act, separate and apart from contract law.

Who the legislation applies to: All individuals, partnerships, associations, labor organizations, corporations, business trusts, legal representatives, or organized groups of persons engaged in an industry affecting commerce that have 20 or more employees for each working day in each of 20 or more calendar weeks in the current or preceding year.

Additional details: One provision of this law requires that employers give an individual employee at least 21 days to consider a release or waiver of claims presented by the employer (that is, a company's offer that includes a promise not to sue the company for age discrimination). This time period increases to a 45-day mandatory consideration period for employees terminated as part of an employment termination program. In either situation, this law also requires that employees be given seven days after signing the release/waiver to change their minds and revoke their agreement.

ADA: Americans with Disabilities Act of 1990, amended in 2008

What the legislation does: Among other things, ensures that people with physical or mental disabilities have access to public places and public services. Also requires employers to provide reasonable accommodation for applicants and employees with disabilities and prohibits employment discrimination on the basis of disability.

Who the legislation applies to: Almost any private-sector employer that has employed 15 or more employees for 20 or more weeks in the current or preceding calendar year, as well as state and local governments, employment agencies, and labor unions.

Additional details: Employers in recent years have taken major steps to accommodate otherwise qualified disabled employees by outfitting the workplace with certain features (for example, wheelchair ramps) specially designed for disabled people or modifying schedules or training programs with an eye toward the special needs of disabled people. The Americans with Disabilities Act Amendments Act (ADAAA) of 2008 amended the ADA to greatly increase the coverage of the statute, including by determining disability without regard to mitigating measures (such as eyeglasses and medication) and counting impairments that are in remission if they would substantially limit a major life activity when active (for example, epilepsy).

See Facts about the Americans with Disabilities Act online for details about major provisions of the ADA and ADAAA.

FIND ONLINE

COBRA: Consolidated Omnibus Budget Reconciliation Act (1986)

What the legislation does: Provides certain former employees, retirees, spouses, former spouses, and children the right to temporary continuation of health coverage at group rates.

Who the legislation applies to: Employers with 20 or more employees are usually required to offer COBRA coverage and to notify their employees of the availability of such coverage. COBRA applies to plans maintained by private-sector employers and sponsored by most state and local governments.

TIP

Unquestionably, healthcare is an extremely important part of the world of human resources. I cover the topic more extensively in Chapter 11 and Chapter 12.

The Equal Pay Act of 1963

What the legislation does: Generally prohibits discrimination in pay between men and women on the basis of sex for work requiring equal skill, effort, and responsibility and that is performed under similar working conditions.

Who the legislation applies to: All employers covered by the Fair Labor Standards Act (refer to the later section about the Fair Labor Standards Act) and, thus, all enterprises with employees who engage in interstate commerce; produce goods for interstate commerce; or handle, sell, or work on goods or materials that have been moved in or produced for interstate commerce.

FMLA: Family and Medical Leave Act (1993)

What the legislation does: Grants to eligible employees the right to take up to 12 weeks of unpaid leave per year for one or more of the following reasons:

>> Because of the birth of a child and to care for the newborn child within one year of birth.

>> Because of the placement with the employee of a child for adoption or foster care and to care for the newly placed child within one year of placement.

>> To care for a spouse, parent, or child with a serious health condition.

>> Because of an employee's own serious health condition that makes the employee unable to perform the essential functions of their position.

>> Because of any qualifying exigency arising out of the fact that the spouse or a son, daughter, or parent of the employee is a covered military member on covered active duty (or has been notified of an impending call or order to covered active duty) in the armed forces. In addition, a qualified employee who is the spouse, son, daughter, parent, or next of kin of a covered servicemember is entitled to a total of 26 weeks in a single 12-month period to care for a seriously ill or injured servicemember.

The FMLA also prohibits an employer from interfering with the employee's FMLA rights or from retaliating against an employee for exercising or attempting to exercise any FMLA right.

Who the legislation applies to: Generally, the FMLA covers any individual or entity "engaged in commerce or in any industry or activity affecting commerce," employing 50 or more employees for each working day during each of 20 or more calendar workweeks in the current or preceding calendar year. Public agencies also are covered regardless of the number of employees they employ.

Additional details: Under the FMLA, employers have posting obligations and a series of notice obligations to give to employees at various points. The content and timing of these notices are complicated. A lawyer can assist in this area.

FIND ONLINE

For details of the major requirements of the FMLA, see the Family and Medical Leave Act Fact Sheets online.

FLSA: Fair Labor Standards Act (1938)

What the legislation does: Generally, establishes minimum wage and overtime pay standards, restricts and regulates the employment of minors, and requires certain forms of record keeping. Also prohibits retaliation against employees who file complaints under the FLSA, have instituted or caused to be instituted a proceeding, or have testified or are about to testify in a proceeding under or related to the FLSA; in most courts, internal complaints to an employer are also protected.

Who the legislation applies to: Most private and public employers.

FIND ONLINE

You can find the FLSA minimum-wage poster, titled Employee Rights under the Fair Labor Standards Act online. Every employer of employees subject to the FLSA's minimum wage provisions must post, and keep posted, a notice explaining the act in a conspicuous place in all its establishments. Visit the Department of Labor's website at `www.dol.gov/whd/regs/compliance/posters/flsa.htm` to download other versions of the poster.

WAGE-THEFT PREVENTION LAWS

Some states have enacted, or are considering enacting, wage-theft prevention laws. Among other things, these laws require employers to provide a notice containing specific wage information (for example, rate of pay, designated payday) to new nonexempt employees at the time of hiring, and possibly to existing nonexempt employees under certain circumstances.

California and New York are two states that have enacted these kinds of laws. Forms addressing California's law can be accessed on the California Department of Industrial Relations website. The California Notice to Employee is available in several languages and can be downloaded at www.dir.ca.gov/dlse/lc_2810.5_notice.pdf. The California Department of Industrial Relations also provides an FAQ sheet addressing the California law at www.dir.ca.gov/dlse/FAQs-NoticeToEmployee.html.

Forms addressing New York's law can be accessed on the New York Department of Labor website. For example, the Pay Notice for Hourly Rate Employees, which is available in several languages, can be downloaded from the following website, along with many other forms related to the New York law: dol.ny.gov/notice-pay-rate.

FUTA: Federal Unemployment Tax Act (1939)

What the legislation does: Stipulates that employers must contribute to a government tax program that offers temporary benefits to employees who have lost their jobs. In most cases, includes both a federal and a state tax.

Who the legislation applies to: Generally, companies that paid wages of $1,500 or more in any calendar quarter.

Additional details: The current maximum tax imposed is at a rate of 6 percent on the first $7,000 paid annually by employers to each employee.

HIPAA: Health Insurance Portability and Accountability Act (1996)

What the legislation does: Establishes rights and protections for participants and beneficiaries in group health plans, including protections for coverage under group health plans that limit exclusions for preexisting conditions; prohibits discrimination against employees and dependents based on their health status; and allows a special opportunity to enroll in a new plan to individuals in certain circumstances. HIPAA is commonly known for its privacy rule. The law established, for the first time, a set of national standards for the protection of individuals' health information, including standards for individuals to understand and control how their health information is used.

Who the legislation applies to: Covered entities include all employers, employers' health plans, healthcare providers, and healthcare clearinghouses.

I provide more information on healthcare in Chapter 12.

IRCA: Immigration Reform and Control Act of 1986

What the legislation does: Among other things, requires that employers attest to the immigration status of their employees and bans employers from knowingly hiring illegal aliens — and establishes penalties for such behavior.

Who the legislation applies to: Any individual or company, regardless of size or industry.

WARNING

Determining the legality of the employee's status is the employer's responsibility. Indeed, the IRCA introduced the Employment Eligibility Verification Form (Form I-9). Matters related to immigration and security are even more important since 2001, when the Department of Homeland Security was established and the Patriot Act was passed.

NLRA: National Labor Relations Act of 1935

What the legislation does: Relevant to this chapter, Section 7 of the National Labor Relations Act (NLRA) protects employees' right to engage in "concerted activities for the purpose of collective bargaining or other mutual aid or protection" to improve wages, benefits, or working conditions (including via social media) without fear of retaliation.

Who the legislation applies to: Most employees, whether the workplace is unionized or non-unionized.

Additional details: While most employees are covered by the NLRA and receive the protection of Section 7, individual complaints about working conditions are not "concerted" under the statute. Further, employees can lose protection by making statements about their employers that are egregiously offensive or knowingly and maliciously false, or by publicly disparaging the employer's products or services without relation to a labor controversy.

Pregnancy Discrimination Act of 1978

What the legislation does: Prohibits employers from refusing to hire a woman because of pregnancy and requires that pregnant women are given the same work modifications and medical-leave benefits that are available for employees with temporary disabilities, or similarly limited in their ability to work.

Who the legislation applies to: Employers with 15 or more employees who work 20 or more weeks a year, including privately or publicly held companies; employment agencies; labor unions; and local, state, and federal governments.

Additional details: The act covers both married and unmarried women. Also, both female employees and pregnant spouses of male employees can receive pregnancy benefits. (The spouse receives benefits if she is covered by the husband's health plan, but the employer isn't required to pay for a spouse's leave of absence, which is the duty of the spouse's employer if she is working.)

The Rehabilitation Act of 1973

What the legislation does: Certain employment-related provisions of this law impose an affirmative-action obligation on federal government employers to seek out disabled individuals for employment, require federal contractors to take affirmative action in employing and advancing the employment of qualified individuals with disabilities, and prohibit discrimination on the basis of disability by private and governmental recipients of federal financial assistance. In 1998, Congress amended the Rehabilitation Act to require access to electronic and information technology that is provided by the federal government for people with disabilities. The law applies to all federal agencies when they develop, procure, maintain, or use electronic and information technology.

Who the legislation applies to: Entities that possess a certain connection to the federal government (for example, those that contract with the federal government or those that receive federal financial assistance).

Additional details: In general, requires written affirmative-action programs from employers of 50 or more people that supply or service (nonconstruction) federal contracts worth $50,000 or more.

Sarbanes-Oxley Act (2002)

What the legislation does: Requires publicly held companies to be more straight-forward in reporting their financial results and how they were calculated. Also requires more stringent company controls to ensure the ethical behavior of all employees. Also prohibits employers from retaliating against employees because the employee provided information or assisted in an investigation regarding an alleged violation of Securities and Exchange Commission regulations, or any federal law protecting shareholders of publicly held companies from fraud.

Who the legislation applies to: Publicly held companies and private firms that are considering becoming public companies through an initial public offering of their stock.

Additional details: Sarbanes-Oxley requires the establishment of a company code of ethics for its senior financial officers. By extension, many companies seek to uphold the spirit of the law by requesting that their HR teams update and commu-nicate the firm's code of conduct for all employees.

Title VII of the Civil Rights Act (1964)

What the legislation does: Prohibits employers from discriminating against employees and applicants for employment on the basis of race, color, religion, sex, or national origin.

Who the legislation applies to: Employers with 15 or more employees for each working day in each of at least 20 calendar weeks in the current or preceding calendar year, as well as employment agencies and labor organizations, but excluding the federal government.

Additional details: The Civil Rights Act of 1991 amended Title VII and provided for the right to trial by jury on Title VII discrimination claims and authorized recovery of a broader range of remedies, including emotional distress and punitive damages (while imposing caps on such relief under Title VII).

The WARN Act: Worker Adjustment and Retraining Notification Act (1988)

What the legislation does: Requires 60 days' advance written notice to affected employees (or their bargaining unit), as well as state and local rapid response/dislocated worker agencies, of mass layoffs or plant closings that will result in employment losses.

Who the legislation applies to: Employers with 100 or more employees.

Additional details: Many states have their own "mini-WARN" provisions that provide additional employee protections and administrative requirements for mass layoffs and/or plant closings.

> » **Understanding at-will employment and avoiding wrongful discharge**
>
> » **Dealing with discipline, employee grievances, and disputes**
>
> » **Knowing how to deal with terminations and layoffs**
>
> » **Keeping your employees safe and healthy**
>
> » **Addressing unlawful harassment and workplace violence**

Chapter **18**

Handling Difficult Situations

Regardless of how good a job you've done in organizing the human resources function in your company, and regardless of how diligently you handle your day-to-day challenges, it's wishful thinking to expect your organization to be entirely free of personnel-related concerns. Even your best team members will make mistakes from time to time. So will your best managers and supervisors.

Inevitably, you or the managers in your company will be obliged at some point to take some sort of corrective action — including termination — against an employee whose job performance or conduct falls short of company expectations.

Of course, at least with respect to job performance issues, you're rarely the one responding directly to the problem — the ultimate responsibility for evaluating job performance lies with the employee's immediate supervisor or manager. Nevertheless, as the person responsible for HR in your company, you still have a crucial role to play. You have to make sure that job performance and workplace conduct issues are handled promptly, intelligently, and fairly — and in a way that doesn't diminish productivity, accelerate turnover, or deplete employee morale. And perhaps most important, you (more than likely) have to make sure that your company's disciplinary and termination policies minimize your company's exposure to wrongful discharge and other lawsuits.

In this chapter, I look at a more challenging aspect of HR management — but with an upbeat message. Most human resources problems are preventable and/or solvable, as long as you're alert to the early danger signs and you respond promptly with a clear sense of purpose.

WARNING

This chapter provides you with a significant amount of legally sensitive information, prepared with the assistance of the law firm Ogletree Deakins Nash Smoak & Stewart, P.C. But this area is not one where you can afford to be your own lawyer. Employee disciplinary action, termination, and layoffs are matters that require advice tailored to your particular company, location, and situation. My advice: Work with an attorney when navigating challenging situations.

Establishing an Ethical Culture

Here are ways to reduce difficult workplace situations:

>> **Prevent them from happening in the first place.** You can never hope to avert all employee improprieties and poor judgment, of course. But establishing a culture based on ethical behavior and strong leadership can go a long way toward diminishing these situations in your organization.

>> **Focus on prompt correction of issues raised.** As soon as an employee identifies a concern, the organization has an opportunity to correct the issue, mitigate any harm, and find a way to re-engage the employee in a positive way.

>> **Become an organization that emphasizes the critical importance of employees' ethical behavior in all their interactions.** This should be evident from the tone at the top on down. People will always find ways and excuses to commit wrongdoing, just as they'll always be capable of making honest mistakes. But including integrity and consideration of others among your organization's core values not only prevents many unpleasant situations from occurring but also helps you develop a reputation as a business that people want to work for.

It's very important that managers be every bit as accountable as employees. Your company should have a formal code of conduct that isn't buried on a shelf but is actively reinforced by all your managers. When employees hear one set of values but see another enforced — or, for that matter, neglected — by managers, the inconsistent messages can confuse them or cause them to question your commitment to your basic principles.

Fleshing Out the Meaning of At-Will Employment

Many private employers in the United States have long operated under a doctrine generally known as employment-at-will. Employment-at-will (sometimes referred to as termination-at-will) means that, in the absence of any contractual agreement that guarantees employees certain job protections, you (as an employer in the private sector) have the right to fire any of your employees at any time and for any (or no) reason — so long as the reason is not improperly related to an employee's protected status. In other words, you may terminate an employee with or without cause, with or without first exhausting all progressive discipline steps (if they exist), and with or without notice. At the same time, your employees have the right to leave at any time, for any (or no) reason, even without giving notice.

The concept of employment-at-will is specific to the United States. Other countries have their own sets of requirements concerning termination.

However, over time, the doctrine of employment-at-will has been substantially narrowed by other statutory and common-law protections preventing termination for a host of reasons. For example, you can't terminate an employee's employment because of their race, color, religion, sex (including pregnancy, sexual orientation, or gender identity), national origin, age (40 or older), disability and genetic information (including family medical history), veteran status, or use of protected leave under the Family and Medical Leave Act (FMLA). Other federal and state laws provide additional protections. Further, if your company is unionized, your employees' jobs are likely subject to contractual constraints.

Courts recognize and uphold the employment-at-will doctrine in particular cases so long as the employer's actions do not violate certain state law public policies and so long as the parties have not agreed otherwise (for example, by agreeing that employment is for a specified term, that employment can be terminated only for good cause, or that an employee can be discharged only after all progressive disciplinary steps have been exhausted). You can't terminate an employee for filing a worker's compensation claim, or for refusing to forge reports to the government or to violate antitrust laws, for instance. So, yes, your company still has the right to set behavioral standards, take corrective action when those standards aren't met, and fire employees who don't perform their job duties. However, you must be sure that in the process of carrying out these practices, you're not running afoul of public policies.

Staying Out of Court

Wrongful discharge continues to be a common theme of employment litigation. Even more sobering is the fact that plaintiffs win many wrongful discharge suits that reach a jury trial largely because juries tend to favor employees over employers. How does a company protect itself? In short, protection comes from preventive action. Here are some key principles to bear in mind:

» **Review all company recruiting and onboarding literature to ensure that no statements, implicitly or explicitly, "guarantee" employment.** Be especially careful about using terminology in employee literature and in conversations with employees (especially prior to hiring) that suggests an increased level of job security beyond employment-at-will, such as words like permanent. Courts have held that terms like this, which relate to duration of employment, can create an implied contract of employment through normal retirement age. If you need to differentiate between classes of employees, regular or full time are better terms. The term probationary should be used with caution for similar reasons; some courts have concluded that, after an employee is no longer on probation, the employee has moved into a more secure employment relationship such that the employer must have good cause to terminate the employee (and can no longer terminate at-will).

» **Coach and educate managers to maintain careful, detailed records of all performance problems and the disciplinary actions that have been taken in response to those problems.** Keep in mind that the verdict in many wrongful discharge suits hinges on whether the jury believes that the discharged employee was given "fair warning." Juries don't like it when they think an employee was surprised when terminated.

» **Make sure disciplinary and dismissal procedures are handled consistently with your organization's stated disciplinary and termination policy.** To be safe, your disciplinary and dismissal procedures should include a clause permitting the company to skip disciplinary steps or to impose more severe discipline or termination as circumstances warrant. Even when your policies allow for employer discretion, though, ensure you consider whether you've consistently applied the policy to another employee in a similar situation.

>> **Make sure that all the managers and supervisors in your company are well versed in your company's disciplinary and termination procedures.** Train them and confer with them on a regular basis to ensure that they're following procedures. If you discover that they aren't, talk with them immediately, letting them know emphatically that failure to follow proper disciplinary and termination procedures is unacceptable and can prove extremely costly. Seek legal advice whenever you're uncertain about any aspects of your company's disciplinary or legal policy.

>> **Be aware of how your actions may be misconstrued.** Be sensitive to the possibility that an employee who leaves your company voluntarily because they're unhappy with a change in assignment or work practices may be able to convince a jury that the change in assignment or work practices was a deliberate attempt on your company's part to force the employee to quit.

Developing Progressive Disciplinary Procedures

Some companies utilize a formalized disciplinary process, one that reasonably and systematically warns employees when performance falls short of expectations. A progressive discipline system is one in which problematic employee behavior is addressed through a series of increasingly serious disciplinary steps. In the previous chapter, I outline the importance of ongoing performance conversations and this approach provides a focused way to capture poor performance as well as good performance.

A formal progressive disciplinary procedure tends to work best in highly centralized companies, where personnel decisions for the entire company are made within one department (most likely HR), which makes sure that each step of the disciplinary process is implemented properly. The advantage is that the rules and regulations of job performance are consistently communicated to everyone. The disadvantage, however, is that you may be restricted to adhering, lockstep, to your established disciplinary system, even in a situation when you would prefer to immediately terminate an employee. If your company doesn't abide by these self-imposed rules, it could be found to have breached an employment contract.

On the other hand, some companies don't utilize such a process. A formalized disciplinary process doesn't work as well for decentralized organizations, where personnel decisions are made within each office or department on a case-by-case basis in accordance with a company's general expectations. In these situations, ensuring that each office or department follows the same disciplinary procedure can be difficult.

If your company isn't required to have a progressive discipline system (for example, under a collective bargaining agreement) but elects to implement one, the policy should be very carefully written and administered. If not, the company may find itself having established a contractual arrangement where the company is required to exhaust each progressive step of discipline before it may terminate an employee. In this situation, a decision to jump immediately to employment termination or harsh discipline can amount to a breach of the contract and expose the company to damages to the affected employee. You may want to consult with legal counsel to create or review your company's policy.

If your non-unionized company elects to adopt a formal disciplinary process, you may want to create some or all of the following phases:

>> **Verbal warning:** The first step in a typical progressive disciplinary process is informing the employee that their job performance or workplace conduct isn't measuring up to the company's expectations and standards. The employee's manager typically delivers this initial communication verbally in a one-on-one meeting. Just because this step is called a "verbal" warning, don't make the mistake of failing to document it. In fact, details from this and all later conversations should be documented. The report doesn't have to be lengthy; a few bullet points highlighting the main topics are perfectly acceptable. However, in this and each successive step, ensure that the organization can clearly articulate the problematic behavior and clearly instruct the employee on how to improve or avoid the behavior in the future, along with providing a time frame for correction.

>> **Written warning:** This phase applies if the performance or conduct problems raised in the initial phase worsen or fail to improve within the established time frame. The recommended practice is for the manager to hold another one-on-one meeting with the employee and accompany this written warning with a memorandum that spells out job performance areas that need improvement. Once again, the manager needs to make the employee aware of how their behavior is affecting the business and what the consequences are for failing to improve or correct the problem. The manager needs to work with the employee to come up with a plan of action (written, if possible) that gives the employee concrete, quantifiable goals and a timeline for achieving them. The manager should be prepared to regularly follow up with the employee on the progress of improvement.

>> **Final or "last-chance" written warning:** The penultimate phase of discipline, sometimes documented in a performance improvement plan (PIP), usually takes the form of a written disciplinary communication from a senior manager. The document informs the employee that if the job performance or workplace conduct problems continue, the employee will be subject to termination. Particularly with a PIP, very specific performance correction steps are laid out,

along with specific deadlines by which the steps must be accomplished. What you're doing here is using the PIP as a tool to assist the employee in gaining (or regaining) an acceptable level of performance — and notifying the employee that failure to meet this standard will lead to termination.

If a union contract applies, this step also may involve a suspension, a mandatory leave, or, possibly, a demotion.

>> **Termination:** Termination is the last phase in the process — the step taken when all other corrective or disciplinary actions have failed to resolve the problem.

This description of progressive disciplinary steps is a general guideline and is not intended as a substitute for legal counsel.

REMEMBER

NO WARNING NEEDED — IMMEDIATE TERMINATION

In the absence of a collective bargaining agreement or written employment agreement stating otherwise, certain employee infractions and misdeeds are so egregious that they justify immediate termination — even without going through the normal disciplinary steps that you otherwise may follow. Your onboarding literature and employee policies should provide examples of offenses that may lead to immediate dismissal (but also should expressly state that the company reserves the right to take any disciplinary action, including termination, at any time it chooses, regardless of whether the offense is listed). Here's a list to get you started:

- Stealing from the company or from other employees

- Possessing, using, distributing, or selling illegal drugs (note, state law may prohibit discipline for off-duty possession or use of drugs legalized under state law, though illegal under federal law (such as marijuana)

- Exhibiting blatant negligence that results in damage to or loss of company machinery or equipment

- Falsifying employment-related or company records

- Violating confidentiality, trade secrets, and similar agreements

- Misappropriating or misusing company assets

- Threatening other employees or managers

- Engaging in activities that represent a clear conflict of interest

- Misrepresenting or lying about job credentials

However you decide to structure your disciplinary plan, the process itself — in addition to being fair — should meet the following criteria:

>> **Clearly defined expectations and consequences:** Every team member in your company should be aware of the expectations and standards that apply companywide and to their particular job. These expectations and consequences should be introduced during the onboarding process (see Chapter 10) and then reinforced in one-on-one meetings between the manager and the employee. Your standards should be attainable and, to the extent feasible, measurable. Employees also need to know how not meeting these standards and expectations affects the company's operations.

Your company needs to communicate standards and expectations early on in the employee's tenure. The same principle applies to workplace rules. Where an employer has imposed upon itself binding progressive disciplinary procedures, some courts may hold that the employer can't fire employees for violating rules of which they were unaware. (At the very least, the employee's lack of knowledge of the rule will be held against the employer in most unemployment compensation proceedings.)

>> **Early intervention:** This nip-the-problem-in-the-bud principle is that an employer steps in as early as possible when an employee's job performance or workplace conduct isn't satisfactory. Again, this is why ongoing performance conversations as I discuss in Chapter 16 are so important. Failing to provide pointed performance feedback early on can hurt you in two ways:

- Employees can interpret the lack of any intervention as an implicit sign that they're doing just fine.

- If you act against another employee who is having similar problems, you leave yourself open to charges of favoritism or discrimination.

WARNING

The discipline needs to be appropriate for the offense. Or, more specifically, the discipline needs to seem fair to employees and, hopefully, to a jury. If your company is ever called upon to defend its actions, one issue that has a profound bearing on the final ruling is the congruence between the severity of the offense and the type of discipline. The general principle here is that you need to draw a clear distinction between those offenses or performance issues that warrant lower-level disciplinary action and those that are sufficiently serious to warrant immediate dismissal. You also need to factor into all disciplinary decisions — termination, in particular — the overall performance and discipline record of the employee and whether other employees in similar situations have been subjected to similar discipline.

>> **Consistency:** You need to apply your company's policies and practices consistently — no favoritism or bending of the rules allowed! Solid, legitimate, nondiscriminatory reasons are the only justification for deviation.

>> **Rigorous documentation:** The phrase get it in writing takes on extraordinary importance in any disciplinary process. Cumbersome though it may be, the supervisors and managers in your company must get into the habit of recording all significant infractions and problems, along with the steps taken to remedy those problems. Lacking detailed documentation of what the company has done throughout the disciplinary process seriously weakens its case, regardless of whether the firing was justified.

When deciding whether to terminate an employee, you should review evaluations, warning notices (if any), personnel policies or work rules, witness statements, witness evaluation notes (notes by the employer representative conducting an internal investigation in which they are documenting their impressions of the credibility of the witness being interviewed), and other relevant documents, such as customer complaints, production reports, and timecards. If the documentation is not deemed sufficient, ask the manager for more information and hold off on taking action until you've determined that you have a sufficient record to support the action you've decided to take. At the same time, be aware that adding papers to the file with new documentation of old performance problems that have never been addressed with the employee may undercut the credibility of the disciplinary action.

FIVE QUESTIONS TO CONSIDER IN EMPLOYEE DISCIPLINE

Whether the format of employee counseling is oral or written, effective and defensible employee discipline should address five subjects:

- **What's wrong?** This is the most critical and difficult portion of any disciplinary communication to develop. Here's where you clearly and concisely tell the employee about the defects in their performance. Beware of three pitfalls: First, determine whether there are other employees who share the same deficiency but who are not subject to the same discipline. Selective discipline for "sins" that others also commit (but for which they are not disciplined) is difficult to sustain. Second, avoid jargon and confusing acronyms (for example, "Numerous late and defective GST forms and FFR reports"). Third, avoid conclusory statements where the employee cannot understand the precise problem (for example, "Your performance undermined our productivity goals"); instead, be specific, explaining the cause-and-effect relationship between the unacceptable behavior and the unacceptable consequence of that behavior.

(continued)

(continued)

- **What does it take to correct it?** This is the second most critical portion of any disciplinary communication. Don't leave the employee with only an explanation of the defects in their performance. Provide an equally clear explanation of what it takes to correct the deficiencies. Again, beware of three pitfalls: First, the corrective steps may not require training. For example, an employee may understand their duties well but perform them carelessly. If so, you may be able to say nothing more than that they must adhere to known policies and procedures. Second, if the corrective steps require training, be sure that the employee receives it and that you document it. Third, if the corrective steps involve close monitoring by a supervisor or manager, make sure that the supervisor or manager is available to provide it. Otherwise, the employee may claim later that "no one helped me during the entire period of my PIP."

- **How long does the employee have to correct it?** This section may be short. It may be no longer than "You must demonstrate immediate and sustained correction of the deficiencies that we have identified." Do not use the word *improvement* in place of the word *correction*; there is bound to be improvement, but your expectation is correction. If discipline is linked to improvement, the employee can assert that they satisfied your expectations. Also, if you specify a period of correction, such as 30 or 60 days, always make it clear that you, as the employer, may shorten or eliminate this period. If the communication is in writing, be sure to insert the phrase: "The company reserves the right to shorten or eliminate this review period if there are repeat or additional performance deficiencies."

- **What are the consequences of failure to correct it?** Clearly communicate the specific consequences that the employee will face if they fail to correct the problem. If written, this portion of the disciplinary communication also may be short (for example, "Failure to [immediately] correct these deficiencies may result in more severe discipline, including discharge, without further progressive counseling").

- **Is anything impermissibly clouding the manager's judgment?** At times, the manager and the employee have a history outside of HR's knowledge and the company records. It's important to evaluate the motive behind the disciplinary action, including the potential for favoritism or unlawful retaliation. For this reason, HR is an extra set of eyes on the disciplinary process.

Defusing Grievances

An effective, well-balanced disciplinary process does more than provide a means for dealing with employees' problem behavior. It also gives them an opportunity to speak up (and be heard) when they're not happy with the way things are going in the workplace. Their complaints are technically known as grievances. Here are suggestions on how to implement a grievance procedure:

>> **Offer complaint-reporting options.** As a general rule, instruct employees to bring their complaints to the attention of their immediate supervisors. If the complaint involves the supervisor, however, employees should have the right to address the matter with someone outside the established chain of command. In many circumstances, directing complaints through a different channel, such as a trained and designated member of the human resources department, may be appropriate.

>> **Stress the importance of a prompt response.** Everyone in the company who's responsible for receiving employee complaints should make it a point to address the complaint as promptly as possible. Ideally, an employee should know within 24 hours that you've received their complaint and are handling it. Don't worry — that doesn't mean you have to provide a complete answer in a day. But a swift initial response demonstrates your concern and commitment to resolving the issue. Of course, determining how long a problem takes to resolve depends on how complicated the issue is.

How swiftly your organization responds is critical when the complaint involves alleged sexual harassment or discrimination. In such cases, all supervisors and/or managers should be trained immediately to notify you or others in an HR role. They should likewise be trained to promptly escalate complaints of serious workplace safety or health violations or criminal activity. Ignoring any complaint that deals with serious issues greatly increases your company's exposure to legal action.

>> **Report back to the employee.** Whether the complaint is substantiated or not, you need to keep the employee who registered it informed of what you're doing to deal with the situation. If you ultimately find that the complaint isn't substantiated ("We have no evidence to suggest that someone is poisoning our water supply"), explain why you feel that more action isn't warranted.

If the complaint is justified, indicate that corrective action is being taken. Depending on the circumstances, such as workplace safety, you may even want to communicate the nature of the action to the complainant. On the other hand, given privacy considerations, you want to be careful in terms of communicating the nature of the disciplinary action taken against another employee.

>> **Protect the employee from retaliation.** Assure employees that if they follow the company's recommended procedure for filing complaints, they won't be penalized for doing so — regardless of the nature of the complaint, as long as it's offered in good faith. When handling a complaint, remind all parties involved of your company's antiretaliation policy. And if you need to resolve a dispute between an employee and a supervisor, caution supervisors about taking any actions that may be perceived as retaliatory — such as unfavorable work assignments, an inappropriate transfer, or a demotion — while an investigation is underway or shortly after its completion.

Your organization needs to distinguish between complaints of alleged unlawful harassment or discrimination and complaints of other, day-to-day workplace issues. In this section, I address the latter — the day-to-day personnel problems and workplace issues that may arise. In contrast, for complaints of sexual harassment or harassment based on another protected characteristic, or of discrimination, your company needs to have a separate antiharassment/antidiscrimination policy and an established procedure for raising complaints under such policy. Also, there are specific features that must be embedded in such a policy in order to ensure that it complies with applicable federal and, possibly, state or local laws.

Settling Disputes: Alternative Dispute Resolution Programs

Left unresolved, conflicts often escalate into major disruptions. But if you can resolve these disputes, you can create the kind of atmosphere that fosters open communication and innovative thinking. The key is to settle any workplace dispute fairly and quickly.

Whenever possible, settle disagreements or disputes at the local level. Some organizations establish an open-door policy, where team members are encouraged to raise concerns or disputes with their supervisors, HR, or other company leaders who are trained on how to handle these issues and are sensitive to when a reported concern must be escalated for higher-level attention.

There may be times when it's not possible to resolve matters internally, and a team member's legal claim against your organization is threatened or initiated. For many companies, *alternative dispute resolution* (ADR) is an appealing alternative to the costly and unpredictable court action in wrongful discharge suits. ADR involves the same options as traditional conflict resolution strategies: mediation or arbitration. Both mediators and arbitrators typically have legal backgrounds, a vital skill given the extremely sensitive and potentially expensive implications of the termination process. Although federal law favors the use of ADR, some state laws impose restrictions on the types of disputes that may be arbitrated or the elements of an ADR program.

Mediation and arbitration programs can also be created and implemented in-house by an organization's own management team or ombuds office. Even then, however, the actual mediation or arbitration meeting or hearing is processed best by an outside firm or professional who specializes in these areas.

If you elect to implement a mediation or arbitration program, you should consult a knowledgeable and experienced attorney.

Terminating Employees: It's Never Easy

Even when you have ample cause for doing so, terminating employees is difficult — not only for the employees losing their jobs and the supervisors making the decision, but for coworkers as well.

You can do only so much to ease the pain and disruption that firings create. You can do a great deal, however, to help ensure that your company's approach to firing meets two criteria:

>> Protects the dignity and the rights of the employee being terminated

>> Protects your organization from legal and/or retaliatory action by a disgruntled former employee

The standard (and recommended) practice in most companies is for the immediate supervisor to deliver the termination notice. The message should be delivered in person and in a private location. Depending on the circumstances, it's generally beneficial for the company to have a third person also attend the meeting, such as another supervisor or member of the HR department. This person can serve as something of a neutral presence as well as a witness, provide moral support for the company representative, and, if necessary, help manage the situation if it becomes emotionally charged. Do not involve coworkers. (*Note:* Some union contracts require the presence of a specific individual, such as a union official.)

Regardless of why an employee is leaving your company, keep the termination meeting as conclusive as possible. It's not subject to negotiation. This is a meeting that is, in essence, a one-way meeting, in which a conclusion about the employee's termination is communicated and not up for challenge or reconsideration. All this means that you need to prepare prior to the meeting. The following list covers some issues to consider:

>> **Legal notices that must be given to terminated employees:** Some states impose obligations on employers to furnish certain information to employees upon their termination, such as written notice of the change in the employment relationship, information related to unemployment benefits, and conversion rights related to group insurance policies. You need to check applicable laws before the termination meeting.

>> **Final payment:** Ideally, any employee being dismissed should walk out of the termination meeting with a check that covers everything they're entitled to, including severance if your organization has a policy allowing for an unconditional severance payment under the circumstances (see "Easing the burden," later in this chapter). Some states, such as California, impose penalties for failing to pay an employee all wages (including accrued, unused vacation

benefits) due at the time of termination. Make sure you know what applicable state and local laws require.

>> **Security issues:** Think about company security, including keys, building or facility access cards, and company credit cards. Prepare your IT department in advance as to when to deactivate the employee's logins and passwords and access to company facilities, systems, and files.

>> **Company-owned equipment:** Be prepared to ask the employee to return any company-owned equipment immediately. If the equipment is off-site (equipment or laptop in the employee's home, for example), arrange for its pickup or for it to be sent back to the company in prepaid packaging to make it easy for the former employee to send you back your valuables.

>> **Workplace violence or aggravated behavior:** You may want to contact your company's and/or building's security services, if such services exist, to inform them that a termination is occurring and that you'll let them know if you need assistance.

>> **Extended benefits information:** If your company is subject to COBRA regulations (see Chapter 17) you're generally obligated to extend the employee's medical coverage — with no changes — for 18 months. Who pays for the benefits — your company or the employee — is your call; you're under no legal obligation to pick up the tab. Make sure, though, that you provide all the information the employee needs to keep the coverage going. The employer is responsible for this paperwork and often employers will outsource this to a third-party administrator (TPA). Also, prepare in advance so you can resolve all questions regarding an employee's 401(k), pension, or stock plan during the meeting, providing up-to-date information on what options, if any, the employee has regarding those benefits. Otherwise, advise the employee of the name and contact information of your benefits representative so they can obtain this information after the meeting.

>> **Notification of outplacement or other support mechanisms:** If your company has set up outplacement arrangements (or any other services designed to help terminated employees find another job), provide all the relevant information, including company brochures and the level of services the company does (and does not) provide. Some companies arrange for an outplacement counselor to be on-site to serve as the first person the terminated employee talks to following the termination meeting.

Avoiding common firing mistakes

The following guidelines can help you avoid some common mistakes in connection with employee terminations:

» **Is there a rule, policy, practice, or performance standard?** Be sure to identify a rule, policy, practice, or performance standard that an employee violated that warrants the discharge. Sometimes what seems to be an obvious standard just doesn't exist. For example, although an employee may have "stolen" parts from a distribution center, there may be no express policy regarding the parts that the employee "stole" if, for example, they were taken from the dumpster in the parking lot.

» **Did the employee know the rule, policy, practice, or performance standard?** An employer may have a policy on a particular subject, but the company never disseminated it or it was never disseminated to the particular employee. It's not true that only policies or standards that are distributed to employees in writing can support an employee discharge, but you should explore the possibility that the employee legitimately did not know of (or understand) the policy or standard at issue. At the same time, some behavior is so outrageous that an employee can't legitimately claim that they didn't know they were doing something wrong (though these situations are not the norm).

» **Did the employee break the rule, policy, or practice or fail to meet a performance standard?** Be sure to carefully analyze the situation. Think objectively about whether the circumstances are convincing. Also consider a related issue: Is there a plausible excuse? For example, an employee late to work five times in one month may explain that on two of these days, they stopped to talk to a supervisor in the parking lot before heading to their desk. Because of the need for careful analysis at this step, make sure that, in most cases, the termination meeting doesn't double as the interview of the employee to get their side of the story.

» **Is termination appropriate?** In deciding to fire an employee, you need to consider whether other employees who have engaged in similar behavior were terminated. Often, there are nuances that seem to justify a termination in this instance, even if termination has never (or seldom) occurred previously. Think critically about whether the nuances may be difficult to rely on if the person sues. On the flip side, there also can be instances in which an employee has committed a terminable offense for which others have been terminated, but for which termination in this specific case may be too harsh or appear too callous (for example, the employee was distracted by a close family member's illness). This isn't to say that termination may not still be appropriate — you just need to think about how the termination "plays" to an outsider and how you can show that the punishment was justified, despite the excuse.

In addition, consider whether the otherwise terminable conduct was considered "protected activity" under the law. For example, an employee's attendance policy violation may have been the result of the employee's protected use of leave under the FMLA, and termination for such absences wouldn't be permissible.

Delivering the news

No perfect script lets employees know that they're being discharged, but the news should be delivered as soon as the termination meeting starts, immediately after opening greetings are exchanged.

Give the employee a succinct explanation for the termination, even if you've had a previous discussion about problems and infractions. When told nothing, employees are more likely to assume the worst about the company's reasons and motives. Tact and sensitivity are important, but so is honesty. Keep the conversation short and to the point. Don't try to fill in awkward silences, and don't apologize for taking this step. Remember, too, that some states require specific information be provided to employees at termination.

WARNING

Remind managers that whatever they say during the termination interview (for example, "It wasn't my idea — management is just trying to cut back") can come back to haunt your company in a wrongful discharge or similar lawsuit. Managers should be trained to state the specific reason for the company's termination decision and not offer additional explanation, even if they disagree with the decision. If the manager doesn't feel confident about how the discussion is to be handled, they can conduct the termination discussion with you, the HR professional, in the room.

Keep any discussion of the employee's shortcomings brief — one or two sentences at most. The termination meeting is not the time to engage in a lengthy discussion of the employee's faults, even if the employee challenges the basis for the decision and tries to engage in extended discussion about the merits of the decision. If you've followed the process described, it's best to let the decision speak for itself.

Putting in place a post-termination protocol

If your company hasn't developed one, work with your management to develop a disciplined, clearly defined procedure for what happens after you discharge an employee. Make the break as clean as possible — albeit with respect to the feelings and dignity of the person being fired. Harsh and humiliating though the practice may seem, accompany the dismissed employee back to their workstation, give the employee a chance to collect their personal belongings, and escort the employee out the door. If the company has confidentiality agreements, remind employees — in writing — of their legal obligations, ideally by handing them a copy of such agreements. Also, advise employees that they're no longer authorized to access the company's computer systems and any online accounts.

TIP

Generally speaking, holding the meeting early in the week and at the end of the workday is best. If you conduct the termination meeting on Monday or Tuesday, you make it easier for the dismissed employee to get started immediately on a job search and for you to begin searching for another employee. By delivering the news as late in the day as possible, you spare the employee the embarrassment of clearing out their office in front of coworkers.

Asking the employee to sign a waiver of rights

Some companies ask a discharged employee to sign a written waiver or release of legal claims in exchange for a financial payment or other extra consideration. Often called a *severance agreement,* some employers require employees to sign this document and return it by a specified date as a condition for receiving severance payments. Note that this payout is separate from any wage-related compensation regulated by state or federal law, such as accrued benefits or regular compensation. Due to the differences in the time requirements between when final pay must be given to the terminated employee and when payment under a severance agreement may be due, it is quite possible that two separate checks will be involved.

Although some people believe that employers who present waivers of rights while terminating employees can communicate — merely by presenting the waiver — that they're worried about the legality of their actions, it's quite common practice in many companies and a useful business tool. Keep in mind, though, that your legal counsel should closely review such a document and that, typically, the employee should be encouraged to consult legal counsel as well. State laws require, or prohibit, various provisions for such release agreements, making legal counsel particularly important. In fact, it's a good practice to discourage employees from signing the document during the termination meeting — if they do, they may argue later that they signed the document while under duress, a legal doctrine that could justify setting it aside as invalid.

WARNING

If your company asks an employee to release claims of age discrimination under federal law, Congress has established a series of requirements that must be met, including certain language within the document itself and certain time requirements. Otherwise, the release is considered an invalid waiver — even if the employee accepts the financial payment for the release. Also, the federal Fair Labor Standards Act and some state laws impose limitations on the release of wage claims, and confidentiality provisions are increasingly regulated by state law. Consult legal counsel for help in these technical areas.

Easing the Trauma of Layoffs

Layoffs differ from firings in a variety of ways, but one critical aspect comes to mind: The people being let go haven't necessarily done anything to warrant losing their jobs. Layoffs occur for a number of reasons, which can include

>> Seasonal shifts in the demand for the company's products or services

>> An unexpected business downturn that requires the company to make drastic cost reductions

>> A plant or company closure

>> An initiative that restructures work practices, leaving fewer jobs

>> A merger or acquisition that produces redundancy in certain positions

Generally, in a nonunion, private work environment, when someone is laid off, there is no expectation that they'll be returning to work. Some companies use the term in a different sense, however. When business is slow and they don't need the entire current workforce, some firms (particularly those operating in a unionized environment) notify workers that they'll be placed on furlough for a period of time and will be offered the opportunity to return to work on a certain date or in stages. Some companies (especially seasonal businesses and those for which losing a major project creates a significant worker surplus) call this arrangement a "layoff" or "seasonal layoff" even though they plan to bring people back to work if and when conditions allow. Depending on the nature of the business — and its affiliation with unions or public- versus private-sector obligations — many companies today avoid suggesting that a layoff is temporary because it can be difficult to determine with certainty whether or when employees will be recalled to work. Layoffs (sometimes called *reductions in force, position eliminations, restructuring, downsizing,* or *rightsizing*) are far more common when they refer to employee terminations that are final. One thing that all these approaches have in common, however, is that they're involuntary and generally are considered to be no fault of the people affected.

I say employees generally are laid off through no fault of their own because sometimes a business must eliminate a certain number of positions in a department or business line, and the decisions about who will be selected may be based on evaluations of the employees' relative work performance. In such cases, employees with weaker job performances may be placed at the top of a layoff list, whereas those with stronger job performances may be protected from layoff.

Whatever the reason for a layoff, the pressure on the HR function is the same. You need to help your company navigate this difficult turn of events with as few long-term repercussions as possible. The following sections guide you through the process.

Analyzing whether layoffs are the right strategy

Carefully consider whether layoffs will be effective in achieving your business objectives — whether your goals are to reorganize operations, reduce operations, or eliminate unprofitable business units or lines. When weighing the possibility of layoffs, make sure that the management team is considering more than the bottom-line implications and is thinking about the impact on customers and remaining staff members. Layoffs may turn out to be inevitable, but management should be aware that the short-term, cost-cutting benefits of layoffs may well be offset by the following factors:

>> Severance and outplacement costs for the laid-off employees (including accrued vacation and sick pay)

>> The impact on your company's future unemployment compensation obligation

>> The effect on morale and productivity

>> The impact on future recruiting and new employee training efforts, in light of the skill and knowledge loss

Knowing the federal and state law

If the number of full-time employees in your company meets or exceeds 100, your layoff strategy needs to consider the federal Worker Adjustment and Retraining Notification (WARN) Act. As I explain in Chapter 17, the WARN Act requires that covered employers give 60 days' advance written notice of a mass layoff or plant closing. A mass layoff is a reduction in force that is not a plant closing and that results in employment losses within any 30-day period for 500 or more employees or 50 or more employees if they represent at least 33 percent of the active, full-time employees at that single site of employment. For this purpose, an employment loss includes a reduction in hours of work of more than 50 percent during each month for six months or more.

Employers covered by the WARN Act don't have to give 60 days' advance written notice in the event of smaller layoffs. Beware, though, that multiple related layoffs occurring within a 90-day period may be aggregated to reach the threshold number required to trigger WARN Act obligations. Also, more than one-third of states have their own mini-WARN laws.

WARNING

Congress has repeatedly considered proposed laws to amend the WARN Act to require, for example, notice farther in advance (for example, 90 days). These matters can be tricky, so consult your legal counsel.

WARNING

Be prepared to defend the rationale behind your layoff criteria. Be careful, too, that in the process of carrying out this more strategically driven approach, you're not laying off a disproportionately high number of employees who are in any group protected by equal employment opportunity legislation. Legal counsel can help with a privileged analysis of your data to provide advice and guidance for the final decisions.

Easing the burden

Moral considerations notwithstanding, it is in your company's long-term best interests to do whatever is reasonably possible and fiscally responsible to ease both the financial and psychological pain that layoffs invariably create. You may want to consider offering severance packages (and indeed, you may have a written policy or practice obligating you to do so). If so, most employers offering severance benefits require a release of legal claims from the employee in exchange for the separation benefits. But you can take additional steps — for example, help in résumé writing, financial planning, networking, and so on — that won't cost you much money but will, nonetheless, help employees get back on their feet again.

Hiring outplacement specialists

Outplacement firms are companies that specialize in helping dismissed employees (usually middle managers and above) move through the transition and find new employment. In a typical outplacement program, managers who've been let go get an opportunity to attend seminars or one-on-one sessions in such areas as career counseling, professional goal setting, and job-hunting basics (preparing effective résumés, networking, interviewing, and so on). Among the services offered by outplacement firms to job seekers are office space, access to a phone and voicemail, internet access, assistance in developing or revising résumés and crafting cover letters and online job inquiries, and administrative help for a predetermined period of time.

TIP

Outplacement, which is paid for by the former employer, can get expensive, particularly if your company is dealing with large numbers of dismissed managers. But it's one of the best ways to help those managers who've been with your company a long time and need the support. In major companies that conduct large-scale layoffs, outplacement services tend to be the rule, not the exception. Also, outplacement firms offer varying levels of services. It may be beneficial to offer at least a basic set of services to displaced employees versus none at all.

ALTERNATIVES TO LAYOFFS

If the purpose of the layoff is to cut down on costs (as opposed to reduce redundancy), you may want to explore options that, at the very least, can reduce the number of people who need to be terminated:

- **Temporary pay cuts:** Reducing salary costs is probably the simplest and most direct way to cut staffing costs without cutting staff. The key to this strategy is to ensure that everyone — including senior managers — shares the pain. Many companies, in their efforts to ensure equality, vary the percentage of reduction according to the amount of salary an employee is earning, with higher-salaried workers surrendering a higher percentage of their regular paychecks than their lower-salaried counterparts.

  Downside: No matter how justified the cuts and how many jobs you save, some workers will resent losing pay — and the decision to cut back on pay may induce some workers to quit. Keep in mind, too, that employees who agree to pay cuts will expect the salary to be restored — and then some — when the business turns around.

- **Work schedule reductions:** This option is worth exploring for companies that have large numbers of hourly workers. You maintain the same hourly rates, but employees work fewer hours per shift or per week. As an inducement to accept the lower take-home pay, most companies pledge to maintain benefits at full-time levels (so long as insurance carriers allow it).

  Downside: Reduction of hours per shift or per week doesn't achieve financial savings for exempt salaried employees and managers who aren't paid by the hour. You may be able to reduce exempt employees' hours and pay by eliminating entire workweeks. If you want to reduce exempt employee work hours and salary by eliminating less than a full workweek — for example, one day per week — you should consult an attorney.

- **Workshare or short-term compensation programs:** Depending on the state laws under which your organization is operating, there may be legislation to help reduce hours (and, thus, costs) but avoid layoffs. Approximately half of states have implemented some version of short-term compensation (STC) programs, authorized by federal legislation passed in 1982. In temporary economic downturns, STC programs allow employers that otherwise may be forced to lay off a portion of their workforce to instead apportion work reductions across the broader workforce. Affected employees receive unemployment insurance benefits on a prorated basis commensurate with the extent of their partial layoff. For example, rather than lay off 30 percent of employees, an employer might reduce the work hours of all employees by 30 percent; generally, the employees could then receive 30 percent of the unemployment benefits to which they would otherwise be entitled.

(continued)

(continued)

Downside: All 50 states participate in the unemployment insurance system, but only approximately one half have STC programs, and until relatively recently, STC programs were rarely used — at least partly because employers were unfamiliar with them. However, such programs are garnering increased attention, particularly given the Covid-19 pandemic, even at the federal level, with more states moving toward establishing them.

- **Exit incentives:** An often-used method of reducing payroll costs is to offer voluntary exit incentives, such as special early-retirement benefits. Because senior employees often are the most highly paid, trimming their ranks can result in significant savings.

  Downside: Senior employees have a high level of impact, and losing too many of them at one time can significantly weaken the leadership of your firm. Remember, too, that under the Age Discrimination in Employment Act, it is illegal, with rare exceptions, to force anyone to retire.

Addressing those who remain

Layoffs are traumatic not only for the people who are laid off but also for those who remain. Apart from the sympathy they may feel for colleagues, remaining workers must generally take on increased workloads. Regrouping after layoffs as quickly and effectively as possible and giving your new, smaller staff a renewed sense of purpose and opportunity is key to your future.

TIP

If, at some point, your company finds it necessary to conduct layoffs, keep the following pointers in mind:

» **Honest, open communication is critical.** Bear in mind that what you don't say to employees can be as disconcerting and worrisome as what you do say. It's important for managers to have team meetings very soon after layoffs have occurred, not merely to explain what's taken place but also to set goals, clarify roles, and, most of all, genuinely listen to concerns.

» **Treat employees as professionals.** Explain why the layoffs were necessary, why current staff members were chosen to stay on, and what you're expecting from them in the future. Make employees aware that their contributions are now more essential to the company's continued success than ever before.

» **Focus on the future.** You need to clearly explain why downsizing was an unavoidable move for your company. In addition to acknowledging the loss that team members may feel, focus on what they're gaining in terms of a stronger, more stable company.

>> **Consult a staffing firm.** Just as staffing services can help your displaced employees find new work, they also can help you bring in skilled supplemental workers to maintain continuity and prevent burnout on the part of remaining full-time staff.

Protecting the Safety and Health of Your Team Members

Employers in the United States are legally obligated to provide a workplace in which neither the environment nor the work practices subject employees to any unreasonable risk in safety or health. Safety- and health-related regulations vary considerably within an industry and according to state or federal regulations. (A good resource is the Occupational Safety & Health Administration, also known as OSHA.) Although the federal Occupational Safety and Health Act law applies throughout the United States, it permits states to implement their own plans with requirements above and beyond the federal regulations. Twenty-two states have adopted their own plans covering private employers. Consequently, no one single standard or list of safety- and health-related regulations applies across the board to every company. At the very least, though, it's your responsibility as your company's HR specialist to make sure of two things:

>> Your company is in compliance with the federal and/or state safety and health regulations that apply to your company.

>> Your company is doing everything that is reasonably possible (independent of your legal obligations) to protect the safety and health of your employees.

WARNING

The safety and health area is a complicated one. When in doubt, consult an attorney.

FIND ONLINE

The online resources include several documents that can help you ensure a safe workplace, including the following:

>> OSHA Information Posting

>> Work-Related Injury and Illness Report Form

Unlawful Harassment: Keeping Your Workplace Free of It

The best way to protect your organization and team members from unlawful harassment is to proactively put in place processes and provide awareness and education — creating awareness and being proactive are the keys. The following sections provide additional information on unlawful harassment and sexual harassment and share insight into how to create awareness and act proactively.

Understanding unlawful harassment

Even though the terms "unlawful harassment" and "sexual harassment" are often used interchangeably, unlawful harassment goes beyond sexual harassment and can include harassment based on race, color, national origin, or religion, and may expand to age, disability, weight, or other protected categories depending on the jurisdiction. (The next section discusses sexual harassment.)

REMEMBER

Simply declaring in writing your organization's commitment to prevent unlawful harassment isn't enough. You need a written policy that spells it out clearly, and you need to state, in no uncertain terms, the penalties for violating the policy. In fact, under the law, an employer may be found not liable for certain forms of harassment if the employer can show that it exercised reasonable care to prevent and correct promptly any harassment and that the employee complainant unreasonably failed to take advantage of preventive or corrective opportunities provided by the employer.

Establishing and enforcing an antiharassment policy is an important part of showing that your organization exercised reasonable care in addressing any harassment. The Equal Employment Opportunity Commission (EEOC) has identified key elements to include in such a policy, such as a clear explanation of prohibited conduct, assurances that complainants will be protected from retaliation, and a process for reporting complaints of harassment (see the next section).

FIND
ONLINE

The online resources include a Sample Policy Statement on Harassment and Retaliation. You should consult an attorney for assistance in preparing your own policy.

Addressing sexual harassment

The definition of *sexual harassment,* on the surface, seems fairly straightforward. Broadly, it means imposing an unwanted condition on a person's employment because of that person's sex. Then again, maybe it's not so straightforward. At issue is the connection between the behavior and the working circumstances and conditions of the person who is being harassed and the role of the alleged harasser. Often, sexual harassment is really about power — abuse of power — in the workplace.

Generally speaking, sexual harassment falls into one of two categories:

>> **Quid pro quo harassment:** The quid pro quo theory rests on the notion that an individual has relied on their actual or apparent authority to demand sexual favors from an employee.

>> **Hostile environment harassment:** Hostile environment sexual harassment, in contrast, is when an individual has been required to endure a work environment that substantially affects a term or condition of employment because of the employee's sex.

The EEOC's guidelines describe sexual harassment as follows: "Unwelcome sexual advances, requests for sexual favors, and other verbal or physical conduct of a sexual nature." The guidelines go on to add additional requirements:

>> Submission to such conduct is made either explicitly or implicitly a term or condition of an individual's employment.

>> Submission to or rejection of such conduct by an individual is used as the basis for employment decisions affecting such individuals.

>> Such conduct has the purpose or effect of unreasonably interfering with an individual's work performance or creating an intimidating, hostile, or offensive working environment.

You don't have to be a linguistic scholar to figure out that these guidelines are loaded with terms that are highly dependent on perceptions and interpretations. People (courts included) have varying ideas of what is implicit and different perceptions about what factors make a workplace intimidating or hostile. As such, these are important concepts that you should understand in order to address this important area in your work environment.

Since the beginning of the #MeToo era, employees have a heightened awareness of unlawful harassment, and employers are well-advised to tread carefully to prevent and correct unlawful harassment. What one person may view as a harmless joke may well be perceived by another as an aggressive and unwelcome sexual advance. Sexual harassment is one area of HR management in which you can never be too careful. To point you in the right direction, this section offers guidelines that may help you develop a proactive — and effective — sexual harassment policy in your organization.

Spreading the word

Your company is responsible for making sure that everyone in the organization — supervisors, managers, and employees — recognizes that harassment is wrong and will not be tolerated in the workplace. Increasingly, states and localities have enacted training and/or policy requirements for sexual harassment specifically, including but not limited to California, Connecticut, Delaware, Illinois, Maine, New York, Oregon, Washington, and Washington, D.C. Some laws require employers to display posters setting forth information about the law and employee rights in this area, whereas other laws require employers to distribute notices directly to employees containing similar information, and still other laws require that employers conduct training of employees in this area. For example, in California and Connecticut, covered employers must provide at least two hours of sexual harassment training on certain topics and within certain time frames. You may want to talk to an attorney or obtain information from your state equal employment opportunity agency regarding your legal obligations in this area.

What the various statues and courts are saying, in other words, is that it's not enough to simply adopt and publish a sexual harassment policy. It's also the company's responsibility to effectively communicate the philosophy and procedures associated with it to everyone in the company.

Publicizing your policy on sexual harassment can be accomplished yearly. Set a date during the same month each year and send copies of your policies to every employee. You also may consider developing an online sexual harassment policy manual and training course that you can deliver to every employee annually.

Creating a reporting process

Employees are not required by law to report unlawful harassment to their employers in order to file a harassment claim with the EEOC or a court. However, it's in your best interest that they do so — and it's critical that your organization establish a reporting procedure for complaints of harassment, generally as part of a broader antiharassment policy. The complaint process must be understandable. It needs to identify accessible people, hotlines, or anonymous toll-free phone numbers to which complaints can be reported (and alternative people in the event that the alleged harasser is one of the designated company representatives who would otherwise receive harassment complaints). There must be assurance that the employer will protect — to the extent possible — the confidentiality of harassment complaints. Aside from its legal significance in helping your organization defend against a claim of unlawful harassment, the existence of an internal complaint procedure is likely to help you correct, and hopefully resolve, alleged harassment-type issues without "help" from the government.

Investigating complaints

Regardless of how frivolous you may consider a harassment complaint, you must take it seriously and investigate it in accordance with your policy. If an incident ultimately spirals into a court case, and it's revealed in testimony that management was aware of the complaint but didn't act on it, you may, as a result, have to pay more in damages.

Every harassment complaint should be documented, and your organization must undertake a prompt, thorough, and impartial investigation into the alleged harassment. When management or HR learns of alleged harassment, it should decide whether a detailed fact-finding investigation is needed (obviously not the case if the alleged harasser doesn't deny the accusation) and, if so, undertake it immediately. As part of the investigation, getting detailed statements from the person making the harassment charges, as well as from the accused and any witnesses, is paramount.

Don't view paperwork as a burden. It can be your company's best defense. Documentation of discipline demonstrates that your company is serious about the problem and the solution. Remember, too, that investigations are both art and science; there's no one-size-fits-all approach. However, even when an investigation requires a less comprehensive approach, you still need to document the activity you've undertaken.

Taking decisive action

If you determine that harassment has occurred in violation of your policy, undertake immediate and appropriate corrective action, including discipline. The type of remedial measures you take should be designed to stop the harassment, correct its effects on the employee, and ensure that the harassment doesn't happen again. These measures don't have to be those that the employee requests or prefers, as long as they're effective.

REMEMBER

Doing nothing or being too lenient can put your firm at great risk and, at the very least, create the impression that you're condoning the behavior. This impression won't do much to help your company recruit or retain good employees and will expose the company (and possibly individual supervisors) to monetary damages.

Addressing Workplace Violence

Violence in the workplace is an issue that no company — regardless of how large or small the company or where it's located — can afford to ignore.

What steps can your company take to provide reasonable protection for your employees? Your best source of information on this matter is your local police department. Most police departments have specialists in crime prevention who can survey your business and make recommendations. Other good sources for crime prevention strategies are your state occupational safety and health agency, which may have guidelines and recommendations on employee safety measures. Also, look to violence prevention experts, insurance companies, or private security consultants.

REMEMBER

You need to take a twofold approach of protecting your team members from the violent acts of both outsiders and fellow team members.

TIP

As much as you don't want to dwell on the unpleasant, it's better to be prepared for both external and internal threats. You can put in place specific policies that can lessen the possibility of emergency situations. To address external threats, consider the following:

>> **Pay your team members by check, not cash.** Better still, encourage direct deposit of pay into employee bank accounts (with appropriate team member consent, of course).

>> **Keep building perimeters and parking lots well lit.** Lighting adds visibility and helps to limit threats.

>> **Limit access to strangers.** Consider implementing an access card system for employees. If appropriate for your business, ask visitors to wait in the reception area until an employee is available to escort them. Identify visitors with a special badge and escort them at all times. Instruct employees to notify the security office about strangers with no identification.

To address internal threats, take these steps:

>> **Establish and communicate to employees a strong, unequivocal policy of zero tolerance for violence.** Include threatening gestures, fighting words, and physical actions as causes for immediate dismissal. This policy should be included in your company's workplace violence policy and employee code of conduct.

>> **Consider providing counseling and other assistance for troubled employees.** You may want to consider offering an employee assistance program for employees with personal, financial, or substance abuse problems. Bear in mind your various legal obligations relative to disabled employees.

>> **Be constantly aware that certain workplace situations have a potential for violence.** Disciplinary meetings and termination interviews are prime examples. Take precautions accordingly.

» **Review and update your weapons policy.** It's important to note that some states provide protections for employees who bring firearms to work, and you should make sure your policy does not run afoul of applicable state laws.

» **Know what protective orders may be available.** Some jurisdictions allow employers to petition the court for a workplace violence protective order on behalf of its employees. Be aware of what your jurisdiction offers, and be prepared to escalate the issue to the appropriate security or legal team members.

6

The Part of Tens

IN THIS PART . . .

Recognize best practices for HR and Talent professionals for leading in an often-chaotic world.

Discover ways to build and nurture key stakeholder relationships.

Navigate the natural paradoxes (tensions) that exist in any business to facilitate different perspectives and arrive at a more inclusive solution.

Chapter **19**

Ten (or So) Best Practices for HR and Talent Leaders

HR leadership is business leadership because the talent in your business makes the business what it is. And because of the shifting expectations of the workforce, the remote nature of work, and the complexities of the always evolving legislative environment, strong HR leadership has never been more important. Amid the changes and challenges, which are likely to only accelerate, you need to keep certain principles in mind. This chapter covers best practices for HR and Talent leaders in any organization. Across each of these principles is a theme of staying connected to the business while continuing to grow as a leader.

Know Your Business

Leading HR professionals know the ins and outs of their business — their why, their mission, how they make money, how they do what they do, and so on. The best HR leaders also stay connected to what's happening in the industries they are a part of. Because of this, they're keenly aware of the ways in which their work fits into their organization's overall business and the organization's differentiators within its space. They do this by understanding the complexities and operating challenges that set their companies apart from their competitors.

An understanding of business finance is helpful. (Quick test: Can you read a P&L statement?) Even more important, the best HR leaders have an in-depth understanding of their company's products and services, the competitive challenges it faces, and the strategic initiatives that are underway to meet those challenges. The best way to gain this knowledge is to participate in as many meetings and discussions involving these initiatives as possible. Set up meetings with line managers or other colleagues to find out about their strategic goals. Ask questions and pay attention to the challenges and opportunities that are getting the most attention in the business — what are leaders talking about and struggling with? Engaging in these conversations puts you in a position to lead business challenges with the right people and talent strategies.

In addition, as your business acumen increases, you will naturally provide more insight into the bottom-line implications of any HR initiative that you recommend — everything from learning and development programs to hiring practices and, difficult as it often is, employee termination procedures. Create simple spreadsheets that show the before-and-after scenarios or work with the finance leaders in your company to establish some concrete ways to attach a dollar value to the contributions your HR efforts are making to the company's bottom line.

Develop a Marketing Mindset

The best HR leaders are good marketers and are effective at making a case for new HR initiatives to all segments of your internal customer base: senior management, supervisors, and staff-level employees. The key is to focus your communication efforts on the benefits these projects deliver. As you're selling HR initiatives to senior management, stress competitive advantage. If your audience is made up of supervisors, stress the operational advantages — how a program can ease their day-to-day burdens.

TIP

As with any marketing initiative, you need to know your audience and base your approach on their needs and concerns. *Remember:* Whenever you're introducing a new initiative to a group of employees who are already under tremendous time pressures, anticipate resistance — even though the new program may be designed to ease those pressures in the long run.

Know Yourself

Self-awareness is the first chapter in the book of leadership. The best HR leaders know who they are and who they are not. They recognize their strengths, their weaknesses, what gives them energy, and what drains their energy.

Often leaders overcompensate for or deny their weaknesses only to lose credibility with others. When leaders show up authentically with humility (acknowledging areas that are challenging for them), they build trust and connection with others.

Knowing what you excel at and what you don't also allows you to plug in and support projects in a way that is most energizing for you (and ultimately the business). And when you acknowledge that you don't have the strengths or expertise needed, you can bring in other leaders, team members, and/or external partners to supplement your strengths. HR (like any business discipline) is multifaceted and ever evolving, so you aren't going to be an expert in all areas. Give yourself grace and never set the unrealistic standard that you know all there is to know.

Adopt a Growth Mindset

As research shows, your mindset drives your behavior, so it's important to pay attention to how you're thinking about and approaching all aspects of your leadership. A growth mindset is open and curious. It's a learning mindset, and instead of getting derailed by failures or setbacks, a growth mindset focuses on what there is to learn in challenging situations. Throughout my career, I've seen HR leaders quickly fall on their sword when senior leadership didn't agree with their approach or perspective, saying things like "I don't get HR." This fixed mindset isn't conducive to growth. In those situations, instead of getting angry, get curious. Identify what you can learn from the situation to improve the next recommendation.

Nurture Your Tribe/Network

HR leadership can often feel lonely — it's not helpful or healthy to vent and talk through sensitive and/or confidential business challenges with internal leaders. An external network or peer group of HR leaders is incredibly valuable to serve as a sounding board and offer thought partnership for leading through challenging situations (although you want to be careful not to share confidential information and instead generalize your challenges it makes sense to do so). Most challenges that HR leaders are faced with are normal, and by talking through them with other HR leaders, you recognize that you aren't alone and that others have navigated similar ground. You can learn from each other's challenges.

TIP

If you don't already have a network of strong HR and Talent leaders, build one. Start locally with online HR groups and pay attention to leaders who are like-minded and/or in a similar business or interest. Ask others to meet for coffee to network and get to know each other. Attend conferences or HR-related seminars and connect with other HR leaders in the process.

After you have a network, nurture it. Take time to meet with members of your network monthly or quarterly to stay connected to best practices and what others are doing.

Build Your Team

HR leadership is business leadership, so whether you're a one-person HR department or leading a team of HR professionals, you're always building HR and talent capability within your organization.

REMEMBER

To ensure you're leading with a team mindset, be cognizant of the following:

>> **Aligning to a vision:** The definition of a team is a group of people working together to accomplish something. Shared values, the organization's mission, and the company's vision all provide a common place of focus for you and your team. With these in mind, the best HR leaders have a clear mission/vision for their HR teams and know what it is they're trying to create. Amidst a challenging situation, having a bigger picture to rally around keeps the conversation focused on where you're going and what the team is working toward.

>> **Engaging in healthy conflict:** Doing so is a valuable part of working within a team environment. Create an environment in which team members feel comfortable sharing a different perspective. Where there's psychological safety and a shared vision, conflict moves the team forward.

>> **Building trust:** This is an ongoing process. Never take trust for granted. It's the key to an open, transparent relationship and takes time to establish.

>> **Building diversity into the team:** Create a team that reflects the people you serve to ensure differences in thought and experience within the team.

Provide Coaching and Focused Feedback to Peers and Leaders

Because of an HR leader's business acumen — understanding the business and having strong relationships — HR leaders are in the best position to coach and provide focused feedback to leaders within the business. Strong HR leaders listen to recommendations and ask questions to make decisions that are best for the business. But in many instances, the role of HR is *not* to be the decision maker, but rather to provide guidance. Many times other leaders in the business will lean on HR to make a difficult decision for them, which prevents those leaders from growing and also owning some of the difficult decisions they need to make — for example, giving an underperforming team member a smaller bonus, taking more time to find a candidate that's within their budget versus going over budget, and so on).

In addition, when colleagues don't follow through on commitments and agreements, strong HR leaders acknowledge this — they hold them accountable for the agreements made. Not only does this establish trust and credibility, but it also supports commitment and getting results within the team.

TIP

When providing coaching and feedback to colleagues, remember to keep the focus on the behavior, not the person. Using this language is helpful: "I noticed that you didn't follow through on. . . ." The key is to highlight the behavior in question without accusing your colleague — using these words allows you to simply state what didn't happen and give your colleague an opportunity to respond.

Be Nimble and Willing to Flex

Flexible leadership is key for HR leaders. There are certainly legalities that require a hard stance, but more often than not, HR leaders are required to flex, see other perspectives, or adopt new perspectives because of the evolving business environment. Digging your heals in doesn't help anyone when the business is trying to move forward. As a business leader, you want to move with the business and support business growth, which requires continually shifting and re-shifting.

REMEMBER

One area that requires flexibility is working to achieve balance between understaffing and overstaffing as workloads ebb and flow. On one hand, you don't want your company to be caught understaffed and unable to take advantage of growth opportunities. At the same time, you don't want to over-hire. The answer is somewhere in between. Strive to adopt a flexible staffing strategy as your permanent business model. By augmenting the efforts of full-time employees with contingent professionals when workloads peak, you can better manage expenses, reduce the possibility of future layoffs (because you haven't added full-time employees beyond your core team), and gain the flexibility to easily staff up or down as demand for your company's services fluctuates.

Continue to Hone Your Craft

Dedicate a portion of your workweek — *every* week — to your growth and development to ensure you remain current on new developments in the field. Here are some ideas on how to stay ahead of the curve:

>> Follow HR and Talent thought leaders on social media.

>> Build and nurture a network on HR leaders.

>> Attend seminars and conferences geared specifically for HR practitioners.

>> Stay informed about legal issues that can affect your policies by monitoring news stories and legal cases that are likely to have HR implications. But don't go too far — be sure to consult an attorney when you're unclear on particular areas or when you're making important employment decisions that may involve legal risk to the company.

>> Pay close attention to your competitors' HR practices — compensation and benefits, in particular. **Remember:** These differences may be giving them an edge in attracting high-performing employees.

>> Take a line position or short-term role in another part of your business to deepen your understanding of the business or build skills outside of your current skill set.

Chapter **20**

Ten (or So) Strategies for Building Relationships with Key Stakeholders

The effectiveness of an HR leader (or any leader for that matter) is dependent upon the success of their relationships. Leadership is a team sport, and the best leaders know that they can't accomplish their goals alone. An HR leaders' ability to support the business's success requires them to understand how *other* leaders are supporting business goals. There is an interdependence between leaders within an organization, and to accomplish goals together and collaborate most effectively, there must be trust in the relationship.

As I reflect on my career in HR, I recognize the power of my relationships *when* I've taken the time to build and nurture them. It's only with intentionality that we maximize the relationships that are most important to us. Following are nine keys for HR and Talent leaders to consider for building and maintaining relationships with key stakeholders.

Recognize the Importance of Relationships

Results only come through your relationships with others, so when building a relationship, you need to identify the value in the relationship and make time to build and nurture it. When you value something, you prioritize it. When you value your relationships, you naturally take the time to build and strengthen them. The best leaders get this and have a mindset that drives trust-building behaviors, which include the following:

>> Asking questions to understand the goals and priorities of your key stakeholders

>> Prioritizing interactions and meetings with key stakeholders (seeing them as primary to accomplishing your goals)

>> Encouraging key stakeholders by taking the time to listen to their challenges and providing supportive guidance and coaching

>> Building credibility with key stakeholders by following through on actions — doing what you say you will do

Know with Whom to Build Key Relationships

The key is to identify your key stakeholders. They're the individuals most influential in helping to accomplish your goals — those are the relationships to focus on in the business. Many HR and Talent leaders spread themselves thin and try to connect with everyone, or they spend time primarily with leaders whose personalities are similar to theirs.

TIP

If you're a new leader within an organization, ask others who they think you need to get to know. Notice who in the business has a lot of influence and credibility and start there. I've found throughout my career that executive assistants within a business are a great resource for information about who to connect with and how best to connect with a particular resource.

It's also important to think about key stakeholders at all levels within the organization. From front line to senior leaders, find out whose influence is most important to the business goals you are working toward. Being intentional about building relationships at all levels also provides good insight into what's happening at all levels within the organization.

And while internal relationships are clearly a priority, also consider external relationships that support goal attainment. Key vendors, customers, and other business partners who are adding value to the organization need to be aligned and communicated with on an ongoing basis to provide maximum value to the business.

Seek to Understand Others' Perspectives

In his classic book *The 7 Habits of Highly Effective People* (published by Simon & Schuster), author Stephen Covey names habit number 5 as "seek first to understand, THEN to be understood." This principle is a cornerstone of any strong relationship because it's a significant trust-building behavior. And yet, throughout my career I've fallen into the trap (and seen other leaders do the same) of sharing my perspective quickly to prove my value or add to a conversation. In other words, I focus on my reply rather than understanding what the person I'm listening to is trying to express. This approach (seeking to be understood first) impedes trust because it focuses all the attention on the one seeking to be understood. Instead, go into a relationship with curiosity and openness, striving to learn about the person you're building a relationship with. Then, after you understand their point of view and the way in which they think about the world, you're much better equipped to respond in a way that connects with them.

I've also seen many HR leaders express frustration when other leaders in the business "don't get HR," and I've challenged that statement and belief because it's contrary to seeking to understand. A much more empowering perspective to reflect on is this: "What do *you* get?" In other words, do you get *their* perspective? That's the key in building the relationship, and it starts with open-ended questions. Following are some simple questions that are helpful in getting to know any coworker or in building any relationship with a new team member:

>> How does your team/department/role support the business?

>> What are your goals?

>> What are your team's/department's/individual strengths?

>> What are you most proud of about the work you do?

>> What are your greatest challenges right now?

>> Where are you stuck?

>> What do you wish you had more time for?

The key to these questions is asking them with a curious spirit. Show up with openness, transparency, and a willingness to learn, and you will do *your* part to create a trusting relationship. And notice that each of these questions starts with *how* or *what*. Asking a question that begins with how or what ensures that the question is open-ended and disarming, which is key in building trust in the relationship.

Align on Shared Values

Shared values can be an incredible source of grounding in a relationship. The key is to take the time to get to know what's important to the people you're working with so that you can find common ground.

For example, an HR leader may be frustrated by the way in which an operations manager is managing (or failing to manage) a struggling team member. Knowing that the operations manager has a strong drive to serve the customer with excellence, the HR leader can leverage this shared value as a starting point for the conversation, saying something like, "I know we both share a strong desire to serve the customer, so what support does the struggling team member need to do this well?" This approach grounds the conversation in a value that both leaders share, so it starts the conversation from a place of unity and connection. Through the process of affirming shared values, the HR leader ensures alignment.

Communicate Proactively

Communication is at the heart of any strong relationship. No one is a mind reader, and in a time in which working professionals are busier than ever, it's mission critical to be intentional and focused on your communication efforts and to communicate proactively. Put yourself in the position of playing offense. Communicate *before* you need to communicate.

REMEMBER

Before sending an email, addressing colleagues at a meeting, sharing information via your internal communication tool, or having a one-on-one meeting with another leader in the business, take the time to get clear on the message, who you're communicating to, and how best to communicate the message. Check out Table 20-1 to help ensure you are considering the best way in which to communicate the intended message to your audience.

TABLE 20-1   Ways to Communicate

What's the Message?	To Whom?	How?
Who is saying what?	What's the cascade/flow?	What's the best medium for delivery?
Is the message clear and devoid of unnecessary tangents?	Is everyone accounted for?	What are the style preferences of my audience?
Is the message prepped for my inquiring audience?	How will I manage the cascade/flow?	How can I be most effective and professional?
	What are their questions/concerns?	What's the timing?

Recognize Conflict and Tension as a Natural Part of Any Relationship

Know that anytime you're building a relationship, tension will naturally arise. You may uncover a past challenge, a conflicting perspective, or any other tension-inducing situation, and *it's completely normal.* Actually, it's healthy. When there's openness and candor in a relationship (evidence of a high-trust relationship), of course, tension and differing perspectives will exist. And when tension arises, press into it. Use it as an opportunity to find out more about the leader you are in a relationship with or building a relationship with. Instead of bowing out, talking with others about the leader, or creating an unfair storyline about the leader, directly talk with the leader about the tension. You may simply say something like, "There is tension between us on this issue; I'd like to talk through that with you to understand your perspective more fully." That's a great way to strengthen the trust in the relationship and gain credibility along the way.

Own Your Actions

You must take ownership for your own actions, as ultimately, you are responsible for your choices. This is a helpful mindset as you're building trust in relationships because it keeps the focus on what *you* are doing, not what the person you're building trust with is doing.

HR has gotten a bad rap for decades, and new HR leaders may come across as having outdated attitudes and perspectives on HR in the businesses they are serving. Recognize biases and outdated attitudes as just that, without making them about you. Show a new style of HR leadership through your actions — that is the best way to change a perspective.

Respond Rather Than React

Between every frustration and your reaction to the frustration is a space, and in that space is where your power lies. In that space, you get to *choose* how to respond every single time. But often, in the heat of the moment, you may not give yourself the chance to stop, pause, and respond rather than react.

REMEMBER

The key is to leverage the pause — give yourself the opportunity to reflect on *how* you want to respond given the situation, the relationships with the people involved, and the information you have.

As you're building and nurturing relationships with key stakeholders, be intentional about responding to them in a way that helps to build trust and supports the goal of strengthening the relationship. Filter the challenge through a bigger picture perspective (the goals you're working on or your values) to ensure that your response is helpful.

Build Trust Continually

You can never take the level of trust in a relationship for granted. The key is to take the time to nurture relationships continuously and maintain a high level of intentionality. Think of the amount of trust in a relationship as you would a bank account — you want to build up your account and monitor it to ensure it's healthy. As I note earlier, conflict and tension will occur, but when there is a good balance in the trust account, deposits won't have the impact they would if the account were empty.

Your path to getting results in the business you serve is through your relationships. Honor them, and they will honor you.

IN THIS CHAPTER

» Recognizing what paradox
   navigation is

» Identifying skills you need to
   navigate paradox

» Understanding the main challenges

Chapter **21**

Ten Skills You Need for Navigating Paradox

There has never been a more important time to be an HR leader — the work environment is complex, and organizations are craving strong leadership. The HR profession must continue to evolve, and HR leaders must build new skills to lead through the complexities. This is why I felt it important to dedicate this chapter to a skill I believe is essential: paradox navigation.

Paradox navigation is the ability to navigate the natural paradoxes (tensions) that exist within organizations (collaboration versus efficiency, strategic versus tactical, long term versus short term). This chapter provides insight on how to serve as a paradox navigator in your organization.

Understand the Impact

In the 2016 HR Competency Model (from the Ross School of Management at the University of Michigan and the RBL Group), a new competency (new in that it was finally named) — paradox navigator — emerged as mission critical for HR leaders.

Researcher highlighted two important findings: 1) Paradox navigation was the competency with the greatest impact on business performance, and 2) it was the competency that had been the most unexplored at that point.

Identify Paradoxes That Need Navigating

Do you remember the days of playground tug-of-war when the balance shifted this way and then that way? The tug-of-war feeling you experienced as a kid plays out today in all aspects of organizational life as leaders navigate the natural paradoxes or tensions that exist within any business. Here are just a few of the common ones:

>> Balancing short-term results and long-term vision

>> Maintaining compliance and innovating

>> Providing structure (control) and empowering team members

>> Navigating the advantages and disadvantages of a centralized versus a decentralized structure

>> Creating healthy competition within the organization while ensuring leaders collaborate and work together

REMEMBER

Just like the two competing forces in a game of tug-of-war, paradox happens when seemingly contradictory activities operate together, and these natural tensions occur daily. Tension and conflict aren't going away — the work world is increasingly complex. So rather than avoid the tensions, press into the challenge.

Emphasize "and/also" Thinking

Paradox navigation focuses on "and/also" thinking rather than "either/or" thinking — long term *and* short term, compliance *and* innovation — the use of the word "and" is purposeful. This mindset takes the pressure off you as a leader because it isn't about picking a side or having an answer. Leaders often put more energy into the tug (either/or thinking) rather than the balance (and/also thinking) and end up making short-sided, exclusive decisions (for example, rushing a decision because of pressure from the CEO or other business leaders).

Make More Inclusive Solutions

Through the development of paradox navigation skills, leaders leverage different perspectives to come to better and more inclusive decisions. For example, as a business leader, I'm continually balancing what's best for the business with what's best for the individual employee (often two distinct perspectives), and I'm a better leader and come to the best solutions when I consider both perspectives — that is the heart of and/also thinking. It's not one or the other; it's both.

REMEMBER

While paradox navigation is critical for all leaders in the organization, HR professionals are in a unique position to navigate paradox because of the breadth of relationships across the business and the broad business knowledge they have.

Stick to Your Guns

Although paradox navigation is a leadership skill that's good for your business, others may not like paradox navigators much for doing this important job because they can be perceived as disruptive and not following along. Serving as a paradox navigator can feel isolating, so you must have the conviction and perseverance to do what's right for your organization.

Demonstrate Empathy

Empathy is the highest form of listening. It's not about solving or fixing; it's about feeling *with* others and validating their feelings. Exhibiting empathy helps navigate paradox because it ensures leaders continually seek to understand and explore more deeply what's happening and why others believe the way they do. Demonstrating empathy also builds trust and strengthens relationships — it keeps the focus on the person being listened to.

Surround Yourself with Diverse Perspectives

Paradox navigators seek diverse perspectives and opinions. They ask for the opinions of people who are different from them. If everyone in a meeting is agreeing on an issue, a paradox navigator will consider a perspective that isn't in the room. For example, if senior leaders are focused solely on what's best for the business, a paradox navigator will speak up and ask whether the solution is also good for employees.

Anchor to a Bigger Picture Set of Values or Vision

Another skill that helps leaders to navigate paradox within their businesses is to anchor to a bigger picture set of values or vision. It's easier to go against the grain when you have a bigger why. Ask yourself, "What would our vision or our core values do in this situation?" to stay grounded in your foundation.

Get Comfortable Being Uncomfortable

Leading through conflict builds trust and credibility, but it's uncomfortable, so paradox navigators learn to be comfortable being uncomfortable.

REMEMBER

The key is to allow for tension without being contentious. Paradox navigators create a safe place for multiple perspectives to exist, and by leveraging many of the skills this chapter addresses, such as empathy and leveraging diversity, leaders naturally engage others.

Continue to Explore the Competency

The complexities aren't going away, so paradox navigation will continue to be an important competency for all leaders. Following is a list of ideas for ways to continue to grow in this area:

>> Read the book *Victory Through Organization* by Dave Ulrich, David Kryscynski, Mike Ulrich, and Wayne Brockbank (published by McGraw Hill). This book highlights the research and the competency model noted previously. A specific chapter is dedicated to the paradox navigator and how you can improve in this area.

>> Talk with your team, leaders in your business, and other HR leaders about this competency.

>> Be bold. You're in your position for a reason, so share your perspective and do your part to navigate the natural tensions that pop up in your business.

Appendix

What's Online

Here's what you can find within the *Human Resources Kit For Dummies* online content:

>> More than 40 documents, including policies, forms, and contracts

>> This is a mix of required forms and sample templates to help you maximize the talent within your business while protecting the business from unnecessary risk.

This appendix details what you can find at www.dummies.com/go/human resourceskit to help you and your organization with some of its basic HR needs.

What You'll Find Online

The following sections are arranged by category and provide a summary of the resources and tools you'll find online. I've organized the forms and documents online by the chapter in which they're mentioned. I briefly describe each document in this appendix, but refer to the actual document for more information.

Note: As is often indicated in the chapters, the forms and draft policies provided are only samples. Different state and local laws may impose different legal obligations, including with regard to the content of the documents and how you use them. An attorney can explain the particular laws that apply to your organization and employees.

Chapter 4

Blank Skills Inventory Form and Sample Skills Inventory Form: The form can serve as a model for an employee skills inventory.

Staffing/Recruiting Firm Evaluation Checklist: You can use this checklist to evaluate staffing and recruiting firms.

Worker Classification Quick Reference Table: This document provides an at-a-glance summary of the differences among worker classifications.

Chapter 5

Blank Position Success Profile and Sample Position Success Profile: This document includes a blank position success profile (often called a job description) so that you can develop your position success profiles, as well as three sample position success profiles.

Chapter 6

Sample Job Posting: This document includes three sample job postings you can use as a reference when preparing your own.

Chapter 7

Rejection Letter: This is an example of a "thanks, but no thanks" letter to an unsuccessful applicant.

Sample Screening Questions for Hiring Managers: This form lists a number of sample screening questions to consider when conducting a job interview over the phone or on video.

Sample Résumés: This document includes examples of well-written résumés and a résumé that could cause you to question the qualifications of the applicant. Keep these in mind when reviewing the résumés you receive for open positions with your organization.

Chapter 8

Candidate Interview Evaluation Form: Use this form to record your general impressions of a job candidate.

Employment Inquiries Fact Sheet: This fact sheet contains suggested guidelines for managers involved in the hiring process. The information is specific to California and may be different for other states.

Nondiscriminatory Interview Question Reference Sheet: You can use this reference sheet to avoid interview questions that could pose legal problems.

Interview Q&A Form: Use this form to write down questions you want to ask a job candidate during an employment interview, to record the candidate's answers, and to jot down any of your own comments.

Pre-Interview Checklist for Hiring Managers: This form lists issues to consider when preparing to interview a job applicant.

Chapter 9

Offer Letter to a Prospective Employee: This sample letter offers a job to a prospective employee.

Sample Reference Check Questions: This document lists several questions you should consider asking when checking an applicant's references.

A Summary of Your Rights Under the Fair Credit Reporting Act: Under the federal FCRA, an employer is required to provide the individual with a copy of the official description of individual rights under the act issued by the FTC at various stages in the decision-making process.

Chapter 10

Employee Handbook Table of Contents: This document is a sample table of contents for an employee handbook. You'll want to customize it to reflect those policies applicable to your company or organization.

Employee Handbook and At-Will Employee Status Acknowledgment: This document is a sample form in which a new employee acknowledges receiving and agreeing to the matters contained in the company's employee handbook. The form also requires the employee to acknowledge that he is an at-will employee.

Onboarding Checklist: This document lists criteria to consider when evaluating the effectiveness of your onboarding process.

Chapter 11

Total Rewards Statement: This form lists all the compensation and benefits that an employer provides to an employee.

Chapter 12

A Look at 401(k) Plan Fees: This document answers common questions that employees have about 401(k) plans.

Certification for Serious Injury or Illness of Covered Servicemember — for Military Family Leave (Federal Family and Medical Leave Act): Employers are entitled to require that an employee's request for leave under the federal Family and Medical Leave Act (FMLA) to care for a covered servicemember with a serious injury or illness is supported by a healthcare provider's certification. The employer may use this optional form for this purpose.

Certification of Healthcare Provider for Employee's Serious Health Condition (Federal Family and Medical Leave Act): Employers are entitled to require that an employee's request for leave under the FMLA due to the employee's own serious health condition is supported by a healthcare provider's certification. The employer may use this optional form for this purpose.

Certification of Healthcare Provider for Family Member's Serious Health Condition (Federal Family and Medical Leave Act): Employers are entitled to require that an employee's request for leave under the FMLA due to a serious health condition affecting a covered family member is supported by a healthcare provider's certification. The employer may use this optional form for this purpose.

Certification of Qualifying Exigency for Military Family Leave (Federal Family and Medical Leave Act): Employers are entitled to require that an employee's request for military family leave under the FMLA due to a qualifying exigency is supported by a healthcare provider's certification. The employer may use this optional form for this purpose.

Designation Notice (Federal Family and Medical Leave Act): When an employer covered by the FMLA has sufficient information to determine if an employee's leave is FMLA qualifying, the employer must provide the employee with notice stating that the leave has been designated as FMLA leave (or that additional information is needed to determine whether the leave is FMLA qualifying) within five business days, absent extenuating circumstances. The employer may use this optional form for this purpose.

Notice of Employee Rights Under the Federal Family and Medical Leave Act: Employers covered by the FMLA must provide employees with written notice detailing the specific expectations and obligations of the employee under the law and explaining any consequences of a failure to meet such obligations. The employer may use this optional form for this purpose.

Notice of Eligibility and Rights & Responsibilities (Federal Family and Medical Leave Act): After an employee notifies her employer (who is covered by the FMLA) of a need for leave, or when the employer acquires knowledge that an employee's leave may be for an FMLA-qualifying reason, the employer must notify the employee of her eligibility to take FMLA leave within five business days, absent extenuating circumstances. The employer may use this optional form for this purpose.

Chapter 13

Employee Opinion Survey: This document is an example of a simple opinion survey an organization can distribute to employees to gauge worker satisfaction and determine areas of needed improvement.

Exit Interview Questionnaire: This form lists questions a company representative can ask when an employee voluntarily leaves the company.

Sample Pulse Survey: This document includes a number of sample questions to ask when conducting a pulse survey of your employees.

Chapter 14

Individual Development Plan Form: Employees can use this form to work with their managers in setting learning objectives and career goals.

Chapter 17

Discrimination Fact Sheets: This document includes fact sheets from the EEOC and Department of Labor (DOL) that detail discrimination guidelines.

Employee Rights Under the Fair Labor Standards Act: This document includes the Fair Labor Standards Act (FLSA) minimum-wage poster, titled Employee Rights Under the Fair Labor Standards Act. Every employer of employees subject to the

FLSA's minimum-wage provisions must post, and keep posted, a notice explaining the act in a conspicuous place in all its establishments.

Equal Employment Opportunity Is the Law: This poster describes the federal laws prohibiting job discrimination based on race, color, sex, national origin, religion, age, equal pay, disability, and genetic information. Every employer covered by the nondiscrimination and equal employment opportunity laws is required to post this notice in a conspicuous location on its premises.

Family and Medical Leave Act Fact Sheets: This document includes fact sheets from the DOL detailing major provisions of the FMLA.

Voluntary Self-Identification of Disability: This is a voluntary form to allow individuals to disclose their disability is they choose to do so. Federal contractors are required to use the form.

Chapter 18

OSHA Information Posting: This document lists the major provisions under the federal Occupational Safety and Health Act (OSHA).

Sample Policy Statement on Harassment and Retaliation: This form is meant to be a sample policy prohibiting harassment of the type your organization should issue to its employee workforce.

Work-Related Injury and Illness Report Form: This form is used for reporting accidents or hazards in the workplace.

Customer Care

If you have trouble with accessing the site, please call Wiley Product Technical Support at 800-762-2974. Outside the United States, call 317-572-3994. You also can contact Wiley Product Technical Support at http://support.wiley.com.

To place additional orders or to request information about other Wiley products, please call 877-762-2974.

Index

About the Author

Andrea Butcher is a catalyst for growth and a visionary — she knows how to lead organizations from big picture to execution. She is a dynamic speaker, executive coach, and facilitator. As the CEO of HRD – A Leadership Development Company, she leads a national team of expert facilitators and coaches to accomplish organizational goals by building and strengthening leadership capability. She is the host of the popular leadership podcast, Being [at Work] and is the author of *The Power in the Pivot: Leadership Lessons from Being [at Work] to Take You from Chaos to Clarity* (Red Thread Publishing).

Andrea's work spans organizations of all sizes and industries all over the world; she has experience in global HR positions, consulting, operations, and executive roles for private and public organizations. Andrea is also the co-founder and President of Next Gen Talent, a program specifically designed to equip emerging HR leaders for success.

Dedication

To the professor who asked me, "Have you thought about a career in human resources?" and to the HR profession — thank you for being dedicated to the well-being of people. Every single employee is bringing their humanness to work each day, and I'm grateful to be part of a profession that is dedicated to creating workplaces that are enriching and supportive.

Author's Acknowledgments

In preparing this fourth edition of *Human Resources Kit For Dummies,* I relied on the advice and assistance of a number of talented individuals whose contributions made this book possible.

Thank you to my dear friend, and the technical editor of this book, Kelly Lavin. Kelly is the co-founder of Next Gen Talent (a nonprofit we created together to equip emerging HR leaders) and the chief people officer at Niche. In addition, thank you to the subject matter experts who collaborated with me on the best practices within specific areas of HR: Megan Nail, vice president, Total Rewards Practice at NFP; Dora Lutz, founder at GivingSpring (expertise in CSR); Thomas Mackey and Art Pizzello (expertise in employee benefits); Phil Strazzulla, founder at Select Software Reviews, (provided extensive insight on HR technology); and Ronda McClurg, vice president, People Solutions at iA (expertise in talent acquisition).

I also want to acknowledge the individuals who made the previous editions of *Human Resources Kit For Dummies* possible, most notably Max Messer. In addition, I'm indebted to Kelsey Baird, managing editor at Wiley, who recognized my passion for the profession and strong HR practices; and to the editors and reviewers whose efforts carried this fourth edition through to completion — thank you to Chad Sievers, Christine Pingleton, Kristie Pyles, and Steve Hayes for your guidance and encouragement throughout the process.

My background and passion is in employee engagement and development, so I relied heavily on the expertise and partnership of leaders at the highly respected law firm of Ogletree, Deakins, Nash, Smoak & Stewart, P.C. Thank you, Bonnie Martin, office managing shareholder in Indianapolis and her fellow shareholder (and co-chair of Ogletree's Benefits Practice Group), Stephanie Smithey — your collaboration was essential to this project. Ogletree, Deakins, Nash, Smoak & Stewart is a leading labor and employment law firm. They provide coverage through 55 offices in 32 U.S. states, the District of Columbia, the U.S. Virgin Islands, and in Canada, Mexico, and Europe. They represent employers of all sizes and across many industries, from small businesses to Fortune 500 companies. As employment issues continue to grow in legal complexity, I believe readers will benefit greatly from their expertise.

Publisher's Acknowledgments

Executive Editor: Steven Hayes

Project Manager and Editor: Chad R. Sievers

Senior Managing Editor: Kristie Pyles

Copy Editor: Christine Pingleton

Technical Editor: Kelly Lavin

Production Editor: Tamilmani Varadharaj

Cover Image: © Ground Picture/Shutterstock